A Golfer's Education

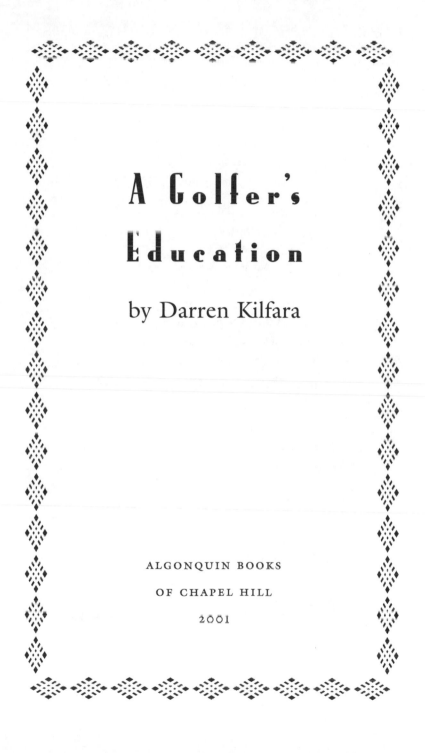

A Golfer's Education

by Darren Kilfara

ALGONQUIN BOOKS

OF CHAPEL HILL

2001

Published by
Algonquin Books of Chapel Hill
Post Office Box 2225
Chapel Hill, North Carolina 27515-2225

a division of
Workman Publishing
708 Broadway
New York, New York 10003

Library of Congress Cataloging-in-Publication Data
Kilfara, Darren, 1974–
    A golfer's education / by Darren Kilfara.
    p. cm.
    ISBN 1-56512-301-8
    1. Kilfara, Darren, 1974–   2. Golfers—United States—
Biography.   3. University of St. Andrews—Golf.   4. Harvard
University—Golf.   I. Title.
    GV964.K49 A3 2001
    796.352'092—dc21
[B]   2001041389

10 9 8 7 6 5 4 3 2 1
First Edition

To my Favorite

Acknowledgments

FIRST AND FOREMOST, I'd like to thank everyone I met in St. Andrews and the rest of Scotland: friends, acquaintances, playing partners and opponents, and everyone else. Without you, there never would have been a story to tell.

Thanks to Nancy Crossman, my agent, for sticking with me from start to finish, boosting my confidence to no end in the progress and making this whole thing happen.

Thanks to all those at Algonquin who have helped carry this book to term—particularly Duncan Murrell, under whose editorship and tutelage I grew immensely as a writer, and as a person.

I never would have started this project without the assistance, inspiration and friendship of so many people at *Golf Digest*, so my hat is off to Jerry Tarde, Roger Schiffman, Ed Weathers, John Barton, Mike Stachura, Pat Murphy and many others (you know who you are!).

Thanks to everyone in the discussion group at GolfClubAtlas.com, for teaching me how little I actually knew about golf course architecture and for continuing to heap enlightenment and entertainment upon me in equal measure. Special thanks to Paul Turner, Mike Cirba and Rich Goodale for their detailed critiques of my drafts; extra special thanks to John Morrissett, for all that and much more besides.

Thanks to the many good people at SSgA, especially Kanesh Lakhani and Sharon Power, for their flexibility and patience in letting me work my writing pursuits into and around my day-to-day responsibilities.

Thanks to Coach Leonard and everyone else with whom I shared the Harvard golf van down the years. Who would have thought it would all come to this, way back when?

Thanks to everyone at HTB for your constant prayers and support.

And thanks to Mom, and to Dad. This book is more yours than I can possibly describe.

Contents

Prologue

COLLEGE LIFE GAVE me many of my most vivid memories, but most of what I remember about the time I spent with my professors and their teaching assistants is blurry. Several years have rolled by since my academic career came to a close, and like most people I tend to remember the best and worst of times, not the dross in between. I can, however, recall meeting the head of the history department late on a spring afternoon in Robinson Hall, one of those columned, ivy-covered, redbrick buildings synonymous with higher learning. It was the middle of what would have been my sixth semester at Harvard University, had I not been otherwise engaged.

I drove up from Connecticut in the morning, parked my car near Harvard Yard and wormed my way toward Robinson through masses of students, teachers and tourists marching in every direction to their own relentless drumbeats. I was anxious. Many students scuttled back and forth between Robinson and Widener Library with monotonous regularity, but I didn't even know what my department chairman looked like. Yet he and I were about to discuss a subject of the utmost seriousness—something that could affect my entire future.

As inconspicuously as I could, I slipped into Robinson via the side entrance, slunk into the poorly lit reception area and sat down to await my summons on an uncomfortable, backless piece of furniture of the kind only found in the reception areas of universities and doctors' offices. The minutes ticked by. I mentally rehearsed my lines—again. Finally, the department head poked his head out of his office. Instinctively, I tried to avoid direct eye contact with him; the tension of the situation was unbearable. I vaguely remember him as a squat, balding man with a strong New York accent, but for all I know he could have looked like Marge Simpson. I wasn't really paying attention to anything but my own predicament.

He beckoned for me to come in and offered me a chair across from his desk. Smiling graciously, he introduced himself and framed our meeting in friendly-sounding terms, but I still squirmed in my seat as he glanced at my open file. Mercifully, the crucial question was not long in coming:

"So you want to spend a year in Scotland at the University of St. Andrews. How will this help your academic career?"

Everyone I'd asked—friends, guidance counselors, tutors—told me not to worry about this meeting. Like most universities, Harvard wants to transform its students into well-rounded individuals; the school values a year abroad as much for the experience as for the formal education. Even the flimsiest argument on behalf of my plan would likely pass muster, people told me. The anecdotal evidence was powerful: a friend of a friend had just come back from Jamaica with a suntan, a semester's worth of credits and a mischievous twinkle in his eye. Surely I could make a stronger case for attending the oldest and arguably the finest university in Scotland.

Anyway, I had a sound plan to present in my defense. I planned to use my time in Scotland to research a thesis. I still had to decide whether or not I wanted to write a thesis and, if so, what I wanted to write about. I didn't actually have to make a final decision about doing one until well into my senior year, but the decision would make itself for me unless I began my research well in advance. And though I vaguely wanted to write about the history of golf, I knew I needed to come up with something specific. So it made sense to spend a year in St. Andrews—not only would I receive excellent instruction from the university's strong history department, but I would also be in the best place to research my thesis. I would have one of the world's best museums and numerous archives on my chosen subject at hand, and many other resources within reach. How could anyone fail to see that a year in St. Andrews would actually be *better* for me than another year at Harvard? Where else would you go to study golf?

I should have been beaming—my case was watertight. But as I sat before the chairman of the history department and tried to answer that all-important question, I was still afraid of being found out as a charlatan. There *was* something silly about telling a tenured, respected professor that the major achievement of your undergraduate career should be 100-odd written pages about golf. A proper thesis topic is something like "The impact of the carpet mite upon the textile industry in Bruges between 1631 and 1634." My best idea was to analyze whether or not the PGA Championship should go back to the match play format.

Of course, my stated reason for going to St. Andrews was a paper-thin façade. All I knew about the British Golf Museum was that it got lots of advertising on television during the British Open every summer. And I doubted I would even be writing a thesis. The university appealed to me because I had to take only two classes a semester—and spend only four hours in the classroom every week —to get a full year's worth of credits toward my college degree. That meant I'd have plenty of time to take advantage of this: as a resident of St. Andrews, I could buy a year's ticket good for unlimited play on all six of the town's golf courses—including the Old Course, the oldest and most famous 18 holes in the world—for £90, or around $150.

A hundred and fifty bucks won't even get you around the front nine at Pebble Beach—once! The first time I looked at that figure in pounds sterling and converted it to dollars, I was sure that I'd miscalculated or that the original figure was a typo. But it was indeed correct, and it made possible the year I *actually* wanted to spend in Scotland. My time in classrooms would be incidental to my real education on the Old Course and other timeless courses throughout Scotland. Whatever I might have said to the history department, I'd always taken my golf far more seriously than my degree.

I WAS THE number four man on my high school golf team my senior year, and I had no real plans to play college golf—not so much for want of desire but for a relative lack of talent. I didn't think my tournament average of just over 80 was good enough. But then my mother, who wanted me to choose Harvard over several other schools, told me that the Crimson practiced and played at The Country Club, Brookline—names that meant nothing to her but everything to her son. I figured that all else being equal, even if I got cut from the team, I'd still get to play a couple of rounds at a three-time U.S. Open venue. So I chose my college because of a golf course, made the team, forced my way into the playing squad with grit and determination, savored every afternoon I could spend among friends on 27 of the most sublime holes you could ever wish to play, and successfully avoided afternoon classes.

I knew all about The Country Club even before I arrived at Harvard, because my father had videotaped the final round and 18-hole playoff (Curtis Strange vs. Nick Faldo) of the 1988 U.S. Open at Brookline. I'd watched the video many times, and I had many others like it (I literally wore out my tape of the 1986 Masters by the time I finished high school). Great major championships, studied and vicariously relived, provided a solidity to my golfing life that my own abilities did not. I hated practicing, but through natural ability I'd shot in the low-to-mid-70s just often enough to raise my expectations beyond what was reasonable. When I fell far short of my unrealistic standards, I easily became moody or petulant. Poor days on a golf course contributed as much to my teenage timidity and uncertainty as anything else. Atlanta Country Club, my home course growing up, was the one place in the world where I repeatedly felt like a failure. Great courses and well-played rounds delighted me like nothing else, but I derived at least as much pleasure from watching and reading about the game as I did from playing it.

In a manner of speaking, I'd already abandoned Harvard for golf—I had to drive to my meeting in Robinson Hall because I was in the middle of a six-month internship at *Golf Digest* magazine. While at *Golf Digest*, I'd crafted my scheme to make golf the focal point of my education. I reexamined volumes written by ancients like Bernard Darwin, classicists like Herbert Warren Wind and neo-traditionalists like Michael Bamberger, anxious to glean as much information as I could about the best golf courses in Scotland. I bought a Michelin map of Scotland, and on it I circled and highlighted the red flags representing those courses worthy of possible study (relatively known quantities like Carnoustie and Muirfield) or exploration (far-flung outposts from Machrihanish to Dornoch to Cruden Bay, and everywhere in between). As I pored over my map late one night, devising the campaigns I was soon to undertake, I imagined I was General Patton, smiling at the thought of glorious battles to come. I analyzed histories of the British Open (or Open Championship, as it's properly known), anecdotal compendiums, a friend's videotape of the 1990 Open, and a number of old yardage books and photographic slides lying around the *Golf Digest* offices. And I reached an agreement to make contributions to *Golf Digest* while I was in Scotland in return for a monthly stipend and reimbursement for some travel expenses.

Couldn't the department chairman see these thoughts etched upon my face? I felt like one of those hapless British soldiers in *The Great Escape:* I had a good cover story with documents to back it up, but I knew that if I fluffed my lines I would be in very hostile territory. And I've never been a very good liar. Still, I believed in the nobility of my cause, and to me that justified everything.

At the tender age of 21, I'd had the good fortune to see much of the golfing world: I had played Pebble Beach, Cypress Point and Shinnecock Hills; partnered professionals like Bob Tway and Steve Jones; walked inside the ropes and into the players' lounge at PGA Tour events; and picked the wonderful golfing minds of Frank Hannigan, Peter Dobereiner, Jerry Tarde, Nick Seitz, Tom Callahan and many others for guidance and inspiration. But as long as I had not seen St. Andrews, nor deeply inhaled the rich scent of Scotland's ancient and mystical golfing traditions, I thought my education was pitifully incomplete. By wangling a year at St. Andrews, I wasn't merely doing myself a favor; I was righting a wrong. And because my "studies" would take place before sunset (rather than after Letterman), I knew I could approach them in a much more leisurely and thoughtful manner than I had ever approached anything at Harvard. I would not let my Scotland trip become some sort of package holiday, with so many Troons and Turnberrys flashing in and out of my horizon in a dun-colored blur. I wouldn't take any shortcuts: Scottish golf would give me a chance to learn how to learn all over again. The thought of that challenge intoxicated me as much as anything else.

So when the history department granted my request to spend a year playing golf in Scotland for credit, when the Inquisition softened its gaze and engaged me in witty banter about Scottish customs, I was more than just relieved; I was exhilarated. I floated across the Yard back to my car, delighted to have outwitted my institutional masters. And as I cruised back down the Mass Turnpike toward my job at *Golf Digest,* there was really only one question to be resolved: where, exactly, would I make that first tee time?

Chapter 1

FINDING MY THRILL

❖❖❖

I STAGGERED TO a halt halfway around Landsdowne Crescent, a block and a half short of my destination, and gasped for breath. How could Edinburgh be this hot in September? It felt like Houston in July—sweat poured down my forehead and arms, and my muscles turned to jelly with astonishing speed. I sank against a black wrought-iron fence, desperate to escape the sun's glare in the mottled shadow of several overhanging branches. Haymarket Station was close by, but both the street and the enclosed park behind the fence were deserted—not a taxi in sight.

I willed myself back to my feet, thinking only of a shower and sleep. Bending over, I gripped my leather duffel bag with my left hand and my bulky suitcase with my right, heaved them a full six inches off the ground and began to wobble forward. Veins bulging from my temples, I made it three-quarters of the way around the curve of the road before my luggage toppled back to the sidewalk with a muffled thud. Peering around nervously, I crept back down the road to where I'd left my rucksack and my overstuffed golf bag carrier and winched *them* over my shoulders, enthralled by the thought of torturing myself again, and again, and again.

In this manner, I huffed and puffed my way to the end of phase one of my Scottish journey. My stinginess bemused me greatly. I *could* have stuck to the legal luggage allowance for my flight from the States instead of cramming everything I could into four bags and gambling that the lady at the airline desk wouldn't compute the sum of their cumulative weights. I *could* have taken a cab from the train station instead of staging my impromptu weightlifting contest. And I *could* have chosen a slightly nicer place to spend my first night in Scotland than Eglington Youth Hostel, which, though eminently clean and well kept, wasn't exactly the Lodge at Pebble Beach. But I was already in hock to Harvard to the tune of five figures, and money was tight. I'd vowed not to touch what little I had before my two-day introduction to Scottish golf: 36 holes at Gullane, and 18 holes at North Berwick.

I've been a connoisseur of golf course architecture as long as I can remember. When I was seven years old, my family went to Hilton Head Island, South Carolina, during one of my school vacations. My father and I played Harbour Town (I shot 107 from the ladies' tees, although my mulligan tally is unrecorded), and afterwards in the pro shop I spied a copy of *Golf Digest's 100 Greatest Golf Courses —And Then Some* on a bookshelf, which my father bought for me. The round at Hilton Head, so different from any of my golfing experiences to that point, gave me an idea of what special golf courses looked and felt like. The book, filled with pictures and lists and diagrams and scorecards and tales of champions and championships past, made me dream of new worlds full of adventure and wonderment. Best of all, I knew that my fantasies could be made real, and since returning from that first eye-opening vacation I'd tried to live out as many of them as I could. As my tastes became more sophisticated my horizons broadened, and the prospect of a day's play at Gullane—itself hardly the stuff of my childhood fantasies—induced in me a restless night's sleep. I'd heard fine things about Gullane, particularly about its No. 1 course, and you can only play in Scotland for the first time once.

The next morning, after what felt like hours spent excavating my golf bag from among the clothing and linens in my carry case, I put most of my worldly possessions behind the front desk of the youth hostel and walked down to the Edinburgh bus station to catch a seat for the 45-minute ride to Gullane. I felt goofy carrying my golf bag through the downtown area of a major city and taking a bus to get to a golf course. I didn't imagine that many of my fellow passengers were rushing out of town for their tee times.

But a bus has its advantages. As we drove through the eastern suburbs, I was delighted to glimpse the white rails of the racecourse at Musselburgh, which meant I'd also spotted the links at Musselburgh, most of which is enclosed by the horse racing facilities. Now barely more than a museum piece, Musselburgh was one of only three courses to host the Open Championship prior to 1892 (the others were the Old Course and Prestwick). My pulse quickened further when I saw road signs to Aberlady and Longniddry—names into which I read important golfing connotations, even though there were none. (Aberlady has no course, and Longniddry a relatively unknown one.) At a bend in the road we passed an elegant-looking links partially etched into a hillside; thanks to my advance research,

I correctly deduced that it belonged to the Luffness club, reputed to be among the few exclusive and snobbish clubs in all of Scotland. Not much farther along, another taller, plateaued hill rose from the ground. It was smothered with golfers, and before I knew it, the panorama encompassed golf holes in every direction. Just short of a smallish-looking village, my bus came to a stop. I was the only person to get off.

I stopped to study the scene, and compared it with my preconceptions of Scottish golf. The size and scale of Gullane Hill notwithstanding, they matched almost perfectly, right down to the weather —gray skies, puffy clouds, a noticeable breeze. Apart from two middle-aged gentlemen who walked past wearing Medinah-logoed sweaters and baseball-style caps, nothing looked like America. Of the vegetation only the odd squat tree rose above ground level. The many fairways I could see were dappled in thin, greenish shades of dun, and the greens were a uniformly brownish shade of green. It was obvious which was the showcase course: unlike the No. 2 and No. 3 courses, which begin on the inland side of the main road, the No. 1 seemed to grow out of the town itself, as if it had sprouted from a seed planted just outside the members' clubhouse and been allowed to grow in a natural direction toward the sea. And since the Scots as a people don't believe in practice ranges, there was barely even room for a putting green between the town and the first tee. This wasn't the same game I played in the States, and it would have been wrong to pretend otherwise. Therefore I found it somehow appropriate that we tourists, fully welcomed but not wholly included, were consigned to the changing rooms, lounge and bar of a visitors' center on the inland side of the road.

The current members' clubhouse, a stately white building that dates back to 1928 but looks at least a century older, was merely one of a row of stately buildings running along the road on the right of the No. 1's first fairway. How many American golf clubhouses sit on public streets, tightly flanked by private houses? I had never been in one, nor seen one, nor even heard of one at any type of golf club in the States, from blue-collar municipal to blue-blooded Brookline. But in Scotland many clubhouses blend in with their surroundings thusly. (In Gullane's case, the buildings flanking the clubhouse are actually older than the clubhouse itself.) I can think of two reasons why this might be so; both of them appeal to me, for they explain in part why I find Scottish golf is so irresistible.

One of them has to do with the golf course architecture. The ancient Scots first coined the terms "outward nine," "turn" and "inward nine" because their courses were roughly linear: nine holes out to a point, nine holes back from there to the clubhouse (the "back nine"). In such a layout, only the first and 18th holes abut the clubhouse area. In contrast, most of the courses designed in America (and elsewhere) in the last 50 to 100 years form loops that return to the clubhouse twice (after 9 holes and after 18), and that means the real estate around the clubhouse must encompass at least four holes instead of two. Such layouts emphasize the importance of the club and its facilities relative to the golf course itself, and they don't leave much room for anything else—least of all buildings that aren't the pro shop, the snack bar or the caddie shack.

The other explanation is rooted more in social history. Golf in America has never been all-inclusive. America's first golf courses were built in the suburbs, away from the major population centers in areas where the wealthy often had large estates and land holdings. More significantly, the "Golden Age" of American golf course architecture (roughly between 1910 and 1930) coincided with the decline of the railroad and the rise of the automobile, and nowadays the vast majority of Americans get to their golf courses by car. Whether in 1909 or 1999, if you couldn't afford a car, you probably weren't high enough on the social ladder to play golf. So American golf clubs have always needed parking lots in the vicinity of their clubhouses, further insulating such clubs from their surroundings with wide moats of concrete. None of these facts are true in Scotland. Links golf predates motorized transport by centuries. Many people still walk from their homes to the first tees, especially at linksland courses near towns and villages like Gullane. You can't be too low on the social ladder to play golf in Scotland. The smallish parking lot at Gullane Golf Club is over the road by the visitors' center because the members don't need one.

Scotland's democratic approach to golf seduced me quickly. An insignificant student with neither influence nor connections, I was able to arrange tee times at time-honored private clubs like Gullane with only a politely written letter and a little advance notice. It would never occur to me to try this in America. While the golf club is very much a fundamental component of the Scottish community at large, in America it tends to serve as an escape from it. America has physically reclusive and socially exclusive country clubs populated by members living in gated communities. In Scotland, people think a town should afford virtually the same access to its golf courses, even the very best ones, as it does to its streets and parks. Sure, you have to pay your green fee, and at some clubs you have to change your shoes in the parking lot. But as I stood on the first tee at Gullane No. 1 and waited to hit my first shot in Scotland, I experienced an overwhelming sense of gratitude at having the chance to hit such a shot in the first place.

And the course . . . I loved every bit of it. I loved the way the conditions challenged my imagination as well as my golf swing. I loved the strategic impositions of the wind, and the obligation to attack on even the most difficult downwind holes for fear of losing ground on the upwind ones. I loved using my putter from any and every spot in the fairway within 20 yards of the green. (I'd always used my putter more than most, but now I could invoke Scottish tradition to justify my technique.) I loved the crispness of the sandy turf and the gentle reverberations conveyed from my divots to my hands along the shafts of my irons. I loved the simple, monochromatic flags on the greens—red for the No. 1 course, white for No. 2, yellow for No. 3—and the tingles of anticipation I felt every time I spotted a new red or white flag on a nearby hole. I loved the quirkiness of the chunky, zebra-striped directional poles—some of them placed to indicate the ideal aiming point to the golfer facing a blind shot, as intended, but some defining an obviously poor line of play, and one or two randomly assigned to holes with perfect sight lines, seemingly apropos of nothing. I loved the taste and texture of what the Scots called "bacon"—less crispy than its American namesake, but also meatier and juicier—as the luncheon roll I ate between rounds melted in my mouth. And I wholeheartedly loved how the breeze politely slackened in the afternoon, allowing me to take advantage of the relatively easy No. 2 course and record three birdies and a one-over-par score of 72. I kept most of my feelings to myself, but the adoration in my eyes must have made my playing partners want to retch.

My FIRST IMPRESSIONS of Scottish golf were so overwhelming, I find it very difficult to trust my judgments of Gullane Golf Club. But I think I'm on solid ground when I say that the most striking aspect of the No. 1 course was its imaginative layout, which incorporated the best features of the Scottish and American styles. It meandered out to the sea and back again, like a linear links, but it twisted and turned so often that from the third to the 13th I never played successive holes in the same direction. This rich variety, rare for a seaside course, overcame the principal drawback of the standard out-and-back layout, namely the monotony of playing as many as nine holes in a constant wind. The variety was strengthened by the incorporation of Gullane Hill into the design. Relatively few links holes can be classified as distinctly "uphill" or "downhill," but Gullane had several holes that fit these descriptions, and collectively they turned a potentially awkward aspect of the terrain into one of its most distinguished features.

The downhill seventh and 17th holes were both thrillingly vertiginous, but several of the uphill holes stand out in my memory. It's tough to design a good uphill hole. Nicklaus has been quoted as saying that his ideal golf course would have 18 downhill holes, and many of his fellow architects seem to view uphill holes as necessary evils: what goes down must come up again. But the fifth at Gullane No. 1, the No. 1 handicap hole, was a big-shouldered 450-yard par 4 that ascended and doglegged to the left with equal intensity, wrapping itself around the hill like a boa constrictor. Gigantic and dignified, it would nobly fortify the defense of par on any course. The 379-yard second was an even better hole. I had to drive into a tight fairway, with wispy, shin-high grasses beckoning on both sides. The approach, rising steeply and curving to a slender green nestled between dunes, somehow preserved my sight lines almost perfectly. A swale loomed just off the left fringe to catch any errant bounces. The green itself was a marvel, slender and canted severely from back to front. It was divided by an otherwise gentle ridge which, as I faced a lengthy putt from bottom to top, impersonated the north face of the Eiger. I couldn't have wished for a more thorough examination of my complete range of golfing skills in all of Scotland—and I'd only played one other hole.

What I loved most of all about the second hole at Gullane No. 1, though, had nothing to do with the golf course itself. As I stood on the green and looked back down the fairway, to my left I could see a pedestrian path carved out of the line of fescue-covered dunes flanking the fairway. The path couldn't have been designed to assist the golfer; even the vilest of slices wouldn't have gotten anywhere near it. It wandered up and down along the dune-tops, and on the rounded peak of the tallest one it passed in front of a wooden park bench. Sitting on it, one could certainly see beyond the second hole, and three other holes of the No. 1 course, and most of the No. 2 course, and all of the No. 3 course, to the fields, woods and buildings of the tranquil countryside beyond. But who might use it?

After holing out, I paused to ponder this question. I envisioned a white-haired Scotsman in woolens, a flat cap and knee-length boots walking his dog along the path on a blustery autumnal day, pausing on the bench to regain his stamina before continuing onward and upward. I could imagine picnickers, young and old, porting wicker baskets full of food and crockery up to the bench, where they might recline on a sunny afternoon and loftily spy upon those struggling to subdue the dastardly second green. As I stared toward the bench, I could also picture myself up there: gazing dreamily upon the ant-sized foursomes in the distance and the furrowed brows of golfers playing the hole beneath me, meditating upon the pluses and minuses of Scottish golf. I chuckled to myself. What minuses?

Chapter 2

PUTTING ON APPEARANCES

❖❖❖

BY THE END of my third day in Edinburgh, with a day still to go before I left for St. Andrews, I could find my way from the youth hostel to the bus station blindfolded. Apart from that, I think I saw a castle somewhere. I can be a terrible tourist sometimes.

My next destination, North Berwick, lay three miles farther along the same bus route I'd taken the day before. This time the bus dropped me off in the town itself, not far from the train station. I had to walk for several minutes to get from the main road to the golf course, which I found annoying, especially for East Lothianshire, where the town of Gullane possesses roughly one golf course for every 1,000 residents. North Berwick, with a population of around 7,000, has only two golf courses. Shocking. I imagine the gridlock between foursomes during the high season must be hideous.

The West Links at North Berwick introduced me to the quirky side of Scottish golf. Gullane's courses were thoroughly Scottish and linksy, but at least they resembled something that the average American club golfer might recognize. They had well-framed bunkers, no hidden hazards, a minimal number of blind shots, relatively smooth terrain with very few rough edges and no holes that were particularly confusing. North Berwick had at least half a dozen holes that made me scratch my head and wonder, What the heck is going on *here*? A number of the fairways looked like moonscapes. I hit a 3-iron off the tee on the par-4 first hole to lay up short of a lengthy chasm. Most of the first green hid behind a half-buried asteroid. I pushed my drive at the second hole onto the beach, nearly into the Firth of Forth (the inlet separating Lothianshire and Edinburgh from Fife and St. Andrews), and was rewarded with the flattest lie I would get all day. At the third my yardage book suggested I should "Drive at gap in wall," a freestanding stone wall that crossed the fairway 135 yards from the green. (A similar edifice directly guarded the front and right sides of the green at the short par-4 13th.) And so it went, hole by bizarre hole.

I was enchanted. I'd seen those sorts of creases, folds, humps and hollows in such abundance only once before, at Yale University Golf Course. *Golf Digest* had a corporate membership there, and every employee could play there twice a week. (When I started working for the magazine, we were allowed to play the course as often as we wished, so I did. The implicit "within reason" in this allowance somehow escaped my attention.) The Yale course was designed in 1926 by Charles Blair Macdonald,* one of those rare golf course architects

---

*As a point of historical fact, Seth Raynor, Macdonald's protégé and a fine architect in his own right, did much of the actual work on many "Macdonald" courses, including Yale. But this isn't widely known—I didn't know it at the time—so I will continue to call Yale a "Macdonald course." The style was first Macdonald's, even if the work at Yale isn't.

incapable of producing a boring hole, green complex or bunker. His spiritual kin among modern architects is probably Pete Dye, the evil genius behind in-your-face courses like the TPC Stadium Course at Sawgrass in Florida and PGA West in California. Macdonald's body of work, which includes incontestably grand courses like The National Golf Links of America on Long Island and Mid Ocean on Bermuda, is more consistently inspired than Dye's. But their shared defiance of convention and flair for excess marked them out as pioneers in their field; love them or hate them, the evolution of golf course architecture owes as much to both of them as anyone.

Most of my teammates at Harvard loathed the Yale course. It looked weird, with lots of corners and near-vertical slopes and misleading undulations, and it played even weirder. I think it scared them. Tournament golf at Yale on a dark, chilly April afternoon is the polar opposite of what you find in golfing holiday brochures. From a scoring perspective, we had to work very hard, mentally and physically, to avoid embarrassing ourselves. But I loved it. The whole course was so *different,* so relentlessly interesting—and it remained that way, even after many playings. Most architects bulldoze or work around funny-looking terrain features, but Macdonald was never afraid to use or even accentuate unnaturalness where he saw fit. He thought "outside the box" before the "box" had been constructed. For that I admire him greatly, although I will admit that some of the bunkers at Yale are so deep and steep-faced on one side, they look better suited for strip mining than for recovery play.

Before I arrived at North Berwick, I had Macdonald pegged as a real American original. (He was born in Canada to a Canadian mother and a Scottish father, but he did most of his work in the States.) Now, I'm not so sure. For one, Macdonald copied North

Berwick's "Redan" par-3 15th on nearly every course he designed in some form or fashion. Essential elements of the Redan, at North Berwick and elsewhere, are a green sloping from right to left and from front to back and a bunker guarding the green on the front left; it plays so well because the golfer can attack even the most inaccessible pin position, just behind the bunker, by drawing his tee shot and using the contours of the green to funnel the ball to the hole. Granted, the Redan is the most-copied hole concept in the world, but Macdonald re-created it so often he should have paid royalties. More curiously, the long 16th green at North Berwick is horizontally bisected by a trench two and a half feet deep. It looks like a feature you'd find after putting through the windmill and into the clown's mouth. As a one-off, it nearly works, but I'm not sure why anyone would want to copy it, let alone dig it twice as deep, which is what Macdonald did on the infamous "Biarritz" par-3 ninth at Yale. And then there's the generally jagged lay of the land to consider at both Yale and North Berwick; ignore the latter's seaside setting, and the two look eerily similar. I don't like Macdonald's work any less for having figured all of this out, but I would feel better if his courses were properly footnoted.

My playing partners at North Berwick, an English member of Royal Aberdeen and a German member of Royal Burgess in Edinburgh, both gave me their business cards and invited me up to their home courses in the future. In my experience, that usually means "in a future life"—it's good form to be polite to one's playing partners, but that's about it. However, over a drink in the clubhouse bar after our round, the German was particularly gregarious. He was a doctor who specialized in sports medicine. I inferred that his practice was thriving, because he said he was staying up the road at the

Greywalls Hotel, the super-posh establishment overlooking the links at Muirfield. At one point, he dipped into his wallet and produced a photograph of himself with one of his client-friends: Franz Beckenbauer, the legendary German soccer player. I was impressed.

"You *must* come to Royal Burgess," he said.

"Sure," I replied, half jokingly. "How does Tuesday work for you?"

"Perfect."

Wow, I thought. That's pretty good. If I keep this up, I will have played every course in Scotland by Christmas.

Royal Burgess turned out to be little more than a well-conditioned parkland course of only moderate character, but my host was so generous, it seems slightly churlish to say that my early visit to Edinburgh was anything less than fulfilling. He explained that though he was based in the Ruhr in Germany, he came back across to Scotland as often as his schedule and his wife would allow. I had to admire his discipline: if I were a doctor with as many Scottish contacts as he had, my patients would never see me.

THIRTY YEARS AGO, Scotland's main eastern rail service detoured through St. Andrews along its route between Edinburgh and Aberdeen, but that is no longer the case, and the golf in St. Andrews is much more peaceful as a result. The rail line used to terminate directly across from the 16th green of the Old Course, and I imagine that the magic of one's initial arrival in the town has been correspondingly diluted. The approach by road from the west still gets your blood pumping; a green carpet in the form of the Eden and Strathtyrum courses rolls along the A91 nearly a mile outside of town, and you can see through to the 18th hole of the Old Course and the famous Royal & Ancient clubhouse from a fair distance. But as an American, train travel was something of an Old World novelty to me, and it would have been really special to actually alight alongside the Old Course itself.

Instead, I stumbled off the train at Leuchars station, spilling my belongings onto the platform in my haste to ensure that nothing would be left behind. I was immediately approached by a red-haired, slightly freckle-faced girl wearing a gray-and-blue T-shirt emblazoned "University of St. Andrews Overseas Orientation Weekend." That's what I was there for, just over a week before the start of term, but I was somewhat disappointed at how easily I'd been spotted.

The girl smiled and quickly divined the source of my bemusement. "We tend to look out for people with slightly confused looks on their faces and lots of baggage," she explained. "Although when I did this last year, one time we wound up picking up someone's luggage by mistake, and he had to chase us all the way to St. Andrews in a taxi."

Her name was Heather. She asked me what school I went to in the States, and I told her.

"Hartford—that's in Connecticut, right?"

I blushed. She seemed very friendly, and rather cute besides, so I let her off lightly.

"Oh, last year I met someone from Hartford University, and I thought he'd said 'Harvard.' So I didn't want to make that mistake again. Oh, dear . . ."

I sat next to Heather in the front seat of the welcoming committee's white minibus. Although there would be more than 100 foreigners joining me in St. Andrews for this crash course on Scottish life and learning, I was the only arriving student on my train, so I had Heather and three other welcomers to distract me on the short ride to town. They tried to make conversation, but I was busy peering out the window, scanning the landscape for any and all signs of golfing life.

At the first roundabout on the edge of town we veered to the right, away from the main road. We circled around and drove back on a side road in the direction from which we had come—and there, dead ahead, was quite possibly the ugliest building I'd ever seen. It looked roughly like two battleships copulating. The thing oozed concrete, windows and obtuse angles. "What on earth is that?" I asked.

"That's Andrew Melville Hall," Heather replied. "That's where everyone is staying this week."

"Superb!" I rolled my eyes and grimaced.

Upon entering "Melville," as it is known to its inhabitants, the first thing I did was inquire about my future housing situation. Many university students lived in rented flats and houses during the academic year, but those who didn't were randomly assigned to one of the undergraduate Halls of Residence scattered throughout the town. I had lobbied for a posting to Hamilton Hall, the imposing former hotel that doubles as the main backdrop to the 18th green of the Old Course, but I couldn't support my application with anything more profound than "It would be terrifically inspiring to wake up every morning and see the Old Course directly beneath my window," so I was lumped back into the random draw.

I thought it a bit sadistic that the Melville staff member who answered my question had a smile on her face when she told me I wouldn't have to move out at the end of the Overseas Weekend. My heart sank. I covered my eyes with one hand and shook my head.

"But the people in Melville are so friendly!" she said.

It's a coping mechanism, I thought.

I soon learned that each of Melville's 250 student rooms had two windows and five walls; its architect apparently won some sort of prize for the way his design blended elements of the avant-garde and the functional. Whispers around Melville insisted that the architect also committed suicide shortly after its completion. (That seemed appropriate, although I've since learned that the architect, James Stirling, died in 1993, 25 years after Melville's doors first opened.) Nevertheless, the building slowly grew on me. Nobody shared rooms there; I would live fully on my own for the first time in my life. Melville's location on the North Haugh was terrible for walking to the golf courses (at least 10 minutes away) and the town center (15 minutes), but it was quite near the soccer fields and some of the other sports facilities. From both the elevated dining room and the lounge you could see out to the Old Course, and beyond that to the sea. And the Melville staffer was right: the people *were* friendly, not that I noticed any of them for a while. It took me a while to start thinking of people as friends and acquaintances instead of potential playing partners.

I SPENT THE rest of the first week selecting my classes, stocking up on school supplies, touring the town and getting acclimatized to the more banal realities of life in the Home of Golf. But apart from my trip to Royal Burgess, I didn't play any golf. I trekked down to offices of the St. Andrews Links Trust as soon as my weekend itinerary let me, but I discovered to my horror that I needed a student identification card before I could apply for my golfing season ticket, and the ID cards weren't being processed until Friday. I faced a serious test of the will: could I go cold turkey until then, or would I pay for à la carte links golf in St. Andrews? My withdrawal symptoms were severe, but I persevered as best I could.

That week, the Old Course stung like lemon juice rubbed in an open wound. I drifted out to it shortly after arriving at Melville, like a kid in a toy store irresistibly drawn toward the stuffed animals. Seeing it for the first time was like meeting a movie star in the flesh: I'd seen the Old Course, on television and in print, hundreds of times before, but that didn't dampen my enthusiasm. I wandered behind the 18th green and joined other tourists spaced along the green picket fence separating the course from the town.

The 18th hole on the Old Course has no bunkers, no water in play, not even any rough. For all that, it remains one of the two or three most instantly recognizable holes in all of golf. For many people around the world, the 18th hole on the Old Course *is* golf. The external landmarks catch the eye first: the tan-gray stone and stern dignity of the Royal & Ancient clubhouse, behind the adjacent first tee; the burnt-red grandeur of Hamilton Hall, behind the 18th green; in between these two, the Martyrs' Monument, a stone obelisk set back from the course which but for its permanence would look out of place; to the left of the fairway, the pointed starter's hut, the distant beach dunes and a glimpse of the sea; to the right, buildings of speckled gray stone, white paint and windows marking the north side of town. White railings toothcombed into the ground at five-yard intervals define the width of a fairway which, shared by the first and 18th holes, is as absurdly wide as everyone says—100 yards across. I looked at it and thought, How could you ever miss *that*? But people do, intimidated by the milling crowds and the history imbued in every divot. In a single foursome of tourists I saw teeing

off on the first hole, one man sliced his drive wildly out of bounds
to the right, and two others topped theirs and watched them drib-
ble down the fairway.

The moguls of the 18th fairway were wilder than I had imagined.
The closer the fairway gets to the green, the more unpredictably it
behaves, tossing and turning like a stormy sea until it reaches the
deep swale guarding the green known as the Valley of Sin—so
named because the price of repentance is steep for the golfer who
leaves his approach short. The fairway can look smooth from a distance, its contrasts muted in early-morning shade, misty haze or
high-noon sunshine. But when I saw the Old Course again in afternoon, with the sun lower in the western sky, the shadows cast by the
slopes danced among the taller, sun-crusted ridges in a swirl of
darkness and light. It didn't look flat then: its inscrutability was
bewitching.

The other hole I had to see immediately was the 17th. The Road
Hole is the toughest par 4 in golf and possibly the one hole in the
world even more famous than the 18th. I approached it in reverse,
walking down The Links road from the 18th green, past the shallow
Swilcan Burn—a walled, narrow stream which, as it crosses in front
of the first green, threatens the golfer on the Old Course with water for the one and only time. Over it stands the cobbled Swilcan
Bridge, upon which are etched the spike marks of nearly every notable professional and amateur golfer through the centuries. (Ben
Hogan never played the Old Course, but I don't think there are any
other notable exceptions.) These timeless landmarks diverted my attention briefly, but the Road Hole drew me back. Its beginning hid
behind the massive, cream-colored Old Course Hotel and the
smaller, dark green faux reconstructions of the old railway sheds that

pinched into the line of play from the tee. Behind its green, 461 yards from the tee, I stood on the hole's eponymous hazard: shots falling off the steep bank at the back of the green roll over a path of pinkish gravel and an intermediate membrane of grass onto a wide stretch of weatherbeaten, cracked concrete. Balls coming to rest on the road, or against the stone wall on another strip of grass beyond the road, must be played as they lie. This single local rule has caused more golfers more grief than arthritis and Pete Dye put together. Yet they would rather miss the Road Hole green long or to the right than to the left, for the Road Bunker, six feet deep on its greenward side and not much wider, deserves its reputation as the toughest sand pit in golf. I couldn't see more than the top rim of Road Bunker from where I stood, peering from the far edge of the road near the wall, out of harm's way. I figured I'd get up close and personal with it sooner than I liked.

Beyond these first, preliminary studies of the Old Course, my self-enforced look-but-don't-touch policy began driving me crazy. Golf radiated through the town from the linksland: St. Andrews has a rich non-golfing history, but the Old Course is the town's meal ticket, the beacon that makes it shine brighter than all but Scotland's biggest cities. On The Links road, North Street and Market Street alone, I counted nine independently owned golf shops selling balls, gloves, clubs and unofficial souvenir merchandise. Other shops on Golf Place, the road behind the R&A clubhouse and in front of Hamilton Hall, sold rare golf books and vintage playing equipment. Every sweater store worth its cashmere vended logoed Old Course products. St. Andrews pubs and hotels identified themselves with the golf industry in many ways, some (like the St. Andrews Golf Hotel) less subtle than others. Even the cemetery was full of dead golfers proudly identified as such; the shrine to Young Tom Morris, near the graveyard's southeastern corner, is an essential part of all proper tours of St. Andrews.

Every time I left Melville, my horizon encompassed the Old Course, but I still dared not pay to play it. No matter how desperate I became, the stupidity of paying two-thirds the price of a season ticket to play one measly round remained inescapable. And while I waited for my store of patience to run out, I did discover an ersatz solution to my plight: in lieu of a proper round, on a sunny midweek afternoon I journeyed down to the Himalayas putting course, which had a green fee I could afford: 50 pence ($0.80).

In Scotland, "putting" is a recreational activity in its own right. Virtually every city, town and village has at least one putting green available for public use. There is a remarkable one in Edinburgh, situated at the base of the deep valley between the main high street and the towering castle, but most are more mundanely sited. St. Andrews has several, most of which are well removed from any of the golf courses; the most central one is adjacent to the bowling green by the bus station. The holes are typically arranged on each green in a circular rotation defined by numbered flagsticks, which are usually painted red, made entirely of metal and less than one foot tall. (Those on the Himalayas course are taller, painted white and made of wood.) The greens are never mowed closely enough to make serious practicing really worthwhile, so friendly competition is usually the order of the day.

What's fascinating about recreational putting is that people who wouldn't be caught dead on a proper golf course flock to it. I played my first round on the Himalayas as a single player sandwiched between foursomes, and normally I would have obsessed about the glacial pace of play. But the quality of the people-watching was so outstanding, I hardly noticed. There were teenagers, boys and girls, dressed in jeans and sneakers and soccer shirts, giggling as they putted from hole to hole. One foursome of female Japanese tourists tried to complete the course without unstrapping their cameras from their necks. Four generations of one family seemed to be represented in one pair of back-to-back groupings; the toddler putted only occasionally, but he waddled around all 18 holes with little or no assistance from his great-grandparents. The backdrop to all of this was quite extraordinary, for only the Swilcan Burn divides the Himalayas from the first and second holes of the Old Course. Some of the putters looked as though they never would have dreamed of using the Old Course as anything other than a thoroughfare or a soccer pitch, and to see them laughing and savoring the delights of something very closely related to golf itself was like watching a parade of diehard Marxists weeping and dancing ecstatically up and down Wall Street. It was moving, and made little sense.

Most of the "putting" greens I've seen have been flat and decidedly ordinary, but the Himalayas green fits neither description. The western half of the course has some of the most steeply graded golf terrain in all of St. Andrews, with all sorts of curvy peaks and ridges jutting upward from ground level. The greenkeeper typically chooses to cut the cups into the depressions between these obstacles, which means that on some holes a disproportionate number of putts funnel into the general vicinity of the cup. I have seen total novices slalom impossible-looking putts into the hole from distances in excess of 50 feet quite often because of this. But such wild mounding also puts quite a premium on lag putting, the expert golfer's science of stroking long approach putts to within tap-in range at worst, and

I became all too aware that poorly-struck or poorly-read putts can drift yards away from the hole with distressing ease.

A group known as the Ladies Putting Club has the Himalayas course to itself during certain hours on some afternoons. I can't get my head around the concept of a putting green with a membership, but its existence says quite a lot about the unique nature of the Himalayas. I couldn't imagine how anyone with an evenly matched opponent and even a remote interest in the art of putting could ever tire of the Himalayas. It isn't "golf" as such, but it's close, and when it comes to value for tourist money, you can't spend a better hour in St. Andrews.

I FELT MUCH better for my Himalayas experience, but the rest of the week still crawled by. As soon as I received my student ID on Friday afternoon, I sped out to the Links Trust offices to get all of my documentation processed. By Saturday morning I had my credit-card-size St. Andrews golfing passport in hand, and shortly after lunch on Saturday afternoon I marched down to the starter's desk for both the New and Jubilee courses. I wanted golf, and I wanted it quickly. I didn't have a tee time, but in St. Andrews that isn't really a problem: every singleton golfer has the right to link up with any twosome or threesome he wishes on the first tee at any time on any course, including the Old. (The New Course hardly accepts bookings at all—except for a small block of tee times allocated every day to out-of-town visitors, it is entirely first-come, first-serve.) But as far as I was concerned, the Old Course could wait. In my condition, I needed meat-and-potatoes sustenance; caviar would have been wasted on me. Besides, the queue for singles at the Old can be quite lengthy, and I needed an immediate fix.

It took me less than 15 minutes to get a game on the Jubilee Course with a trio of local working-class men in their thirties. They spoke with guttural accents that were nearly but not quite decipherable. Two of them wore blue jeans. Nobody else around me seemed to find this odd. I was quite surprised to later learn that the unwritten dress code for local golfers in St. Andrews seems to be "business casual," as defined by one's current or most recent place of employment. (Bankers, professors and certain classes of retirees typically don formal tweeds, cashmeres and the occasional necktie, but blue-collar workers very often wear jeans and occasionally even collarless shirts to the links.) For the first time I felt inclined to crinkle my nose at the come-as-you-are nature of Scottish golf. But then, who was I to insist upon khakis and knitted cotton? And can any sport capable of producing the likes of Doug Sanders, Payne Stewart and Jesper Parnevik really take its dress code too seriously?

We teed off, and at once the wind howled, nearly knocking my cap off my head in disapproval. The adjacent North Sea was dark and choppy, the sky uniformly gray and intimidating. I zipped up my windbreaker as a chill permeated the air. I hadn't really noticed any of this in my haste to get started, but I certainly did after I missed an 18-inch bogey putt at the first. Sinister elements of my imagination began to hijack my round. I soon saw prickly gorse bushes lying poised for ambush by the dozen, on both sides of every fairway and behind every green. Crooked numbers invaded my scorecard, jumping from one box to another seemingly without my pencil's intervention. In disgust, I banged clubs down on several holes.

The wind buffeted my swing plane into submission very quickly. On the short par-3 fifth, I ballooned my attempt at a punched 8-iron high into the air. It was a poor shot; I thought it was lucky to sneak onto the front right corner of the green, about 60 feet from the hole. When I reached my ball, I discovered that a gaping, rounded bunker lay directly in my line. The pin was located on a four-foot-high tier in the back corner of what I now appreciated was an "L"-shaped green. I laughed bitterly. The only way I could sneak my ball anywhere onto the top tier without taking a divot out of the green—a high-risk, low-chance-of-ever-playing-in-St.-Andrews-again-if-a-marshal-sees-you sort of shot—involved using the inner bank of the bunker as a ramp. And I thought the Himalayas were wild. Never has anything on natural grass so obviously screamed "four-putt!" at me, and in the end I took my double bogey gracefully.

I reached the turn in 49 strokes. The wind roared even more venomously; the holes around the turn lay closer to the sea than any others in St. Andrews, and before nature's fury I felt more naked than ever. I started the back nine as follows: 5, 6, 6, 5, 6, 6, 7. I detested the 15th hole, which I immediately nominated as the worst short par 4 I'd ever seen. In any kind of wind it was unplayable by mere mortals. Its fairway didn't exist: all I saw was gorse and tall grass. The green towered above sea level and sloped defiantly from back to front. A short shot would kick left into thick grass or 40 yards backward down a 30-foot-high ramp last seen during the Winter Olympics moonlighting as a ski jump. Anything even marginally long or right would end up in the gorse, with no viable drop zones nearby. I tried to hit a short-iron into the green—as my third shot—and I swear I heard the wind screech, "Yeah, right! Bring it on, punk!" I did supremely well to save double bogey; my playing partners, decent enough golfers themselves, carded two eights and a nine.

We were all trying our best, but it was the sort of day that explains why the Scots are so much keener on match play than most Americans. One can be "three down" without feeling the need to apologize for anything. "Three up" is even better, for it can mask an awful lot of one's own horridness. But a single-digit handicapper will have a bit of explaining to do if someone asks him how he's playing and he has to reveal that he's just moved to a cool 22 over par.

In fact, as I stood on the tee of the pentultimate hole something suddenly dawned on me, and I hurriedly pulled out my scorecard and totted up the figures I had been doing my best to ignore. The resulting calculation caused me to shiver: I needed to finish no worse than bogey-bogey to break 100. And the final two holes were into the wind. I gulped and tried to remember when I had last renewed my membership in the Century Club. Age 13, perhaps, during my days as a touring member of the Atlanta Junior Golf Association? I had no golf swing and very little self-respect left to speak of, but nevertheless I gritted my teeth and with a renewed sense of purpose launched my body into my tee shot on the uphill, upwind, 211-yard par-3 17th. I chose a driver, hit it decently enough, and was lucky to land in a narrow strip between hillocks, three-fourths of the way to my target. I still had a full pitching wedge left into the green, and I hit it pretty well, but I only found the front fringe. Still, after a good approach putt and a tap-in, I was halfway to safety.

The 18th was 437 yards long. Could I cover 437 flattish yards in three shots and two putts? I threw all my weight into another swing with my driver off the tee, and my ball fluttered to earth well short of the two pot bunkers on the left side of the fairway. Another passably struck driver stayed in the fairway and fetched to within 100 yards of the hole. For my third I chose my 5-iron and aimed well to the left of the pin, hoping to ride the quartering wind into the heart of the green. I swung, and for an instant the contact felt good, and the ball began curving the way I wanted. But it kept sliding to the right and flew beyond the green as well, finishing a good 30 yards away from the hole. I sighed and braced myself for the inevitable. My pitch was poor. And my 25-footer didn't threaten the cup.

I shook the hands of my playing partners and trudged disconsolately back to Melville. The click-clacking of my spiked shoes as I crossed a North Haugh parking lot sounded like mocking, staccato applause. Back at Melville I had to go to the bathroom, so I wandered down the corridor and a staircase leading to my new dorm room, dropped my golf bag and crossed the hallway to the communal toilet facilities. Closing the door, I noticed something that caused me to stop and stare at the toilet. There, etched on the toilet's cistern, was presumably the name of the company that had molded that particular bit of porcelain: SHANKS. I scowled.

Chapter 3

SOMETHING OLD,
SOMETHING NEW

❖❖❖

THE START OF the school year was still several days away, but the rhythm of my St. Andrews experience began to settle into a pattern I hoped wouldn't change. The main questions on any given day were three: Would I play golf? If so, when would I play it? And *where* would I play it? I didn't have to worry about with whom I would play it, for the Links Trust starters could take care of that for me. And for the moment, I didn't have to worry about other messy entanglements like classes and homework. I didn't expect to worry much about them anyway, to be honest. The only appointments I really had to keep were in the Melville dining hall; although my first impressions of the facilities therein were somewhat underwhelming, I knew I'd paid for my meal plan already, so I might as well take my chances. Otherwise, I kept my eyes on the prizes my Links Trust season ticket let me claim.

One day after being tortured by the "Jube," as the locals call it, I steeled myself for the New Course, feeling eminently masochistic but still very much hoping to shoot a round in double figures. I birdied the first hole, a short par 4 of just over 300 yards. I birdied the sixth hole, a long and tight par 4 with a fairway flanked by gorse and a ridiculously sloped and tiny green. I birdied the 13th hole, a fun one-shotter soon to become one of my favorite par 3s in all of Scotland. I made a few mistakes here and there, but my swing seemed fine. And the course was extremely pleasant, a solid test loaded with strong holes and fun holes and fun strong holes, receptive to good shots but punishing to bad ones. Against a par of 35-36-71, I shot 40-38-78. I felt like a good golfer again.

The next day, I played the New for a second time. I couldn't find a fairway, and my threesome spent an eternity poking and getting pricked by gorse bushes while searching for my wayward drives. After seven holes, I was 10 over par. I finished the round with a score of 46-45-91: no birdies, four double bogeys and two triple bogeys.

Anyone who has ever read or heard anything about Scottish golf or even watched a few hours of any British Open on television will know that wind is an important part of the links golf experience. But it took me three wildly dissimilar rounds in St. Andrews before I began to appreciate just how much the wind is *the* defining component of golf courses as exposed as those in St. Andrews, without appreciable clusters of dunes or trees to provide the occasional pocket of calm. On a normal day in the flatlands, the wind gets first in your jacket, then in your bones, then in your brain, and pretty soon you've forgotten what a "normal" 5-iron shot looks like. The same swing with the same club can produce a shot that either starts and finishes more or less on line but flies 200 yards and rolls another 50,

impersonates a lead balloon after a 50-yard takeoff, or swerves lat-
erally in a parabolic curve usually seen only in algebra textbooks.

The phrase "club selection" came to mean something entirely new
for me in Scotland. It never really mattered what club I used on any
given shot—forced carries of any distance are rare on links holes,
and on most of them there is room to bounce the ball into the green,
if not necessarily at the pin. So I could achieve the same result from
100 yards with anything from a sand wedge to a 3-iron given
enough thought, shot preparation and the courage to swing with
conviction. What mattered was the care with which I chose my clubs
at the start of my round. The Rules of Golf allow you to carry 14
of them, but I had 15 that I wanted to use: driver, 3-wood, irons
numbered one to nine, three wedges, putter. So I had to take care in
choosing my ideal set composition from day to day. As a rule, on
windy days I omitted my 3-wood, which flies higher than my 1-iron,
and on calmer days I removed my 1-iron, for the opposite reason.
But on some days I rode my luck and cast aside my lob wedge, hoping to be lucky and avoid the perils of St. Andrews's deeper pot
bunkers. It was always a tough decision, and once or twice I com-
promised by leaving my 2-iron behind instead.

Then there is the singular suffering of playing in a Scottish gale:
my putting stroke all but dissolved. Previously an upright, Cren-
shavian glide, my method rapidly devolved into the wristy twitch of
a hunchback searching in vain for a brace against the wind. Sometimes the wind rocked me back on my heels, perpendicular to the
line of play, in unison with my backswing. I searched for more balance, spreading my feet so wide on occasion that I felt more like a
gymnast than a golfer. Then there were the effects of the wind upon
a rolling ball. The science of green-reading, normally an elementary

study in contour, can become a mind-boggling exercise in physics when wind direction and velocity enter the equation. Putts aren't supposed to break uphill. I used to think that stories of the wind's effects on putting were old wives' tales used exclusively by television commentators and poor putters, but no more. I'm a good putter, but I missed more 18-inch putts in Scotland—including four in my Jubilee round alone—than I have in the rest of my mature golfing life.

Eventually Mother Nature and I reached a modus vivendi. I agreed to greatly overclub myself whenever the wind wasn't directly behind me, to accept that sometimes par is a pipe dream and double bogey a good score, and to work tirelessly on my course management skills whenever and wherever possible. Mother Nature agreed that I wouldn't shoot in triple digits ever again. After several weeks of links golf experience and practice, my wind game improved to where any round in the 90s was a disaster. Very generally speaking, my scores settled into three distinct ranges: low 80s to high 80s when very windy; high 70s to mid-80s when breezy; and mid-70s to low 80s when calm. I was happy to get any calm days at all, and surprised to get a pretty fair number of them. I could dismiss the high numbers as aberrations: potentially good scores borne by the wind quite unfairly into hacker territory. But even as I rationalized, the variability of my scores continued to bother me. It still does, even now.

I CONFESS: I have always been addicted to keeping score. As I grew into an adult golfer, I simply could not get my head around the idea that I could play golf noncompetitively, or without a scorecard. Other guys could do what they liked, but I always tried to putt out on every hole in even the most informal of settings. I've always wanted to start and finish each hole with the same ball, penalty strokes notwithstanding, which is why I prefer stroke play over less straightforward formats like the scramble. Even in practice rounds before big high school and college tournaments, I was ambivalent about the common custom of dropping balls and playing them for practice purposes, thinking that doing so meant corrupting the integrity of the game itself. (The Rules of Golf forbid practicing on a hole until you've finished it, and even then you're only allowed to putt and chip around the green of the hole just finished and the tee of the hole not yet begun.) A sage man once advised that one should always practice golf as though playing, and play golf as though practicing. I've always been excessively good at the former, but problems often arise when I go out on a course under tournament conditions and become even more intense, not less.

It is difficult for me to explain how I evolved into a manic scorekeeper, just as I find it hard to analyze how I became so fascinated with military history, why I dislike the taste of most fruits and vegetables, or any of the other peculiarities that make me "me." But because golf is a game that can be enjoyed in many different ways and from multiple perspectives, it's worth discussing why I look at golf the way I do. Why are the birdies, bogeys and worse chronicled in this volume worth chronicling?

I've always been insanely competitive about nearly everything—golf, most other sports, chess, Trivial Pursuit, high school grade point average—that can be objectively measured. But over the years I often found myself playing golf alone, in the company of gentlemen 30 or more years my senior, or with people I have never met before. As a shy teenager, any of these were enough to deter me from seeking competition, and that meant the only opponent available to me was the golf course itself. Sports psychologists say that to shoot better scores, you should try not to keep track of how you stand relative to par during your round, but for me that advice largely misses the point. Where is the thrill of competition when you ignore the opposition until after the game is over? When I equaled par over 18 holes for the first time, I knew full well that I needed to hole a 15-foot birdie putt on the final green. What if I had strolled away from that green and had to do a bit of mental arithmetic before realizing what I had done? Wouldn't my sense of accomplishment have been diminished, my joy at the outcome dimmed?

Much of my golfing experience has come in tournament golf. Par is the sole opponent in such circumstances, where rumors about "the leaders" are rarely trustworthy and the scores of one's playing partners best ignored. I know the old tournament saying: 90 percent of the people don't care what you shot, and the other 10 percent wish it was worse. But I do my best to provide a public service and listen when people tell me of birdies made and shots thrown away in their rounds. I even try to look and sound interested. Because whatever they may think about everyone else, it's amusingly obvious that 100 percent of all tournament golfers care about their own scores.

Another thing about score: it lingers in the memory. I was born in 1974. Am I too young to reminisce? Possibly, but I have been playing golf since I was three, and the old scorecards I keep in a shoebox on a bookshelf at home never cease to delight me. When I was younger, I used to record not only scores but also statistics for each hole I played: fairways hit, greens hit, putts, up-and-down chances converted around the green. I laugh at myself now for having been such an intense child, but that same seriousness made it

possible for me to now look at a scorecard from a course I barely remember and piece together details about what most of the holes
looked like and what it felt like to play them. Score brings into focus
personal milestones, half-forgotten feats, even awful rounds as though
they happened yesterday. But even when I don't really remember
that I did something, I have it on pretty solid evidence that I did.
For sheer narcissistic satisfaction, nothing beats telling yourself
strange and exciting stories about your own achievements.

Score also allows golf to turn chaos into order. On the tee of every
hole, we begin with a barely comprehensible jumble of thoughts
and emotions. We are swing doctors and golf course architecture
critics and sports psychologists and meteorologists and agronomists
and traffic wardens and fathers/brothers/sons (or mothers/sisters/
daughters), all at once. And then our minds drift away, and we become entranced by the natural beauty around us, or wonder how the
Red Sox are getting on today, or remember we left the light on in
the bedroom—hardly the best preparation for what is to come. And
then we swing a club back and forth and propel a white ball forward.
We do everything in a same-yet-different way all over again and
again and again, and when the ball goes into the hole we write down
a number on our scorecards. That number defines a period of between 5 and 20 minutes of our lives. It doesn't say whether or not
we have been good or bad people during that time period, but it
does tell us whether or not we've been good or bad golfers. And after compiling 18 of these numbers, we have enough evidence to tell
us beyond a reasonable doubt whether we can set our minds and
bodies about a particular task, seeing it through for better or worse.

That's one view of the game, though I only wallow in it when I'm
in my more Romantic moods. But the inescapable logic of the score-

card has always drawn me to golf. I can cope with an untidy desk or a cluttered bedroom, but especially as an intense teenager, my mind craved the logical order that score could provide. Par is one of sport's best and most accurate measuring sticks; thanks to the handicap system, one can equitably rank every golfer in the world—man, woman and child—along a continuum. I often wonder how many thousands of golfers are better than me, and when plagued by self-doubt and frustration, it would give me great satisfaction to know how many millions are worse. Because I keep score every time I play, I can efficiently monitor my rate of improvement or decline. Baseball players who get only four at bats per game, defensive backs who face 10 passes every week and tennis players who play three sets a day cannot precisely pinpoint their progress the way I can.

That is, before I started reckoning with the vagaries of Scottish weather. Upon arriving in St. Andrews I took the extreme measure of setting up a simple, computerized database to keep track of my Scottish golf experience, round by round and hole by hole. I called it my Scottish Record, and its existence proved I had embraced my obsession; only a very uptight person could have dreamed it up. Nevertheless, I hoped it might help me answer questions such as: Which specific holes in St. Andrews are giving me trouble? Do I score better on a diet of six rounds a week or two? When would I play my best and worst golf, and would I be able to ascertain why my peaks and valleys occurred when they did? Would I be a better golfer when I left Scotland than when I arrived?

Three rounds later, most of my schemes were in tatters. The same golfer had, in the space of three days on golf courses of comparable difficulty, shot rounds of 28, 7 and 20 over par. Four rounds near Edinburgh the previous week had resulted in scores of 12, 1, 5 and

6 over par. How is it possible for one person to go from +1 to +28 in nine days, or from +28 to +7 and nearly back again in two? Given constant conditions, it isn't. Worse, I can't accurately assess the quality of my 78 relative to my 91, because in the wind, the truth of score becomes subjective. This threw my entire system of logic out of kilter. Looking back, I only know one thing about my Scottish Record with certainty: any day I shot in the low-to-mid-70s, I must have played really well, *but* there also must have been little or no wind. That "but" looms like a gigantic asterisk; Scottish golf is all about mastering the wind, not avoiding it. And every other score leaves me scratching my head—there's no way to tell a "good" 82 from a "bad" one, and I might have played better in a round of 86 one day than in a round of 79 the next. Baseball fans will understand the difficulty of comparing facts when benchmarks and conditions vary. Who had the better year, Roger Maris in 1961 (61 homers in a 162-game season) or Babe Ruth in 1927 (60 homers in a 154-game season)? Who pitched better, Bob Gibson in 1968 (1.12 ERA from an elevated mound during the "Year of the Pitcher") or Pedro Martinez in 1999 (2.07 ERA in the era of the designated hitter and the juiced ball)? You can't be sure.

The Scots have a solution to this conundrum: match play. One can only speculate, but I suppose that the earliest golfers would have derived the truth of their game solely from head-to-head competition. Conditions from day to day and round to round were wildly varied and wholly unquantifiable, especially when the rudimentary layout of the course was itself subject to change. But two golfers in the same group playing against each other didn't have this problem. So why try to measure score against a fixed benchmark like par? Imagine if golfers were rated by their win-loss percentages instead of strokes taken, and you might have a sense of what competitive golf must have been like before the first formal stroke play competition was held, in St. Andrews, in 1776. (The irony of that date isn't lost on me: stroke play golf and America were obviously made for each other.) Things aren't much different today. On windy days in modern-day St. Andrews, there are three options: stay inside; forget about par and struggle against bogey; or measure your progress against friend and neighbor instead of counting strokes. The Scottish golfer chooses the last course of action, hands down.

It is to my discredit that I find the match play format incredibly awkward because it reduces par to an irrelevancy: putts to halve holes struck with an all-or-nothing decisiveness alien to stroke play; scores of bogey and double bogey losing in equal measure to an opponent's par. And what score do I write on my card when my opponent calls my putt a gimme and knocks it away from the hole? I want score to exist even when it doesn't want to. And that paradox places me in strange situations when I try to have the best of both stroke and match play worlds.

To illustrate: Suppose I'm facing two tricky, curving, five-foot downhill putts. Both are identical, except one of them is to halve a hole at match play, while the other is to par a hole at stroke play. Suppose I feel that in order to maximize my chances of making this five-footer, I have to hit it at a speed that would make it go 10 feet by if I miss. What do I do in each scenario? In the match play situation, there is no ambiguity: I have to ram the putt and try to hole it. In stroke play, though, my ultimate objective has to be weighed against the possible consequences of missing. Given a difficult putt, the smart play is usually to hit it at the speed that will produce the best average score. Even if you miss the putt more often than you would if you charged it at the hole, presumably you'll save shots on average. But one cannot serve two masters simultaneously, and this is why I've always been terrible at match play: I can't help but worry about par before I worry about my opponent. I'm compelled by the urge to score. If that means not giving myself the best chance to win or halve a hole, so be it. The sad thing is that I enjoy the good-natured competition and banter of typical, informal Scottish match play. But I've always been so absorbed by my scorecard, I can hardly loosen up enough to enjoy myself.

To MY RELIEF, my stroke play vs. match play struggle did not ruin my first round on the Old Course, which began within an hour of the conclusion of my first university lecture. In due time, I would form an excellent relationship with my history professor; he, like me, was a transplanted American living and loving life in St. Andrews, and his course on Britain in the Era of the Great War was as enjoyable and informative as any I'd taken at Harvard. But during that first session I could think of one thing and one thing only. As soon as we were dismissed, I walked speedily back to Melville, had a very quick bite to eat, grabbed my clubs and went straight to the white starter's hut adjacent to the R&A clubhouse.

My first wait for a game on the Old Course was mercifully short. Within half an hour, I was able to join a threesome of American tourists. I sensed that they weren't interested in head-to-head competition at all, and on this occasion neither was I. I wanted to conquer the Old Course in the same way I'd seen Ballesteros, Faldo and Daly conquer it on television—at stroke play. And as much as possible, I wanted to do it alone; I was polite toward my companions, but for the next four hours I withdrew mostly into myself, into the fantasies I'd created for myself about the round I wanted to play on the Old Course. As with my first round at Gullane, I wondered how my dreams of the Old Course would measure up to my first impressions.

This time, though, my compass mostly malfunctioned. I recognized all the holes plainly enough, and I coaxed fair results out of many of them, but something didn't quite feel right. For all my advance knowledge and preparation, nothing could have prepared me for the sensation of cluelessness that overwhelmed me. In a sense, I would have been better off stepping straight off a tourist bus and onto the first tee, with no idea about what was about to hit me, for then I might have expected to encounter the enigmatic creature that the Old Course always is at first glance.

Score, I thought, should have everything to do with the *collaboration* of mind and body. But even if the body knows exactly how to swing the golf club, if the mind doesn't know where to aim, score always comes down to chance. While the Old has few out-and-out blind shots, the shots where I felt mentally blind were numerous. Important hazards were hidden better than I thought they'd be; equally crucial contours were imperceptible from a distance. The Old posed unique questions, and though I frequently consulted my newly purchased yardage book, I couldn't find many of the answers. Many first-timers like to pay a member of the Old Course's legendary caddie corps to find the answers for them, but even if I could have afforded one, letting someone else do my thinking for me wouldn't really have helped me in the long term. While I still found my fair share of fairways and greens in regulation, I didn't feel as if I'd done much to deserve to find them. At the seventh, where I made my one birdie of the round, I hit my approach shot to within 10 feet of the hole, but rather than rejoice when I discovered my ball was so close to the pin, I was first moved to exclaim, "The green does *that?*" Obviously, I had much to learn.

After 12 holes I was still only two over par. My score definitely flattered me, but that didn't make the correction I suffered over the next four holes feel any less painful; playing into a slight breeze, I double-bogeyed the 13th, bogeyed the 14th, double-bogeyed the 15th, and then hit my first drive out of bounds on the par-4 16th en route to a quadruple-bogey eight. The first three of these scores were as random as the many pars I'd pumped out of the front nine, but I knew I'd been had on the 16th, where a trio of famous bunkers collectively known as the Principal's Nose blocked the straight path to the green. The safe drive would have gone to the left of the bunkers; I knew this, but with false bravado I tried to play down the narrow chute between the Principal's Nose and the fence line to the right and was deservedly punished when I blocked my drive almost into the practice area well beyond the fence. It was a harsh tutorial in strategy, but I took it in stride. A quadruple bogey was a small price to pay if the lesson stayed learned.

And from the two holes I'd already studied, I coerced results that I felt I fully deserved. The Road Hole played into the wind; from the tee, I understood why the 17th was a par 5 until the late 1950s. I faded my drive expertly over the corner of the railway sheds and blasted a second driver from the fairway straight at the green, but I came up 20 yards short. Still, I discovered that when the pin isn't tucked behind Road Bunker, the up-and-down from the fairway is almost straightforward. I lagged my putt nicely up and over the bank at the front of the green; it curled slightly to the left and stopped six feet from the pin. I stroked my par putt sweetly into the middle of the hole.

And I was lifted, not intimidated, by the history of the 18th. I played it straight: drive, short-iron into the middle of the green, two putts. I knocked in my final three-footer and waved cheekily to the "gallery" of casual spectators. I thought of all the Open contenders who would have killed for a par-par finish. Though my score of 82 seemed excessive, my finish led me to pronounce myself mostly satisfied. I'd get to know the Old Course much better in due time, I thought, and I figured I could shoot better numbers as well.

My love for golf has always run deeper and wider than score. I can lose track of this in my self-centeredness sometimes, but events usually jolt me back to a more balanced view. Rarely, though, does a golf course affect me along these lines quite the way that Carnoustie did.

My day trip to Carnoustie in early October was the first of several I planned to make by rail and bus to those noteworthy courses within range of St. Andrews. Carnoustie seemed an ideal place to start: only 25 minutes away from Leuchars by train, it has a championship course that most students of golf course architecture hold in great esteem. Ben Hogan completed his Triple Crown of majors (Masters, U.S. Open, British Open) there in 1953. Tom Watson won the first of his five Opens there in 1975. Tommy Armour, Henry Cotton and Gary Player won there, each giants of his day. Everything—the history, the golf course itself, its convenience— made it a trip worth taking.

But from the moment I arrived, Carnoustie was a real disappointment. In fact, I've never played a highly regarded golf course that has inspired me less or depressed me more. The letdown began with the clubhouse, a garish structure distressingly reminiscent of Andrew Melville Hall. It seemed to me the architectural equivalent of bell-bottoms; thankfully, it has since been replaced by a modern hotel-*cum*-clubhouse, but the old building severely disoriented me. Perhaps that sounds silly, but I really was offended that such an eyesore could welcome me to what was supposedly one of the greatest golfing tests in the world.

From there, I would have thought that the scenery would have to improve once the golf course began. It didn't. For all of Carnoustie's aesthetic sameness, I could have been golfing on a treadmill. I kept struggling forward, hoping that around the next corner or beyond the next rise I'd uncover the golfing paradise Carnoustie had in store for me, but it never came, and after working hard for 18 holes I felt as though the setting had never changed much from when I started. The sea at Carnoustie, though audible, remained just out of view. Smokestacks dominated the grim landscape of the adjacent town. Jack Nicklaus has used the words "primitive-looking," "undramatic" and "banal" to describe the look of the course itself, and I had to agree—nothing jumped out at me, apart from the bunkers and the rough and the diabolically firm greens.

The weather should have been a major boon to me. Calm days at Carnoustie are as rare as solar eclipses, but the conditions I faced were ideal for scoring: mild, overcast, windless. Given how well I played, I was borderline horrified to shoot no better than an 11-over-par 81 at Carnoustie, with nothing but fours and fives on my scorecard. Ironically, the reason for my depression was the overriding emphasis that Carnoustie placed on score. I agree with most critics that Carnoustie is designed to demand the very best of your swing and your golfing brain. Before the most recent Open there in 1999, I could have pointed to Carnoustie's roll call of champions as proof that only the best golfers in the world are capable of winning

there. For that matter, when I consider the abominably high winning score of six over par, Jean Van de Velde's watery collapse at the
72nd hole and the ensuing bogey-littered playoff, I'm pretty sure
that Carnoustie itself won the 1999 Open and that Paul Lawrie was
merely the sole human survivor. (Not since 1947 had an Open golf
course yielded no 72-hole scores under 290.) But if Carnoustie
chews up and spits out the world's best golfers for fun, what does
it do to us plebeians? Exactly. I was lucky with the weather, and I still
felt as though I'd been through a meat grinder.

The respected golf course architect and critic Tom Doak has written that Carnoustie is "not as penal a course as it is made out to be—
it is just depressingly efficient at exposing the weaknesses of one's
game." Which is to say that some courses are longer, some are nar-
rower, some have thicker rough, some have deeper bunkers and
some have trickier greens than Carnoustie—although I seriously
doubt that any championship course combines all of these as devil-
ishly as Carnoustie. I *did* find room for error on many holes at
Carnoustie, but never much. I knew I could nearly always correct
my errors with a good recovery shot, which one cannot say about
courses with excessive water or out-of-bounds. But even on a good
day, I repeated this cycle of failure and attempted recovery ad nauseam over the course of 18 holes, and it wore me down well before
I finished. About Carnoustie, Dan Jenkins wrote, "Every hole starts
out like the one you just played—unreachable." I found only one
relatively easy hole at Carnoustie, the short par-3 13th—and I bogeyed it. Apart from that, Carnoustie seemed to want me to struggle, whether I was playing for score or not.

But unlike many other difficult championship courses, Carnoustie
made no effort to cloak its difficulty with beautiful scenery, quirky

terrain, unusually fast and polished greens or other memorable features. Some golfers may admire the frankness of the course, but I was taken aback. Carnoustie took the essence of resistance to score, distilled it and drip-fed it to me one shot at a time. When I lost the ability or the will to score, it felt like Chinese water torture because there wasn't anything pleasant to distract me. Difficult courses can excite the senses—witness the stunning beauty of Royal County Down, the wastelands of Pine Valley, the topography and native grasses of Shinnecock Hills and Crystal Downs, the greens at Oakmont, even the jagged-edged severity of PGA West. But Carnoustie was simply tough. Period.

I feel like I should apologize for sharing my opinions about Carnoustie; many professionals and hackers alike feel that Carnoustie is both a marvelous test of golf *and* a layout with charm and appeal, and I can see why others might like it. Who knows—if my time at Carnoustie had worked out differently, maybe I would now be raving about its frankness instead of bemoaning its difficulty, and praising its straightforward honesty instead of criticizing its blandness. I've since tried very hard to like Carnoustie. I want to like it, I really do, but my best efforts seem doomed to failure. Maybe I don't like it because it hits too close to home; the people I've always disliked the most have been the ones in whom I've seen my own shortcomings magnified. There must be some truth in that, for my final analysis tells me that even on a calm day, score is just too important, too central to the experience at Carnoustie. And that is something I hadn't thought possible.

Chapter 4

MELVILLE MATES

❖❖❖

ON THE FINAL night of Overseas Orientation Weekend, I learned how to *ceilidh*. The ceilidh (pronounced KAY-lee) is an athletic form of Scottish country dancing popular among both young and old at weddings and the like, and many student societies in St. Andrews traditionally hold ceilidhs during the winter months. As a rule I hate dancing, but the ceilidh caller made each step easy to understand, and much to my surprise I thoroughly enjoyed flinging myself from one end of the Student Union to the other. And when I saw Heather across the dance floor—wearing brown boots, jeans and a very fetching dark green body suit—I broke another habit of a lifetime and asked her if she wanted to dance. She said yes.

The following week I chanced upon Heather in the Melville foyer. She asked me if I wanted to come over to her place for dinner with some friends that Sunday, and I said sure. But when the day came, the novelty of live English soccer on television in the Melville common room overwhelmed my desire to walk to the other end of town, so I phoned her with my regrets. (The word "caveman" comes to mind.) Fortunately, after the match ended, I came to my senses and phoned her back to ask if I could still come down for a while. To her credit, she said yes. I had a lovely time with her and her flatmates and friends, and wound up staying and chatting with her into the wee hours of the morning—well after everyone else had left.

Something had clicked between us, or at least I thought it had. With all the subtlety of a bagpipe sextet, I asked her out on a proper date soon thereafter—to see a production of *Romeo and Juliet* at the Byre Theatre on South Street in St. Andrews. She said yes, again. That made me nervous: three yeses in a row. I figured I was pushing my luck. And sure enough, on the evening of the play, I cut my throat horribly while shaving. Despite my best efforts to tidy myself, an enormous scab formed on my Adam's apple. I knew I should have stuck to golf.

But Heather didn't seem to notice. She was friendly and charming. The production also provided plenty of talking points to keep her distracted: Why were the men all wearing tuxedos? Why were the Capulets speaking in broad Glaswegian accents? Why did Romeo enter the stage during the second act on a moped? The play was enjoyable and surreal in equal measure—and I could say the same about my budding relationship with Heather. Having come to Scotland for the golf, how could I get involved with a girl who had lived in St. Andrews for four years and hadn't swung a golf club once?

I was amazed that anyone could come to St. Andrews for any length of time and not at least attempt to play golf. Who would go to St. Moritz and not ski, or St. Croix and stay indoors? But many of the students had no interest in golf; for them, St. Andrews was a town with a good school, a relaxed ambience, some lovely buildings and a few acres of open land to the west. The setting of the castle and cathedral ruins alone would make St. Andrews a historic tourist destination and an interesting place to be, even without the golf. But not once during my year abroad would I come across another university student willing to own up that he or she had come to St. Andrews first and foremost for the golf. (Slackers from American and British universities blanket the Florida and Ibiza coastlines during spring break, and yet I'm the only one to hit upon the concept of St. Andrews as a nine-month, pseudo-academic holiday? Astounding.) Some non-golfing students I met did feel duty-bound to play at least one round before they left St. Andrews, but not Heather. She'd putted around the Himalayas a few times, but when I asked her if she ever planned to play golf "for real," she gave me a blank look and I withdrew the question.

MY EDUCATION AT St. Andrews, University Branch, began as I expected. The required reading lists were long—the syllabus for my elective course on European Security in the international relations department listed 176 lengthy book excerpts and journal articles, not including the additional 66-work bibliography of "Suggested Reading." (Fat chance.) But I can skim with the best of them. And I had no classes at all on Wednesdays and Fridays. Bliss . . .

Within a few weeks of my arrival in St. Andrews, I'd come to terms with the more banal aspects of life in a midsize Scottish town. To shop for most everyday products, I could either walk to the St. Andrews town center and get a basic version, or I could travel to a bigger city and forage up and down a number of broad-avenued high streets. The same general rule applied to the arts: Edinburgh's theater scene was among the best in Britain, whereas in St. Andrews we had only the Byre; and the tiny, two-screen cinema in St. Andrews couldn't hold a candle to the multiplex to the north in Dundee, where Heather and I saw the new James Bond film on a double-date with some friends who had a car. This principle also held true, in a manner of speaking, for the local history—the castle remnants and museums in Edinburgh are far larger, if not per se "better," than they are in St. Andrews. And even in golfing terms, St. Andrews wasn't wholly unique. Most Scottish towns around its size have either great, good or not-so-good golf courses to call their own; I knew that St. Andrews happened to have all three, but then, so did Gullane, and I imagine the Ayrshire coastline could be gerrymandered into similar clusters near Prestwick and Troon as well.

In my first week of Melville dining hall life, I overheard a lamentation for the reigning Open Champion: "Pity John Daly," the guy said. "A recovering alcoholic stuck in a town in which there's nothing to do but drink." I was tempted to blurt out "and golf," but for the non-golfer his view of St. Andrews rings true. For most students, the pub crawl is not just an adventure—it's a job. There are countless different places and ways to drink in St. Andrews. Some pubs that cater to the locals are hostile to the presence of students and obvious tourists, although countless others welcome both groups with open taps. But no matter where, what and how (or how much), the *why* of drinking in St. Andrews is obvious: the Brits love their lagers, ciders, ales, bitters and spirits. For nine months of the year, beneath its touristy façade St. Andrews is really a college town.

The drinking age throughout Britain is 18. And nearly everything in Scotland apart from the pubs shuts down at six in the evening.

One can be a teetotaler in St. Andrews, though. I know. I've always believed that my first drink could be my last—my father was an alcoholic who lost his lifetime battle against the bottle, an ugly fight at which I had a ringside seat for years, and alcoholism is very prevalent on his side of my family. Against these facts, peer pressure has always been somewhat less than compelling. I recognize that the British pub, cozy and inviting, is a substantial improvement upon the American bar, but beyond a certain hour I can't hear my neighbor's conversation in either. And I still get angry when I see college kids drinking to get drunk, as though he who vomits the closest to dawn receives some badge of courage. Life in St. Andrews was far too pleasant to be spent hungover or in other states of altered reality. So I stayed in many evenings and saved my tests of stamina for the links. This policy probably cost me a few friendships that might have been forged had I responded more often in the affirmative to "Fancy a pint?" But I saved enough money by not drinking to fund several day trips worth of great golf, so on balance I think I came out ahead.

I met a few interesting characters along the way besides. My next-door neighbor in Melville was a ginger-haired geology student named Scott Campbell—or "Scottcampbell!" spoken with a hint of a pirate's accent, as I somehow came to greet him. Give Scott a pair of thick-set, black-rimmed glasses, and he looked a dead ringer for one of the lead singers of the Scottish band The Proclaimers. The abiding memory I have of Scott on the golf course is him saying, "It's a bucket!" as I snaked a lengthy hole-winning putt into the cup on him, which he took in good humor. Scott came from Kirkcaldy, halfway between St. Andrews and Edinburgh, and his hometown soccer team was a small club called Raith Rovers, which he supported fanatically. Raith Rovers had the year before completed the best season in their history, and Scott was enamored with their manager: "Jimmy Nicholl is God," he used to say. "He's GOD. And there's nothing else to say about him."

One winter's day I arrived back at my room to find a newspaper clipping pinned to my door with the scores from an Australian tournament I'd barely heard of. In big letters, Scott had written across the top "IAN BAKER-FINCH MADE A CUT!!!" I think Scott identified with Baker-Finch's struggles at times. But he made a fun playing partner, and a great neighbor.

Another Melville mate was Martin Parry, a "fresher" (first-year student) from Colchester in the south of England. Most of the English students in St. Andrews dressed, talked and acted as though they were attending Oxford or Cambridge. But Martin had a tradesman's accent and always looked as though he'd just visited John Daly's barber. Still, he was a very good golfer. "On the tee, Martin Parry!" I would cry with delight in imitation of Ivor Robson, the longtime first-tee starter for the Open Championship with the distinctive, high-pitched voice. Martin would wave to the imaginary gallery and then pound the ball miles off the tee. I invariably hit my second shots before he hit his. He also introduced me to two polite curses that I use to this day on the golf course: "That shot was absolute toilet" and, in a similar vein, the simply marvelous "Pants!"

(Briticisms: British "trousers" are American "pants." British "plus-fours" are American "knickers." And British "pants" and "knickers" are both euphemisms for what is worn underneath British trousers and plus-fours.)

Melville contributed a soccer team to the second division of the St. Andrews Sunday League, through which I met another motley assemblage of laddish, pint-drinking types. By nature I'm a goal-keeper, which is the only position Americans are really any good at (Kasey Keller, Brad Friedel, Jurgen Sommer and Ian Feuer are among the American goalkeeping imports in recent years by English soccer's top division, the Premiership), so I was enthusiastically drafted into the Melville ranks. We were decent enough, but our emphasis was on fun, friendship and a bit of silliness. Our club name and crest said it all: there are clubs in the English Football League named Ipswich Town FC (Football Club) and Luton Town FC, so we called ourselves Shanty Town FC. And the crest consisted of two fingers pointing upward, fingernails showing (the British version of "the finger") above our Latin motto, *Sunt Haec Tua,* which translated means "Are These Yours?"

Most of my friends golfed with some degree of seriousness, and many of them used golf as a metaphor for everything; I think it was one of my more mature Shanty Town teammates who first noticed my budding relationship and cracked, "So, Darren, are we thinking about losing our balls in the Heather? Eh?" But even if they didn't, they still would have been in the Melville common room with me at the end of September to watch the Ryder Cup. I was pleased to see how much the Ryder Cup mattered to so many people in St. Andrews, even if everyone's interest did make me the equivalent of Davy Crockett at the Alamo: an isolated American among hordes of the enemy. Everyone loves to beat America, and for good reason. Even those Americans who can see beyond their country's borders can often appear or sound brazenly proud of their nationality. This in part explains why the Ryder Cup is an amazing creation. It manages to make Americans look beyond the parochialism of base-ball, football and basketball and actually care about trying to prove that their athletes are the best in the world. The odd Olympics or women's soccer team apart, Americans are usually happy to call their teams "World Champions" even in the absence of competition.

The Ryder Cup is also amazing because it manages to rally Europeans around the European flag more than politics ever will. Britons may be deeply confused by their involvement in the move-ment toward European Union and a single currency, but every alternate September they are united in their warmth toward Spaniards, Swedes and even Germans. The Ryder Cup compels non-golfers to take notice. The world of professional golf and golfers is not universally embraced in Scotland like golf itself, but no televi-sion set in a St. Andrews pub was tuned to anything else during the event's three days. And the usually eclectic tastes of the Melville common room crowd also settled upon the Ryder Cup coverage with unanimity, even though the matches were taking place in the States and hence during prime-time viewing hours. Scott, Martin, the Shanty Town boys and I were all there, sprawled on firm cush-ions and hard-backed chairs with scores of other guys and girls, watching together and feeling claustrophobic.

When Corey Pavin holed a chip shot, I was the only one to sit up, pump a fist and emit a shriek of joy—a stifled shriek, naturally, be-cause I wanted to be around to watch the conclusion. More often, Colin Montgomerie or David Gilford or Costantino Rocca would drain a putt and the student crowd would crow with delight. I heard the otherwise monotonous "U-S-A! U-S-A!" chant mocked with the hilarious cry of "Eu-oo-rope! Eu-oo-rope!" On occasion, as an American putt slid past the hole, a Scottish voice at the back cried

"Sweep! Sweep!"—the humor of which doesn't fully translate unless you're acquainted with technical terms used in the game of curling.

This particular set of matches ended dramatically: no change, then, from every other Ryder Cup since the mid-eighties. The Americans' one-point margin of defeat was thoroughly avoidable. Europe won four and drew one of the matches that went as far as the final hole on Sunday, and if Curtis Strange or Jay Haas had so much as parred the 18th, the Cup would have stayed in America. There was delirium in Melville and beyond; I might have torn my hair out had I not felt so enormously privileged.

For from my armchair in the common room I could see the Old Course—the Old Course!—without changing channels. It was right there, outside the window. I was *that* close to golf's ancient home. And as I sat, I watched golf provide inordinate pleasure to friends and acquaintances whose lives only touched the game at the very periphery. And the next day I could go out and play 18 or 36 holes or more, on the very same turf that inspired the men who inspired the men who inspired the men who had just inspired me, on television. What a place. What a life!

Chapter 5

THE CRUDEN WAY

❖❖❖

MY DAY TRIP to Cruden Bay was supposed to be simple.
I'd arranged this outing for a day on which I had no classes, and
I'd plotted my itinerary meticulously. I bought my rail tickets a day
in advance. I set my alarm clock for 6:45 in the morning and incorporated plenty of leeway into my timetable thereafter. I'd catch the
7:33 bus from the North Haugh to Leuchars, the 8:10 train from
Leuchars to Aberdeen, and the first bus thereafter from Aberdeen to
Peterhead. The latter bus route went directly past the clubhouse at
Cruden Bay Golf Club; I'd checked to make sure the driver would
drop me off exactly where I wanted. Estimated time of arrival:
10:30. Just time enough in October, I reckoned, to squeeze lunch
between two rounds of golf and still finish my 36th hole before
dusk.

Only it didn't quite work out that way. On the appointed morning I groggily awoke to the sounds of silence. I peered at my alarm

clock—7:40. Aaaargh! Now I was wide awake. Jolted into an obscenity-strewn fit, I dashed down the hall for a 30-second shower and shampoo. Back in my room, clothing flew everywhere as I pulled my golfing attire over my still damp body while simultaneously trying to fix a breakfast sandwich. I sprinted out of Melville to the North Haugh bus stop, 400 yards or so away, as quickly as I could with my golf bag draped over one shoulder. My breathless arrival at the bus stop preceded the next bus to Leuchars by less than 10 seconds.

I paid my fare and awkwardly slumped into the nearest available seat. Pulling the local bus timetable out of my golf bag to see which bus I'd caught, I discovered I was scheduled to arrive at Leuchars at 8:10, just as my train pulled in. I crossed my fingers and hoped for the best. In the small village of Guardbridge the bus stopped for an elderly man who unsteadily climbed aboard, took an age to realize that he only had a £10 note for the 90p fare and took two ages to collect the masses of change given him by the driver. We pulled out of Guardbridge behind a car driving 10 miles an hour slower than the speed limit. I felt my face redden with rage as I mentally screamed at everyone in sight. Come on, come on! All ahead full! Ramming speed!

The bus pulled into Leuchars behind schedule. I ran out, slowed to a jog up the stairs, huffed and puffed as I crossed the pedestrian footbridge leading over the tracks to the station and pessimistically descended from the footbridge to discover my fate. The good news announced itself over the loudspeakers at the station: my train was running 10 minutes late. Hurrah! It took me a moment before I realized the bad news: I'd left my train tickets on my bedside table back at Melville. I thumped my forehead in disgust. I had to buy them all over again. And I only just got to the front of the queue at the ticket office before my train showed up.

As part of my pre–St. Andrews planning, I'd sketched out a number of day-trip possibilities along Scotland's east coast. With minimal hassle, almost every notable golf course in Britain can be affordably reached by public transport. This is not a coincidence; the Golden Age of British golf course architecture coincided with the golden age of the railroad, and the brilliance of designers like Herbert Fowler, H.S. Colt, James Braid and Willie Park coexisted with the greediness of railway companies looking to maximize their profits by laying additional stretches of track. Cruden Bay was one such course, a pleasant holiday destination with its own rail connection before World War II; as at St. Andrews, the direct rail link has long since been abandoned. The one line in northeastern Scotland now swerves toward Inverness (and away from Cruden Bay) at Aberdeen. But rail consolidation doesn't mean that the frugal golfer, scared by rising gas prices approaching £1 per *liter* (something like $6 a gallon), can't still get around. Bus routes now pick up the slack for the railroads, so one can still travel almost anywhere without a rental car. No need to be embarrassed, either: bring a golf bag onto any bus or train in Scotland, and nobody will look at you twice.

For the late start on my trip to Cruden Bay, though, I deserved to be flogged. The night before rounds on highly regarded courses, I normally felt like I did as a kid on Christmas Eve. Wound up with anticipation, I'd have trouble falling asleep, and in the morning I'd inevitably wake up before my alarm clock told me to. I wondered if St. Andrews was making me soft. In my rush to get ready, for a brief moment I'd even paused and thought about going back to bed, playing the Old Course instead and worrying about Cruden Bay some other time, if at all. But perhaps my doubts were justifiable. My day trip to Cruden Bay was longer by far than any of the others I had planned. To be sure, I'd read glowing descriptions of the course, but the general overuse and misuse of the term "hidden gem" in modern golf writing left me unsure of what to expect. And in his book *To the Linksland,* Michael Bamberger had complained that while he loved the course, the club lacked "a true and great golf ambience. . . . I never had the idea that golf was central to life in Cruden Bay, as I had in Gullane and St. Andrews."

I needn't have worried. Cruden Bay stirred my soul like no other course in Scotland. It was as different from what I'd previously seen in Scotland as Gullane was from anything I'd ever seen in America. Its scale was enormous, its impact immense. If golf courses were symphonies, Cruden Bay would have been composed by Gustav Mahler. As with Mahler's music, something about Cruden Bay's *Sturm und Drang* appealed immensely to the disaffected, angry young man in me. Cruden Bay is a flawed work; some of its holes were downright weird, many more confusingly quirky. But the composition as a whole was incontestably dramatic, unceasingly moving and, at times, breathtakingly beautiful. And credit must go to its architect, Tom Simpson. As his work at Ballybunion in Ireland also demonstrates, Simpson was a master at coaxing wonderful holes out of turbulent terrain.

Cruden Bay is all about mounds and dunes. Most of the holes lie within one of two bowls of land formed by fescue-covered sandhills. The larger bowl incorporates most of the front nine and the two finishing holes; the other circles all of the land between the 10th and 14th tees. Away from the sea, the hills are packed down and refined; the clubhouse is an extension of a row of houses resting on the inland rim of the larger bowl. But along the waterfront, the virgin duneland is wild, untamed, and awesome in the literal sense of the word. Some of it rises more than 100 feet above the base of the valley. (Cruden Bay made me feel small.) Simpson was content to relegate most of the wildest dunes to the background, but several of them do encroach significantly upon the line of play. The green at the fourth hole, a great mid-length par 3 adjacent to an inlet of the sea and in sight of the fishing village of Port Erroll, is but a shallow perch on a massive vertical dune. The 15th is a blind 239-yard par 3 over a corner of the tallest dune on the course—not a great hole, but assuredly a memorable one. The most dramatic shot at Cruden Bay, one of my favorites in Scotland, is the drive on the par-4 10th, which drops 80 feet down a whin-covered cliff. Even mediocre shots hang mesmerizingly in the air, seemingly in a trance of suspended animation, before plunging to earth—possibly into a burn nearly 300 yards away that can easily be reached with a following wind.

It is in the smaller dunes, though, that Simpson's genius really shines. Modern architects might have been tempted to flatten many of the rises that give Cruden Bay its character. Unable or unwilling to mess with them, Simpson simply routed the course over them and around them. He made a few strange holes along the way; on one of them, the par-4 17th, it looks as if an elephant was buried in the middle of the fairway. Really . . . it *does.* (It could be the last resting place of the Loch Ness Monster, though, or a thousand Jimmy Hoffas.) But more often the mounds made perfect strategic sense, and figuring them out was so much fun! The shame is that a round of golf gives you only one chance at each hole at a time—there were at least half a dozen holes at Cruden Bay that I wanted never to leave.

I PLAYED CRUDEN BAY mostly by myself. No matter how remote its location, I found it difficult to comprehend how a great course like Cruden Bay could ever be virtually empty when six-hour rounds are the norm at so many awful courses with similar green fees. Not that I complained. When I arrived, the teenager behind the counter at the pro shop told me I could tee off whenever I liked. Same again for my afternoon round. It was a gray day, as most days are in Aberdeenshire, and the air was typically heavy and damp. But it never felt like it was going to rain, and the wind wasn't terribly strong. The weather seemed just about perfect to me. Cruden Bay is just up the road from the ruins of Slains Castle, an inspiration to Bram Stoker while he was writing *Dracula,* and the course couldn't feel properly Gothic when bathed in sunshine.

During my first 18 holes I played quite deliberately. I made sure I knew where the greens were on most of the blind and semi-blind holes, paced off many of my yardages and occasionally paused to soak up the atmosphere. I shot 80, 10 over par. The round took less than two and a half hours to complete. Does time pass by more slowly in Scotland than elsewhere? I was never that fast in the States.

In my afternoon round, I started with two pars and came to the third, a short par 4 of only 286 yards from the medal tees. I'd bogeyed it in the morning, and I bogeyed it again in the afternoon, but I didn't feel bad at all. I couldn't remember seeing a better hole of its length. When a hole toys with my mind and gets the better of me even though I know what's coming, I'm filled with admiration. I *can't* get angry. I often want to get even, but that emotion is tribute in and of itself; bad holes make me want to move on quickly, not try again immediately. Good golf course architecture elevates the game to a higher plane of thinking. Other sports may place as many demands upon your sporting brain as golf does, but with nothing else is the shape and size of the playing field so important. And the best holes, the ones you have to approach as a puzzle-solver as much as a sportsman, are those that operate like the third at Cruden Bay.

Two mounds on the third hole feature prominently: a small one pinches into the fairway 50 to 70 yards from the green on the left, and a much larger one (more like a small dune, really) guards the green to its front and right. The fairway twists between these two mounds in the shape of a backward question mark. Both were covered with gnarly, ball-eating fescue grasses when I played the course; each would have dictated my strategy off of the tee to some degree no matter where the green was situated. But Simpson's first architectural masterstroke was to cant the green along the reverse slope of the larger mound on the right, meaning that although the green fits the shape of the dune (from front-left to back-right), it also slopes naturally away from the dune (from front-right to back-left). The advantage therefore lies with the golfer who hugs the left edge of the fairway with his tee shot, even if his approach shot is thereby made blind by the mound on the left. A sideslope won't cancel all of the spin on a landing ball, whereas a downslope often will.

The second masterstroke was to keep the hole short. Especially in today's power-hungry golf world, it takes a supreme act of self-discipline to restrain oneself and select a medium iron on the tee of any par 4, but after careful consideration I'm fairly certain that this is the only reasonable play for me. If the hole were 80 yards longer, there would be nothing particularly intellectual about the tee shot, but as it is, of the four strategic options available on the tee, the three straightforward ones are mistakes waiting to happen:

1) The most obvious error is to take a driver and blast it at the

tiny gap between the two mounds, trying to drive the green with little chance of success. I fear that many unsophisticated golfers would try to do this anyway, get hung up on one of the mounds, make bogey at best and then complain how stupid the hole is for not letting them "let the big dog eat." (One shouldn't expect more from a pig than a grunt, but such comments are becoming more and more commonplace on American golf courses, and they make me fear for the future of golf.)

2) A variation of the first mistake is to take a driver but aim slightly left, trying only to carry the nearer mound. A stretch of fairway wraps around the green to its left, and a pitch into the green is much simpler from that side. But the risks of the big hit—including out-of-bounds on the left—still hugely outweigh the potential rewards. The appearance of subtlety is in no way proof of intelligent strategy.

3) The most subtle of the three pitfalls is the one that got me twice. I saw through the obvious errors and chose a long iron, opting to play out to the right into the longest part of the fairway. I was tempted by the extra room on offer and by the relatively open sight line into the green from the right, but most of all I was tempted by what seemed a relatively safe chance to get within 50 yards of the green on a par 4. I, for one, am rarely within 50 yards of the green on any par 4 for my second shot. I instinctively feel as though I should be somehow advantaged when I am. In the morning I missed the fairway and had to scramble for my five, but in the afternoon I hit my tee shot successfully into the fairway, and it *felt* as though dodging the minor risks involved in the forward layup should have led to the reward of a birdie opportunity. But they didn't. Instead, I was left with a blind half-wedge shot to a green

sloping fiercely away from me. I would have been lucky to keep the ball on the green if I'd have targeted the hole. With the pin at the front of the green, my best play might even have been to lay up short or to the left of the green with my second. Of how many 50-yard shots from the fairway can you say that?

My only lament is that the third hole at Cruden Bay would be even better if it were on the back nine somewhere, because then the first two "mistakes" might become reasonable options under certain circumstances, especially in match play for the trailing golfer needing a spark of inspiration. But there are so many other holes at Cruden Bay as delightfully tricky as the third, I can hardly complain. I could pontificate upon the unique merits of the second, fourth, fifth, sixth, seventh, eighth, 13th and 14th holes at equal length. In fact, the only uninspiring hole for me at Cruden Bay is the ninth, a par 4 along a featureless stretch of farmland at the top of the course—but as it quickly transitions the course from one of its bowls to the other, it isn't really a waste of space. All the others are quirky, brilliant or memorable. Many are all three.

AFTER MY BOGEY on the third hole in my afternoon round, I proceeded to bogey the fourth and double-bogey the fifth. On the sixth tee, I took a deep breath and cleared my head. Thereafter, I settled into a nice groove of scoring. Two fantastic shots on the tough par-4 seventh netted a birdie. A lengthy putt for another birdie at the 10th got me back to three over par for the round. The day was humming along nicely.

As I reached the 11th hole, a 139-yard par 3, I finally discovered that I wasn't alone on the golf course. Two men in their thirties were teeing off, and one of them motioned to me that I could play through if I wanted to. Great day, great course . . . I decided I'd be happy to slow down and share the day with someone, to savor it even more in the company of a few savvy locals. So I asked if they wouldn't mind an extra playing partner, and I was pleased when they said they'd be happy to have me.

I thanked them for their courtesy and quickly introduced myself. "Have you guys both hit already?" I asked.

"Aye," one of them answered. "The tee's all yours."

I teed up my ball and made two quick practice swings—quicker practice swings, I noticed, than the ones I'd been making when I was playing alone. I laughed silently to myself and wondered, Why do you feel *any* performance pressure in a situation like this? I made one more deliberately slow swing to shake the tension out of my arms.

Resuming my normal preshot routine, I briefly stepped back behind my ball, mentally pictured my shot and focused upon an aiming point. Then, stepping back up to the ball, I took my customary waggle and swung. The ball began 10 yards to the left of my target, drifted back on line with the pin, landed on the green, bounced once . . . and disappeared.

"No," I said, dumbstruck. I felt my mouth twist into a goofy, delirious smile. "That couldn't have just happened. Could it? Did it?"

I looked over at my newfound companions, both of whom beamed with understated mixtures of awe and curiosity. One of them said, "It looks like it did to me." But we couldn't be sure, for a small rise short of the green just obscured the bottom of the flagstick.

Time seemed to stand still as we walked from the tee to the green. I babbled nervously about myself to my companions, unsure of how to react to what I'd just seen. I wanted to sprint ahead at full tilt to the flag, but something held me back. I put down my golf bag by a bridge over the burn guarding the front of the green and took out my putter and sand wedge—just in case. Then I clambered up the bank of the plateaued green and tiptoed gingerly to the pin. I peered over the edge of the cup . . . and exhaled. My first-ever hole-in-one!

THE GENTLE MIST of the early afternoon, the smell and taste of the salt spray from the North Sea, the dark but placid skies of mid-autumnal coastal Scotland—and the image of a ball, *my* ball, slicing through the air, onto the green, into the hole on one bounce. I freely confess it: I've spent an embarrassingly large proportion of my life daydreaming about one swing of an 8-iron and the result it produced. For several months, I wavered between reality and the 11th at Cruden Bay. It isn't hard to realize why.

The hole-in-one. In a sense, the ace is the heart in the body of golfing mysticism. It is "one," it is everything, it is perfection, it is why we play the game. It is such a bright, shining concept that its very brightness makes it difficult to comprehend. You can't make lower than a one on a hole. Your odds of making one on any given hole is one out of X, where X is a number with a whole lot of zeros. One wonders why we even bother trying at all; I've concluded that it's stupid to enter the lottery, and yet I keep playing par 3s. That we all do this proves that no golfer can be, in the strict sense of the word, a "perfectionist" without going clinically mad. Ball-striking is all about relativity, about rationalizing, about lowering our standards to a point at which we can gloat about our flaws. The television voice describes a shot as "perfect"; we know full well that it isn't, because we can plainly see the ball lying above ground, tens of inches away from the hole or the corner of a dogleg. But we allow the voice to pass with barely a flicker of acknowledged disagreement, because we are conditioned to accept such half- and quarter-truths.

Even the pros think this way. While at the 1995 Nestlé Invitational I heard Nick Price explain to a fellow journalist that when he's driving the ball well, he picks a spot as tiny as the tooth of a fairway bunker rake as an aiming point. By focusing his powers of concentration upon such a precise line, he said, he readies himself as well as he can to play the shot. Ah, I responded, but what happens when you hit the ball as little as five yards off-line, even when the ball stays in the fairway? Doesn't it make you mad?

Price brushed the question off. "As long as the ball goes in the fairway, who cares?" he said. "The *real* goal is to drive the ball in the fairway, right?" At that time, Price had won the previous two major championships, was the top-ranked golfer in the world and was also widely acknowledged as the world's best ball-striker. And yet even he accepted the proposition that he mentally deceives himself, fully ready to accept the imperfection that inevitably follows.

But the hole-in-one, that happy cohabitation of intent and result . . . that *is* perfect. Or is it? Among the sensations I can recollect from the experience of my maiden ace is the exact feel of the contact between clubface and ball, transmitted through the vibrations of the club's shaft to my hands. On a colder day, the vibrations would have painfully shocked my left hand, so low on the clubface did I contact the ball. The swing plane of my follow-through was outside-to-inside, which would normally produce a slice even without the help of a three-quarters left-to-right wind. Luckily, my clubface was slightly closed at impact—this negated the slice swing with a touch of over-the-top hook spin and proved ideal for holding the ball against the wind. And even more luckily, my shot hit the pin and dove directly downward instead of skipping through the green or careening sideways. Even granting that I factored in the likelihood of an off-center contact when I made my club selection, could such a symbiotic combination of coincidence and luck be fairly labeled "perfection"?

I've since compared my ace, and the thought process behind it, to another shot—one I made during my senior year at Harvard on the par-3 seventh hole at The Country Club. I'd blocked my tee shot into the bunker short and to the right of the green. Apart from a fairly good lie, nothing about my recovery shot looked easy. If I carried the ball even onto the front edge of the green, it would doubtless rocket well past the pin, for the hole was cut on a downslope and the green was very fast. But I had to carry several yards of tangly rough to reach what was only a thin cordon of fairway-fringe on my line to the hole. And the green broke in two directions: quickly to the right at the start, then gently to the left at the end. In retrospect, I can imagine Johnny Miller commentating, "Anything within 20 feet of the hole would be very good." But I trusted myself to make no worse than bogey no matter what I did, so I focused upon hitting the ideal shot instead of what might have been the smart one. I landed the ball exactly where I wanted to, just beyond the rough. The fringe nearly slowed it to a stop, but as it fell onto the green the ball picked up the scintilla of speed it needed to reach the downslope. At a veritable crawl the ball slid down the hill, broke right, then left, and with its final rotation it toppled into the hole—it didn't even touch the flagstick, so impeccable was my touch. The shot took nearly 10 seconds to travel 50 feet from start to finish, and if it hadn't have gone in, it would have stopped stone-dead next to the hole. Not only did the intent match the result, the execution deserved it. I'm fairly certain that this shot was, by *any* reckoning of the word, "perfect."

This comparison made me wonder: in golf, can there be degrees of perfection? If two shots from the same spot both go into the hole, can one be better than the other? In absolute terms, was my bunker shot better than my ace? Different golfers will answer these questions differently. I'm a golfer who hits his irons off the heel or the toe with far greater regularity than I do the sweet spot, but I have a knack for saving par by getting up-and-down from strange places anywhere within 100 yards of the hole. And I've birdied more than a few holes in my day by sinking chips, pitches and indeed bunker shots. As such, I've become conditioned to value the absolute nature of the scores I make—the cliché that there are "no pictures on the scorecard" rings true to me. I suspect that most golfers are similarly right brained; the inconsistency of our swings promotes chaos, so our value structures combat this by creating order. By asserting that all aces/birdies/pars are intrinsically alike in some important way, we feel better about ourselves—even if we usually construct them with the help of lengthy putts, freakish bounces or the "pulled slice" that finishes upon the exact vector we were hoping it would. It was Gary Player who said, "The more I practice, the luckier I get," but I prefer the converse statement: the luckier I am, the less I have to practice.

Not all of us are like this. One of my ex-teammates from Harvard is a prime specimen of the left-brained golfer; I vividly remember him telling me, "I wish you were forced to take two putts on every green. Make golf a pure ball-striking contest." Joel can spend hours on the practice range without batting an eye, stripes every club in his bag with laser-like precision, loves the feel of a pure contact more than any result it might bring him (he says "At least I hit it good" a lot), and idolizes the way Ben Hogan played golf with a fanaticism bordering on the bizarre. Joel is no less passionate about the game than I am, but his passion exhibits itself in ways I am not fully capable of understanding. For example, while Joel and I often look as if we aren't having fun on the golf course, for me this usually means I'm not (my score is probably soaring toward the 90s), whereas Joel's appearance can be deceiving. He derives a significantly higher proportion of enjoyment than I do from the self-discipline and "soul-searching" (his term) he inflicts upon himself in attempting to make each and every swing as pure as it possibly can be. He can look ashen-faced and deadly serious while in the throes of golfing ecstasy.

How Joel and I think has a lot to do with how we play. Joel is what I would call a "ball-striker," a player whose entire game revolves around hitting fairways and greens in regulation. In contrast, I am the ball-striker's polar opposite—the "scrambler." I know I don't hit the ball straight enough to compete with the ball-striker on his terms, so I've cultivated my short game and my powers of recovery to help compensate for my other failures. Both the scrambler and the ball-striker can become very good golfers, and while there are many more of the latter than the former on the PGA Tour, John Daly is a perfect example of someone whose touch around the greens and ability to scramble probably does more for him in winning tournaments over 72 holes than sheer power does. While Daly might not think in exactly these terms, it stands to reason that a player who cannot rely upon pinpoint accuracy (relative to his peers, of course, for even at his alcoholic worst Daly hits the ball much straighter than most of us could ever hope to) would have to regard himself more as a scrambler than a ball-striker.

Is one of these types superior to the other? I would say no, but

Joel might say yes, even if I pointed out to him that Nick Faldo and Seve Ballesteros, the archetypal late-twentieth-century examples of the ball-striker and the scrambler, have spookily similar résumés. (At the start of the 2001 season, Faldo had won three Opens, three Masters and 39 other tournaments around the world; Seve had won three Opens, two Masters and 61 other tournaments around the world.) Joel tends to treat the way I play golf with varying degrees of contempt, bewilderment and amazement, even though (or perhaps because) I'm a better short-game artist and more imaginative in bad winds and weather than he is, and even though he's suffered through several of the worst bouts of the putting yips I have ever seen in person. I can't say I agree with him, but I can see his point: par is predicated on taking two putts per hole, not one or none. And he's not alone — golf equipment companies prefer to advertise the virtues of staying out of trouble, not getting out of trouble. The modern golfer's virtues are those of the ancient Olympians: *Citius, Altius, Fortius*. Seve was an anomaly. Faldo, at his best, was a near-perfect refinement of that which we are taught to seek.

I suspect Joel would have been downright embarrassed to have made my hole-in-one at Cruden Bay. He would have apologized, probably once per hole on his way into the clubhouse, for getting so lucky. I think he might have felt genuinely distraught about using such dishonest means to achieve what is, let's face it, the dream of many a golfing life. And if I pointed out to him that the average handicap of the male ace-maker in America (14.6) is only a few notches lower than that of the average male golfer (16), he might just swear off the concept forever. I can hear him now: "*Anyone* can make a hole-in-one. What does making one prove about your ability as a golfer? Nothing." And he'd be exactly right.

My bunker shot fills me with more pride than my ace because it's the sort of shot that all golfers can relate to, including people like Joel. Mine was the shot Joel would have hoped to hit in the same situation; for that matter, Seve would have been proud to call my shot his own. I don't mean to sound immodest in saying that. Quite the contrary: I am overcome with awe to think that relatively bad golfers like me are ever allowed to experience the sensations of perfection. Great golfers routinely glimpse perfection, and they dwell in a world where near-perfection is an achievable standard. Yet nearly everyone who plays the game for any length of time will eventually do something singularly skillful—make a great swing, hit a stunning bunker shot, hole an outlandish putt—and will be able to look God in the eye and confidently assert, "Tiger would have done worse."

But any hole-in-one is still a class apart. Joel still hasn't made an ace, a fact that does not change the truth that he will beat me over 18 holes several times for every time I beat him. He is relatively stronger at ball-striking than I am at scrambling, and vice versa; he is also stronger mentally than I am, and as such there is no doubt in my mind that he is the better golfer. But I'll always have that day at Cruden Bay, and he won't. I'll always note with relish that my maiden ace came on one of my favorite courses in the world, one that had become special to me well before my 29th hole of the day. I'll recall with eerie delight how my ace came so soon after hooking up with that twosome; they waited for me as if destined to view the supernatural, and I was saved at the last possible instant from the ultimate fish story, a hole-in-one with no witnesses. And I can say, "I aced the 11th at Cruden Bay," without any elaboration, to nearly anyone and receive a suitably worshipful response. These thoughts aren't rational, but as they say, I'd rather be lucky than good.

Chapter 6

It's All Dunhill from Here

❖❖❖

THERE ARE TWO ways to walk from Andrew Melville Hall
to the history department building on The Scores, the northernmost avenue in the town proper. The direct route goes straight
through town and takes about 10 minutes to walk. The indirect
route proceeds across the cracked concrete that gives the Road
Hole its name and runs parallel to the 18th hole of the Old Course
before intersecting The Scores behind the green. It took me about
11 minutes to walk. I can't count how many times I was ever so
slightly late for class.

The indirect route is marginally faster on Sundays because the
Old Course is closed for play, a tradition born in the days when St.
Andrews was the ecclesiastical center of Scotland and golf a pursuit
that interfered with archery practice. When golf isn't being played
on the Old Course, anyone can use it as a public park, within reason
(i.e. no sandcastle-building in the bunkers and no rugby-playing on

the greens). On warmer days, some picnic on it; on windy days, kites often fly above it. I reveled in the realization that I could use the most famous golf course in the world as a shortcut. Imagine walking up to a Pinkerton at the gates of Augusta National and asking, "I'm trying to get from Waffle House to the liquor store. Mind if I cut across Amen Corner?"

One mid-October Sunday, I took the Old Course detour back to Melville at sunset, and not for the first time I paused at the Road Hole road to soak up the atmosphere. To the west, gray clouds scratched their way across a brilliant yellow sky; to the east, the R&A clubhouse stood guard, as always in the evening sublimely floodlit to a crisp, rusty brown. It was picture-postcard stuff, truly, but for two annoying distractions. Behind the wall adjacent to the road, the silhouette of a monstrous spectator stand reminded me that the Old Course was about to be repossessed by the professionals. And to its right stretched a lengthy structure, more elaborate but also erected from scratch during the first two weeks in October. Complete with front façade, electric lighting and paintings on the walls, the latter would serve, I soon learned, as the main hospitality tent of the Alfred Dunhill Cup—an event on the European PGA Tour's October calendar with a unique format and a distressingly high noise-to-signal ratio.

On Monday morning, while crossing the Old Course on Grannie Clark's Wynd (which is the name of a road, not a disease), I noted that scores of flagpoles had been erected in the vicinity of the first, 17th and 18th holes. I counted 44 flags flying: 29 carried the Alfred Dunhill Cup logo in dark blue and white, which left only one each for 15 of the 16 competing nations—Taiwan's was nowhere to be seen. Trooping around the Old Course at that moment were dozens of amateurs who had paid a significant amount of money to try to *qualify,* I was told, for the Wednesday pro am, in which the marquee four-ball was scheduled to include Ernie Els and Sylvester Stallone. As I searched for the press tent to collect my *Golf Digest*-sponsored media credentials, I passed through the Alfred Dunhill Cup's smaller-scale version of the Open's "tented village." A merchandising feast to warm any sponsor's heart, it included a souvenir shack selling the finest items from the "Alfred Dunhill Collection" and a display board featuring the best entries to an Alfred Dunhill–sponsored primary school art competition. The latter might have been more endearing to me if only it didn't seem so fascistic—surely a child's crayon drawings should be displayed on a refrigerator, not serve as propaganda for a "luxury goods" company specializing in tobacco and smoking accessories.

This, then, is the problem with the Alfred Dunhill Cup, as assessed by a relative outsider before the competition had actually begun. Is it worthwhile for St. Andrews to take the Old Course out of the hands of its day-to-day patrons, the people who love the game and arguably make St. Andrews the special place that it is, and put it even for one week in the possession of the game's sleazier elements, the moneymen, the sponsors? Those people attract the legions of professional golfers to St. Andrews, many of whom view the Old Course as little more than another tournament venue, or worse. In the lead-up to the Cup, I attended a press conference at which England's Mark James explained how he learns nothing from the Old Course no matter how many times he plays it—he called it *"Groundhog Day* on grass." Most of us treasure every second we can spend on the Old Course. Should James and his compatriots be allowed to keep the rest of us off the Old Course at all?

Although the Alfred Dunhill Cup has been a mainstay of the St. Andrews autumn calendar since it was first held in 1985, it is only well known in America by the sorts of aficionados who write letters to their local congressmen if their cable provider won't give them The Golf Channel. The year I was in St. Andrews—an important distinction, for the event's organizers seem keen to tinker with its format almost annually—each of the 16 participating countries selected three golfers as its team, and the teams were then seeded and divided into four groups of four. Thursday, Friday and Saturday were reserved for round-robin matches to determine the group winners, who advanced to the semifinals. The semifinal and final matches were scheduled for Sunday, with the two morning winners returning shortly after noon to finish a 36-hole day by struggling against each other and the waning daylight hours of mid-October.

A match between nations consisted of three individual games contested at the medal-match play format, with tied games going back to the first hole for a sudden-death playoff. In medal-match play, two players go head-to-head, and the lowest gross score after 18 holes wins. For example, in Friday's group match between the United States and Sweden, Lee Janzen trailed his crucial game against Per-Ulrik Johansson by three shots going into the 17th hole. In match play, the game probably would have ended on the 16th green in a 3&2 victory for Johansson: three holes up, two holes to play. At this reckoning the competitors would shake hands and walk straight into the clubhouse, bypassing the two holes that are not to be missed by all normal visitors to the Old Course. But in medal-match play they played on, an arrangement which suited nearly everyone—especially Janzen, who still possessed slim hopes of recovery, and people like me in the grandstand behind the Road Hole, waiting patiently for the train wrecks that would inevitably come. Johansson graciously obliged everyone by finding the cavernous Road Bunker by the 17th green with his second shot. He had to play out sideways and wound up making double bogey. Janzen made par, and we rediscovered that phenomenon unheard of in match play, the "two-shot swing." Janzen then wedged to within 12 feet of the hole at the last and made birdie. And over to the 19th hole they went.

Despite such attractions, I'm pretty sure that, for the Alfred Dunhill Cup, the Old Course is the wrong place at the wrong time. With regard to the latter, I polled a number of players in the pressroom before the tournament started, and the verdict was nearly unanimous: St. Andrews in October can be an excruciatingly cold and windy place. Wednesday's weather exemplified their concern. A warning on a wall in the pressroom predicted "isolated gusts of around 45 miles per hour" coupled with a steady, horizontal drizzle. Stallone begged out of the pro-am—very un-Rambo-like, I thought —and Sweden's Jesper Parnevik was the only pro of 35 starters to break 70. I asked Zimbabwe's Mark McNulty if he could possibly enjoy himself on a day like that, and he shrugged his shoulders and said, "Oh, this is *nothing.*" It didn't feel like nothing to me. Then again, the two previous years had seen even worse wind, rain and sporadic subfreezing temperatures from day to day. South Africa's Els, Taiwan's T.C. Chen, Sweden's Anders Forsbrand, New Zealand's Grant Waite and England's Howard Clark each failed to break 80 on the opening Thursday the year before . . . and all five golfers *won* their respective matches.

And nothing against the Old Course as a great test of golf, but it's hard to deny that it's singularly unsuitable for spectators. You need a photographer's armband to get anywhere near most of the greens. At most professional tournaments, the crowds flank each green on three sides, only slivers of rough or sand between. At the Old Course, most of the greens are shared between two holes and attacked from opposite directions, which removes spectators altogether from two sides. And with few exceptions, each successive hole overlaps the one before it quite closely on the outside; the walks from green to tee on the Old Course are thereby the shortest in the world, which is great if you're a golfer but rather less so if you're a spectator, ushered away from the greens by the tees. When the Open comes to St. Andrews, this spatial deficiency is partially improved by a proliferation of grandstands—at least one is erected at nearly every hole, and a little bit of elevation does much to restore the viewer's sense of perspective, even if one does need binoculars to locate the cups. But for the Alfred Dunhill Cup, the only two grandstands were at the closing holes. And the Old Course has no large dunes and precious few knolls adjacent to the fairways to compensate.

As THE TOURNAMENT began on a warm but still breezy and cloudy Thursday, I tried to devise a spectating strategy that would surmount these quirks of the Old Course. The best idea I had was to follow one twosome all the way around the course, concentrating upon a single story line rather than a single hole. In so doing, I would lessen my desire to see exactly *how* the pars, birdies and bogeys were being made; the *what* itself would be sufficient to keep me going. As a preliminary experiment, I decided to follow the mid-morning match between Andrew Coltart of Scotland and Chen Liang-hsi of Taiwan. Two years earlier Scottish newspapers had put the Alfred Dunhill Cup on their front pages when the host nation lost its match against golfing minnows Paraguay; I was mildly intrigued by the prospect of such a national embarrassment happening again. Coltart seemed the most likely individual victim on a team that included Colin Montgomerie and Sam Torrance.

Coltart promptly rattled off four birdies in his first six holes—so much for that theory. Professional golfers can be disgustingly good at times. Given the strength of the wind, Coltart's iron play was virtually flawless. He went on to shoot a bogeyless 66, the best round of the day, and defeated his Taiwanese opponent by seven shots. I probably would have enjoyed watching that match to its conclusion, but my master plan sprung two important leaks. First of all, any spectator walking around the periphery of the Old Course will quickly tire of the cry to "Hold, please!" The pedestrian paths bordering the Old Course are made of crushed seashells, and they drain superbly in wet weather. But with hundreds of people treading upon them, they sounded like someone had just poured several gallons of milk into a vat of Rice Krispies. The noises distracted *me;* the guys actually on the golf course must have felt as if they were sandwiched between groups containing Arnold Palmer, Jack Nicklaus and Tiger Woods. I was extremely self-conscious; no matter how slow and even my steps, I felt I was always one crunch away from being screamed at by a marshal or, worse, a caddie.

More frustratingly, when I reached the 7th fairway, I abruptly found myself in a cul-de-sac. The 7th and 11th holes on the Old Course famously crisscross one another, forming with the 8th, 9th and 10th holes what is called the Loop. The architectural merits of this crossing have been debated for centuries; while the logistical problems posed by this quirk of the layout can hardly be considered ideal, in its defense it has given golf a uniquely strategic par 4 (the

7th) and one of the great par 3s in the world (the 11th) to play and ponder. All well and good for the golfer. But what was I to do? I could have doubled back and crossed over the 6th and 12th fairways, waiting for clearance to do so at a designated crosswalk; by the time I caught up with my group, it might have reached the 8th green. I could have raced quickly around the 11th, 10th and 9th and hoped to rejoin Coltart in that fashion. Or I could have remained on the seaward side of the course and watched across two fairways for two-plus holes before joining up with my group at the ninth green. After choosing any of these options, I also would have had to somehow cross the course to get from the 11th tee to the 12th. Were a young Scot and an anonymous Taiwanese worth that kind of hassle? I turned around and walked back toward the town.

HEATHER CAME TO spectate with me on Friday morning. She'd never voluntarily watched golf before in her life, either on television or in person. Her interest seemed a good sign for our relationship, but as we tiptoed around the edges of the action, searching in vain for good vantage points, I couldn't imagine her perceptions of golf were improving. She saw lots of little men in the far-off distance rotating their torsos. Barely knowing where to look, much less how to follow a white speck against a gray sky, I'm not sure she saw a ball in flight even once. After about two hours, she had lost interest and bade me farewell. What could I say? I wasn't terribly gripped by the proceedings either, so I made a beeline back to the media dining tent. There, I sat down to watch some of the continued coverage of the event on Sky Sports.

Normally I'm a big fan of televised golf. Golf tournaments can be watched in person from a variety of perspectives, but the leaderboard narrative can only be properly followed and understood from a distance. Even at the Alfred Dunhill Cup, to see a match between countries unfold in its entirety you need to be in three places at once, and only television makes this possible. But television commentators are prone to hyperbole, which is why my retreat to the press center proved an inadequate remedy. Never mind the £100,000 reward per head on offer to the winners of the competition, and the even larger sums of appearance money paid to entice the top players to St. Andrews in the first place: the Sky Sports crew only wanted to talk about national rivalries. England played Argentina on Friday, and both the Falklands War and Diego Maradona's "Hand of God" goal in the 1986 World Cup soccer tournament featured heavily in the discussion. Nice though the thought is, did 18 holes of medal-match play between Barry Lane and Vicente Fernandez have anything to do with settling nationalistic scores? Did anyone back home in Germany and Taiwan *really* care about the Sven Struver vs. Chung Chun-hsing contest, except perhaps their immediate family members?

The event elicited varying degrees of patriotism from the players themselves. Some, such as the upstart defending champions from Canada, were obviously fired up and ready to fly their respective flags. But Greg Norman talked of the "obligation" the big-name players had to represent their country on the St. Andrews stage. Nick Faldo and Bernhard Langer declined to attend at all, leaving gaping holes in the teams of their respective countries. And though John Daly would have loved to come back to St. Andrews in the wake of his Open victory, the PGA Tour wouldn't release him from a previous commitment to another event. Just for a laugh, I asked Mark James during his Wednesday press conference to compare the patriotic pressures of the Alfred Dunhill Cup to those of the Ryder Cup. He stared blankly at me for about 20 seconds, as if I had just asked him what kind of tree he would be if he were a tree. Then he put his head in his hands for another 10 seconds before emerging, staring straight at me, and commenting, "I wouldn't like to compare this tournament to the Ryder Cup—it's a different type of competition." I smirked back at him.

By Friday night, the novelty of having professional golfers around town had begun to wear thin. The golf seemed mildly interesting at best, strongly irrelevant at worst. I hadn't played golf myself in nearly a week—only the Jubilee remained open during tournament week, and I wasn't about to voyage there during Dunhillesque weather. One of Heather's flatmates even reported that she herself had spent the night in the room of a well-known and married Tour player on Thursday night, which was more than I really wanted to know (although she insisted that "he was a perfect gentleman" and nothing had happened). I would have happily let the week end then and there. And then I met Kenny.

I STAYED UP way too late on Dunhill Friday. I was in the computing center adjacent to the university library in the center of town until four in the morning, following the progress of my beloved Atlanta Braves in the National League Championship Series via the Internet. Even by my student standards, and even though the Braves won, it was a bit ridiculous.

I sped back toward Melville with the chastened air of a man knowing he'd behaved badly. The damp and chilly night air further quickened my progress. I wanted to get home, get five or six hours' sleep quickly, get ready for two more days of golf-watching as pain-lessly as possible. As I approached the intersection of North Street and Golf Place, I saw the form of a man slumped against the stairs at the entrance to the Dunvegan Hotel. Roused by my footsteps, he twisted to look at me, and my mind flashed back to shaky, after-dark encounters I'd had with hoodlums and panhandlers in Harvard Square. Had fatigue not dulled my reactions, I'm sure I would have crossed to the other side of the road as soon as I'd seen him. But I was too slow-witted to make a polite getaway.

I crept toward him nervously. Bloated, unshaven and unkempt, he had been drinking, and he shivered in the cold. He rose unsteadily to his feet, introduced himself, and slurred an explanation for his presence. He'd come up from Glasgow that morning to watch the golf, he said. His car was parked somewhere near the 18th hole, but he didn't think he could make it that far. No local hotels were open for business at that hour. All he wanted was a place to sleep. Could I help him out?

I didn't know what of Kenny's* story to believe. He didn't look like anyone I'd seen in the Road Hole grandstand that afternoon; he looked much more suited for a homeless shelter than a St. Andrews bed-and-breakfast. At that moment he certainly wasn't capable of driving, but he could have crept back to his car and slept in it—if it existed. Alcohol seemed the prime cause of his predicament. I shouldn't have felt much sympathy for him.

I don't know why I decided to take him back to Melville with me. But I did. I hobbled with him along the North Haugh, Kenny drunkenly gushing with thanks the whole way. I talked our way past the Melville night porter—"Just a friend," I said. I took a pillow and blanket from my bed and laid them out on the floor for him. I was nowhere near prepared to assume the mantle of Good Samaritan,

---

* Kenny isn't his real name.

yet there I was, several hours from daybreak with a total stranger on the floor of my dorm room.

He wouldn't sleep, either. Worse, he got up from the floor and tried to get into bed with me, hugging me and even—I think—trying to kiss me. I gently but firmly pushed him away, but then I started to get really scared. What on earth was I doing? I offered to trade my bed for the floor. Maybe all Kenny wanted was the comfort and warmth of the mattress. But he effusively declined—and then tried to get into bed with me again. I again pushed him away and repeated my offer. I don't know which of us was more confused. But getting any rest myself was by now the least of my worries.

Eventually I deduced that Kenny only wanted some companionship. I'd been to a night shelter before, and I knew that friendly conversation is almost more valued by a homeless person than a bed and a hot meal. So we started talking—about golf, by far the safest topic available. Surprisingly, Kenny had plenty to say. He thought American captain Lanny Wadkins should have picked John Daly for the American Ryder Cup team instead of Lanny's pal Curtis Strange. ("How can you not pick the reigning Open champion?" he asked, not unreasonably.) He questioned the European Tour practice of awarding appearance money to its stars, although he agreed that the sponsors have every right to want to give it out. One of his fondest memories was of his brother acing the third hole on his home course and then hotfooting it directly to the clubhouse to buy everyone drinks—"What was the point of playing on any further, you know?" Kenny used Wilson Staff irons, but he had no preference when it came to golf balls; he nearly got his brother in trouble during a visit to his club for buying a bucket of balls for £6

($10) from a kid who should have known better than to hawk his wares on club property.

The sudden lucidity of Kenny's speech and thought astounded me. At the time I was reading *Football Against the Enemy*, Simon Kuper's brilliant sociopolitical examination of how frighteningly important "football" (i.e. soccer) is to people around the world. Of the poor man in Naples, Italy, Kuper says, "He first buys himself something to eat, then goes to the football, and then he sees if he has anything left to find a place to live." Soccer as an opiate for the masses I could just about believe. But golf? Kenny had obviously been at the tournament. He described in first-person terms shots in the same Ian Woosnam vs. Michael Campbell game I'd watched that day myself, and I'm sure his narrative would have lacked fluency and enthusiasm had he only seen it on television. This means he must have paid at least £10 at the gates for admission; judging from the smell of his breath, he must have spent at least that much again on alcohol. But he was unwilling or unable to pay for a night's shelter. On many levels, this is madness. To the question "What is there to do in Scotland other than golf and drink?" the standard joking answer is "What more do you need?" It's a good line, but I never imagined anyone would take it literally.

And yet . . . the best golfers in the world are in Scotland a maximum of four weeks a year. They come for a tournament at Loch Lomond in July, the week before the Open. They stay in Scotland for the Open—if it's being played at St. Andrews, Carnoustie, Troon, Turnberry or Muirfield. Some now come in August to the Scottish PGA Championship, an event christened in 1999, but it coincides with a more prestigious tournament in the States to which the entire European Ryder Cup team is invited. And some come to the Alfred Dunhill Cup in October, but the field is small, its quality mixed. So, essentially, Scotland is guaranteed only two full-field European Tour events each year—one of which is an afterthought on the world golf calendar. By contrast, each year four full-field events are held in Spain, one of which is the season-ending World Golf Championship event, and three are held in Germany. This is scandalous. Messrs. Olazabal, Garcia, Langer and Cejka may be marginally popular in their home countries, but this doesn't sound like the principle of supply and demand at work on the European Tour to me. Perhaps Kenny was proof that the Scots, deprived of the chance to see their heroes as frequently as they want to, will go to great lengths in extreme circumstances to see them as often as they can.

Or perhaps the issue is much simpler than this. Maybe Kenny had just run out of luck for one terrible night. I don't know. But Kenny showed me that the Alfred Dunhill Cup mattered to someone. Rightly or wrongly, it mattered a lot. And as soon as it mattered to someone, anyone, the Alfred Dunhill Cup became much more than a glorified corporate shindig.

BEFORE I COULD get back to the Old Course to explore this theory, I had to figure out what to do with Kenny. He finally fell asleep, but I never did. Not that I would have gotten much rest anyway, such was my growing apprehension, but Kenny's snoring sounded like a cross between Darth Vader and a maraca. Soon enough, though, it was morning. And as Kenny knew I had a job to do—"I have to get up soon and cover the tournament," I told him— I was able to shepherd him outside before nine o'clock without making him feel unwanted.

He again thanked me profusely and gave me what he said was his address in Glasgow. As he began ambling back toward the Old Course, he insisted I look him up on my next trip there. I tried to smile. Earlier in the darkness I had felt as pure, spiritually, as I had in a very long time. But as I watched Kenny disappear into the distance it occurred to me that I would prefer never to see him again. The bonds between golf and reality, I thought, are ambiguous enough without Kenny's mix of golf, alcohol and misplaced priorities. On Alfred Dunhill Cup Saturday morning, I was happy for my St. Andrews to remain emotionally sanitized.

THE OLD COURSE is revered in part for the way it elicits greatness from great golfers. Picture Costantino Rocca, falling to his knees and pounding the ground in ecstatic relief after retrieving a duffed pitch with a miraculous putt to tie John Daly on the final hole of the 1995 Open. Or Seve Ballesteros, punching the air with unrestrained delight after his closing birdie putt in the 1984 Open toppled into the hole and virtually clinched victory. Or Jack Nicklaus, taking off his sweater on the final tee of the 1970 Open playoff and then driving through the green, 346 yards away. One can go back still further, to black-and-white newsreel footage of the 1930 British Amateur showing Bobby Jones chasing the third leg of his Grand Slam and winning his final match before being engulfed in a sea of flat caps and tweed jackets. These scenes are indelible, and in their own time their impact reverberated far beyond the narrow confines of the Old Course.

What would the Old Course be without such moments? It would still be the acknowledged birthplace of golf, and it would still make for an intriguing and memorable day on the links, but would it feel just as magical as it does now? I don't think it would. During any round on the Old Course, a decent golfer is bound to replicate perfectly at least one or two shots struck by giants of the game anywhere along the spectrum between Tom Morris and Tiger Woods. Is this buzz available anywhere else? I somehow doubt that any course could ever provide the depth and the richness of experience that St. Andrews can. More qualified people than I have argued that in a purely architectural sense, the Old Course has been surpassed on numerous occasions in the last 150 years; panels of experts, convened by the major golf magazines of America and elsewhere, consistently tell us that Pine Valley is the best course in the world. The merits of its design are unquestionably outstanding, its setting in the New Jersey scrubland hauntingly beautiful. Also, unlike St. Andrews, getting a game at Pine Valley is harder than breaking into Fort Knox, so anyone lucky enough to be offered one should immediately cancel all plans and book any necessary flights. But how can Pine Valley's one Walker Cup and one *Shell's Wonderful World of Golf* television match begin to compete with St. Andrews's 26 Opens, 15 British Amateurs and countless minor tournaments over the years? You don't have to be a historian to realize that for the golfer who has seen neither, exposure to the Old Course fills a much larger gap in a golfing education than a round at Pine Valley.

The Alfred Dunhill Cup ranks well down the list of events ever held in St. Andrews. But it still gathers great golfers upon the Old Course, and as long as anyone cares about it, the competition gives the Old Course meaning. More than that, the Alfred Dunhill Cup creates golfing history, even if on a small and localized scale. The event gives the public another chance to experience the tension and drama that come when great golfers make great (and not-so-great) swings on a great golf course. These moments, and the awareness that the Old Course has been accumulating them for centuries, give St. Andrews its historical flavor. As soon as I loosened up and figured that out, I began to have a great time watching.

With the help of a little sleep deprivation, I managed to chill out just as the golf started to heat up. Philip Walton had birdied the 18th to beat Lee Janzen by a shot on Thursday. On Saturday, with Ireland's advancement to the semifinals in his hands, Walton faced a sudden-death playoff down the first hole against the Swede Parnevik, and his prospects didn't look good. The flagstick was barely four yards beyond the watery grave of Swilcan Burn, yet Parnevik had wedged his second shot to within six feet of the hole. From my location, in a small gathering to the right of the green, I had the best possible view of Walton's approach. Golfer and spectator knew with equal clarity what was required, and as is always the case at the first hole of the Old Course when the pin is close to the burn, the margin of error was minimal. Walton swung, and we collectively held our breath. The ball landed just over the burn, took one bounce and spun to a halt . . . inside Parnevik's ball, just four feet from the hole. To a man, we cheered loudly. Parnevik then missed, perhaps stung at unexpectedly having to putt first. Walton calmly stroked his putt into the hole for the birdie that clinched Ireland's position at the top of Group One. A few feet away from me, one of Walton's teammates, Darren Clarke, beamed a smile of joy and relief, his eyes glistening. As Walton stepped off the green, the two Ulstermen hugged; I thought I heard Clarke shriek in tearful delight through the applause. Theirs was an embrace of minute importance in the long annals of the Old Course, but it meant a lot to me.

Likewise, Andrew Coltart was a revelation throughout the week. He won two of his group-stage matches; only Ernie Els got the better of him. On Sunday morning, he slogged his way past Walton in the rain and helped his more illustrious teammates book a place in the final against Zimbabwe. And in the afternoon he blitzed past Tony Johnstone with a wonderful 67 that included an ace at the par-3 eighth. His four-shot triumph sparked the home nation's popular 2–1 victory, and at the post-match press conference Johnstone was magnanimous in defeat. "He made putts, he made holes-in-one, he might have made off with my wife, I don't know," Johnstone jested, and when asked how he felt after Coltart's ace, he said he was thinking, "Maybe I should give him a good kick in the nuts, even things up a bit." We all laughed, and right then it felt as if the Alfred Dunhill Cup was definitely a good thing.

Thanks to the media dining tent, I ate as well during Alfred Dunhill Cup week as I did at any time during my stay in St. Andrews —I wasn't quite above taking advantage of a sponsor's munificence after all. The presentation ceremony, at which the Alfred Dunhill Cup was presented to the host nation for the first time, included a bagpipe procession that swirled up the final fairway in the fading light and brought a tear to one or two eyes in the gallery. I played the Old Course shortly after the Cup concluded, and with the pins still cut in their Sunday spots I birdied three of the first seven holes on my way to matching the outward par of 36, which felt excessively rewarding. These were also good things.

But normalcy in St. Andrews is pretty nifty, too. All five courses fully reopened for play within a day of the tournament's conclusion. I was glad to see the tents and grandstands disappear, to have my view from the Melville dining hall unblocked. My ears rejoiced when the constant jackhammering noises finally ceased. The good life in St. Andrews carried on as before—and I could live it on my terms, not Alfred Dunhill's or anyone else's. Weeks after the title sponsor's presence had been eradicated from St. Andrews, I couldn't help thinking about what Colin Montgomerie had said at the final press conference when asked to compare his feelings at winning the Alfred Dunhill Cup to those of winning the Ryder Cup: "Pretty similar. Very similar, actually. And at least we get paid this time."

A pause. "Please don't quote me on that," he added, since he'd been joking about that last bit. I think.

Chapter 7

THE WORD ON THE STREET

❖❖❖❖❖

THE FINAL DAY of Alfred Dunhill Cup week coincided with the university tradition of Raisin Sunday. At the beginning of the academic year, third- and fourth-year students adopt incoming first-years into "academic families" as their "academic children." "Academic parents" help to familiarize their children with the university and the local pubs. Academically incestuous relationships are known to spring up as well, often at the behest of lecherous academic fathers.

Raisin Weekend is the pinnacle of the dysfunctional academic family life. Children go to their mothers' houses for afternoon tea, at which gelatin made with vodka instead of water is a popular hors d'oeuvre. Early in the evening, the fathers collect their children from the mother and take them out for the vilest possible night on the town. Alcohol is consumed by the gallon. Some students target the Old Course; flagsticks are popular souvenirs in the dorms, and in the darkness more than a few couples over the years have endeavored to give the Valley of Sin in front of the 18th green a more literal meaning. Throughout the night, a minibus affectionately known as the "Pukemobile" drives around town, collecting incapacitated students and taking them home or, in extreme cases, to Nine Wells Hospital in Dundee. Hangovers notwithstanding, the children must wake up early on Raisin Monday morning and report back to their mothers' houses, where they are made to change into outrageous costumes before being escorted to St. Salvator's Quadrangle. There, Raisin Weekend climaxes in the mother of all bun fights as the children paste each other with shaving cream, flour, raw eggs and other savory substances. Covered in muck, the children finally slink back to their halls of residence, where older students will have helpfully let the showers run cold.

Not all students partake of academic family life. Foreign transients like me, in our third or fourth year of university but our first year at St. Andrews, don't really fit the system at all—which suited me perfectly. Physical self-abasement has never appealed to me, and moral considerations aside, I'm far too cowardly to enjoy breaking the law. (Sneak on a golf course without paying a green fee? Never. I'm so afraid of getting caught in the act, I can barely hold a golf club, much less swing it.) My idea of anarchy in the U.K. was slipping onto the Old Course in the darkness of the Monday night of Alfred Dunhill Cup week. In this brave act I was preceded by an 8-year-old boy and a 10-year-old girl, a brother and sister who lived in one of the houses adjacent to the Old Course. I was walking along the 18th fairway, on my way into town, when I saw them tossing a frisbee back and forth not far from the Valley of Sin. Their innocence touched me; seemingly oblivious to their surroundings, in a sense they were but playing in their front yard. Fascinated, I wandered over to talk to them and play with them for 10 minutes, waiting all the while for armed members of the Alfred Dunhill security force to descend and whisk me away to be buried neck-deep in a pot bunker. I felt liberated, but compared to the antics of Raisin Sunday, my Dunhill Monday was like a quiet evening in a monastery.

Heather did sweetly offer to foster-mother me, and on Raisin/Dunhill Sunday evening she kindly presented me with a lollipop, but after midnight I found myself once again alone, walking from the center of town back to Melville. I was happy enough to be heading home and to sleep—and at a reasonable hour relative to when I'd met Kenny two nights earlier. Ready to swap my passive roles as spectator and reporter for something more participatory, I looked forward to playing the Old Course again in the morning. But I hadn't made much progress home when I discovered that just as the St. Andrews linksland isn't exclusively reserved for golf, in St. Andrews golf isn't exclusively reserved for the linksland.

Along North Street I spotted one of my bespectacled colleagues from the St. Andrews University Golf Club. I said hello—and noticed he was holding what appeared to be a pitching wedge. Scratching my head, I then heard the unmistakable thwack of a golf ball being struck on the far side of the road.

"Nice shot," my friend called out. A young woman skipped over, took his pitching wedge and handed him a 6-iron.

"What the . . ." I was truly confused.

"Ah, I should explain," said my friend. "Darren, meet Miss Scarlet. Scarlet, meet Darren."

Scarlet said, "How do you do?" I stood motionless, silent and dumbstruck.

"My name is Opus," my friend continued. He winked—that

wasn't the name by which I knew him. "You will notice that a meeting of the St. Andrews Street Golf Society is now in session. So glad you've come along our match has been needing a referee. Will you please join us? It would be an honor."

The Street Golf Society. That was a new one. St. Andrews has all sorts of student societies, from the mainstream sporting, academic and arts organizations to the Tiddlywinks Society and to the Tunnock's Caramel Wafer Appreciation Society (recently in the news when a former member auctioned off a poem Ted Hughes wrote on the back of a Tunnock's Caramel Wafer wrapper). But I didn't remember reading about the SGS in my Overseas Weekend university prospectus. For once, curiosity got the better of timidity. I volunteered my services immediately.

"Excellent," said Opus. "We're just underway—we teed off at the University Library a short time ago. The hole is a vodka bottle in Miss Scarlet's room, which is on the fourth floor of New Hall."

I mentally plotted our route. New Hall is adjacent to Melville. I figured the "hole" to be a slight dogleg-left of approximately 1,800 yards, not counting the elevator ride. Its par was beyond my comprehension.

Opus took the 6-iron and walloped a shot up the left side of the "fairway." His swing wasn't as elegant as I'd seen it in the past. I examined his club, a forged blade that had clearly seen better days. It looked as if he had used it to take divots out of North Street before. I wasn't sure the R&A or the USGA would have deemed it fit for play, but I let it slide without comment. He passed it back to Scarlet and received the pitching wedge in return—the competitors had only the two clubs between them. Scarlet played her next shot, and I remarked that her swing looked quite good.

"Scarlet is the Ladies' Captain of the SGS," Opus offered by way of clarification. Scarlet grinned. She seemed marginally the more sober of the two. The match figured to be quite competitive.

I asked if I was responsible for scorekeeping as well as refereeing, but both players responded in the negative (which was probably just as well, given the circumstances and my propensity to obsess about score). We walked along to where each of the shots had wound up, and we found them both quite quickly. I was surprised. I remarked that searching for balls tends to be easier in daylight.

"Maybe," said Scarlet, "but I've never played a Street Golf match in the daytime. Opus?"

"Nope. Even at night, you see one police car and you're diving for cover. Last match I played there was one squad car on patrol—he must have swung past us three separate times within half an hour. Bloody nuisance." I gulped.

It had been drizzling on and off all day, and the gutters were clogged with rainwater; this proved a serious hazard while we remained in the town. Opus's next shot started on a good line but gradually drifted away with the slope of the road to the right and into a puddle. I offered him a casual water drop, but strangely he refused, preferring instead to splash his way out. With a mighty heave, he chopped into the water. Not only did he soak himself; his ball traveled no more than 10 yards before sinking into another puddle farther along the same gutter. I raised my eyebrows in confused amusement.

"We are not thick," Opus insisted self-righteously. He defended himself, citing Street Golf's traditionalist origins. "When golf first started, there wasn't a hole and shit. You just played out to a point and played back." For the first time, Opus sounded distinctly tipsy. "We're playing 'gowf.' Yeah, that's it, we're playing 'gowf.' No casual water drops in 'gowf.'" He beamed triumphantly. As he reached this conclusion, Scarlet half-shanked a shot up the wrong road (and toward the Road Hole, actually), narrowly missing a parked Mercedes.

We searched for Scarlet's ball, but the Pilmour Links road wasn't as well lit as North Street and the ball proved unfindable among the "gorse bushes" (parked cars). But Opus had come with a pocketful of replacements, so after the allowable five minutes of searching had elapsed, Scarlet and I returned to the spot from which she had played her previous shot. She stretched out her arm horizontally at shoulder height and dropped her ball correctly, as per the Rules of Golf. It plinked around several times on the macadam road surface, and when it came to rest I pronounced it "in play." Her replayed shot was a corker, zooming past Macintosh Hall along Links Crescent into the halogen gloom. A majestic stroke, it nearly reached the roundabout at the western edge of town.

At the roundabout a friend of Scarlet's joined our group and graciously accepted a posting as spectator-*cum*-marshal. His timing was impeccable, for the second stage of the match began just after he arrived, at which point Opus and Scarlet briefly went their separate ways. As the buildings of the town center gave way to the fields and trees of the North Haugh, a thick grove of saplings at the southwest corner of the roundabout barred the direct line to New Hall. Opus chose to skirt around the trees to the left, and the marshal followed him. He took the 6-iron. Scarlet decided upon a frontal assault, attempting to carry the trees and/or burrow beneath them, and I joined her. She was left with the pitching wedge.

Opus's plan and club selection seemed better than Scarlet's, but I would soon learn that in Street Golf strategy is usually a poor substitute for execution. As Scarlet successfully navigated a path through the trees, we heard a booming *gong* that sounded as if someone had rung the Liberty Bell. I dashed over to investigate. Opus stood upright, holding the 6-iron at right-shoulder arms and peering from side to side with a perplexed look on his face. The marshal looked like he was about to wet himself. He explained that Opus had struck a full-blooded shot flush against a metal lamppost along the street. The ball rebounded backward, narrowly missed the marshal and ended up 20 yards behind where it started. By the time the three of us composed ourselves and finally caught up with Scarlet, about 100 yards short of New Hall, what looked a formidable lead had been trimmed to only one shot.

Under other circumstances, play would have continued into New Hall via the front door, the hall foyer and the elevator. Being Raisin Sunday night, though, the hall wardens were vigorously guarding the front entrance. Opus, Scarlet, the marshal and I held an impromptu conference to address the situation, and we proposed and seconded an extraordinary ruling: upon striking a shot into any part of the New Hall façade, Opus and Scarlet would be permitted to pick up their balls and bypass the course until reaching such point at which the match could safely be resumed. Opus played a nice pitch against the outer wall of the New Hall lower common room from around 40 yards; his ball dropped into a small bush, and he tiptoed up to collect it. Scarlet, from half as far away, aimed for a concrete section of the same wall but pushed it slightly . . . and struck glass. We instinctively dropped to the ground as one. Mercifully, the window didn't shatter. Scarlet decided she could retrieve her ball the following morning.

We stood up, brushed ourselves off and crept around to the front entrance. Smiling sheepishly, we marched through the foyer and past the unsuspecting New Hall dignitaries. Once in the safety of the elevator, I reopened my golf umbrella and allowed the 6-iron and pitching wedge to tumble out on the floor. Our stratagem had worked beautifully. Opus pressed "4," and as the door closed, the two contestants each dropped new balls, again correctly from shoulder height. The balls pinged off the hollow-sounding floor of the elevator. When the door opened, the third and final stage of the match began. Opus still clung to his one-shot lead.

New Hall has 450 rooms, all interconnected by a complicated system of long, carpeted corridors. Scarlet's room was at the opposite end of the Hall from the elevator. Clearly, the match was far from over. As we progressed diligently through the lengthy series of hallways and swinging double-doors that the marshal and I held open for the players, I spotted a tactical variance: Scarlet enjoyed playing dainty shots of much touch and precision along the walls, whereas Opus preferred to bash the ball as hard as possible and play for the multiple carom. The deflections off the walls were soft and friendly, but when Opus crashed his ball into the oaken doors of the student rooms, a thunderous crack echoed down the corridor. One of his efforts struck a door not far away from one of the New Hall sub-warden's rooms; as we stood around, debating the merits of Opus's shot selection, the sub-warden opened her door, fire in her eyes, and charged up the hall to ask us what the heck was going on.

"Don't you have somewhere to be?" she growled. "Because there are a lot of us trying to sleep, and it would be a good thing if you would get there as quickly as possible."

She quickly stormed back into her room and emphatically closed the door. As soon as she was out of earshot, the two competitors began to snigger.

"We call her Hitler," explained Scarlet.

I wouldn't call Opus's shotmaking technique moral, especially given the hour, but it certainly proved effective; as we neared the finish line, he eased his way into the lead by several shots. Scarlet's chances of salvaging something from the match hinged upon two contingencies. First, Opus had to negotiate a precipitous ledge leading to a fire escape stairwell: a push or a pull might have trickled down five flights of stairs into the New Hall basement. This alone could have given Scarlet victory, for Opus didn't seem alert enough at this stage to invoke the unplayable lie rule on his behalf and claim the stroke-and-distance penalty to which he would have been entitled. But both players expertly crossed the chasm with well-directed shots, so this point became moot. Second, Scarlet could have claimed a half were the match to be abandoned. Not that she would have wanted one, but an abandonment is always a possibility in Street Golf. With only the final corridor to negotiate, Opus clattered a shot into the door of yet another sub-warden, prompting a scurried dash back down the corridor by the lot of us. But the sub-warden failed to emerge, and with that, Opus's victory was assured.

Scarlet opened her door to reveal a bottle of Smirnoff poised in a corner at the foot of her bed. Opus graciously let Scarlet "putt" out first with the 6-iron, and then with a bladed wedge from 15 feet Opus finished the contest with a delicate stroke into the bottle via one final deflection against the base of Scarlet's wall. The final score: Opus 37, Scarlet 42. Only five shots the difference, and the course successfully completed—both causes for celebration. Immediately the bottle was open and flowing freely.

Opus slumped onto the bed in glorious exhaustion, but his rest was only momentary. After a swig of the bottle, he began regaling me with tales from the history of Street Golf. The best hole he'd ever played, he said, took 72 shots to complete, from a flat in Eden Court to a fruitcake in another friend's New Hall room. I lapped it all up—until I glanced at my watch. Four-thirty in the morning. I'd come to Scotland to experience golf in *all* its splendor, but this was getting a little ridiculous.

Chapter 8

NORTHERN LIGHTS

❖❖❖

IN EARLY NOVEMBER, Heather and I traveled to Inverness. I'd sortied north of St. Andrews only twice before: to Cruden Bay, and afterward to Stonehaven.

One of the witnesses to my hole-in-one had invited me to play at Murcar, a well-regarded links course near Aberdeen, four days after we met at Cruden Bay. An hour before my train's departure, I called him up and discovered that he'd forgotten about me and had to be at work in 30 minutes. Rather than waste my rail fare, on a whim I quickly made arrangements to visit Stonehaven, a golf course I'd previously seen from the train, just south of Aberdeen, sandwiched between the railroad and the sea. I was annoyed to discover that the course had seven par 3s, no links atmosphere and precious little architectural merit. What had drawn me there were its holes, visible from the train, perched above the water on Pebble Beach-sized cliffs—but even those failed to impress, for an impenetrably thick fog rolled in from the sea as I played the opening hole and remained for most of my round. On the third, an uphill par 4 near the shoreline called "Kingsacre," I teed off into the murky whiteness and covered at least an acre looking for my ball; after 20 fruitless minutes, I finally employed the "expanding square" search technique taught to carrier pilots for naval reconnaissance. The ball was in the fairway. I had to laugh.

But Inverness was a serious proposition. Heather was heading home for a week during the university's fall midterm break, and she'd invited me to meet her parents. On such pretexts are golf vacations founded: Inverness, the largest town in the Highlands, looked a perfect base of operations for linksland patrols to the north and east. Only after I'd happily plotted a golfing itinerary did I grasp the implications of Heather's invitation. I liked how our relationship seemed to be blossoming, but a week with her parents would have been an escalation of the nuclear missile variety. To be on the safe side, I booked myself into several bed-and-breakfasts.

Our train ride north heralded the introduction of a new Scotland. The Scottish coastline is often tempestuous and moody, but the Highlands north of Perthshire were uniformly tranquil and friendly. The late-autumn colors of the Highlands were astonishing: I never imagined that faded reds and purples and yellows and dun-greens and grays could shine so brilliantly. Hills boldly rippled with heather and broom curved gently into one another to form a treeless horizon. Even the mountains had smooth edges. Dusted with heather, the rounded red-gray peaks stood sentinel over the valleys like lovable giants; as the train bobbed and weaved between them, they tried immensely hard to look stark and fearsome, but the effect almost made me giggle. Were they human, I would have called out

"Come here, you big softy!" to one of them and given it a big hug. Colloquial language reflects this friendliness. The Scottish pastime is called hill walking, not mountain climbing. And they are called the Monadhliath mountains; even bereft of meaning, like so many other place names in Scotland "Monadhliath" looks and sounds like centuries of wordsmanship at work, its Gaelic complexity perfectly evocative. One can instinctively discern that the Cairngorms, to the east, don't look like Monadhliaths.

Heather's parents, Ian and Alison, and her younger sister, Laura, waited for us on the platform at Inverness train station. Each of them greeted us with a hug and a jovial "Hullo!" and rattled on in a stream of alien dialect at a speed that made it impossible for me to comprehend. Heather's family moved five times while growing up, and her accent must have crawled closer to the front of her mouth with each successive migration, for it now sounded faintly American. Heather's parents, though, hadn't left Glasgow until they were both in their thirties, and their words exploded into life from their throats in voices at once hearty and impenetrable. I glanced nervously at Heather, who whispered to her mother, "Slow down!"

We drove to Invernesian suburbia and their house, one of many boxy, same-but-different houses spaced two yards apart from each other on a meandering side street. Every house was part stucco, part wood and part brick; the designers' attempts to juggle these three materials created the only appearance of originality. Inside, a false fireplace rested against one wall of the living room. Vertical venetian blinds covered the panoramic living room windows. Off-whites, light browns and earthy yellows patterned the walls, kitchen tiles and furniture; in the bathroom, olive green graced the toilet and sink.

Ian and Alison dialed back their voices to an intelligible frequency and sat me down at the dining room table for tea. Still apprehensive, I asked for a cup; Ian poured, and Alison offered the sugar bowl. I withdrew the spoon . . . and the sugar fell through a large hole in the spoon's center. Hmmm, I thought. How odd. The room fell strangely silent. Was I committing a terrible faux pas? I tried to scoop out sugar quickly into the cup using the tip of the spoon. Laura tittered ever so slightly, and that snapped the spell—everyone burst out laughing. Relieved, I laughed, too. I felt honored to be made the butt of a practical joke so soon. People normally take days to ferret me out.

THE NEXT DAY we drove farther north, across and beyond the rich, rolling farmland of the Black Isle. Very kindly, Heather and her family elected to spend the day at Dunrobin Castle in Golspie, just over an hour north of Inverness. They wouldn't have bothered, I don't think, had they not already offered to chauffeur me to and from a seaside village, just south of Golspie, called Dornoch.

I had pitched a travel story to *Golf Digest* on the "hidden gems" of Scottish golf. Little-known links courses with curious names and mysterious reputations dot the coastlines of the remote northern and western Scotland, and I wanted to tackle every test the "Highlands and Islands" region could throw at me. But of them all, I reckoned Royal Dornoch Golf Club might alone make the long trip worthwhile. Its charms, only recently discovered (in the same sense that Columbus "discovered" America) by traditionalists like Ben Crenshaw and Tom Watson, had become renowned in certain circles. The great architect Donald Ross served an apprenticeship at Dornoch, and Dornoch's crowned greens inspired his greatest creation, the No. 2 course at Pinehurst in North Carolina. I knew very little about Royal Dornoch's appearance (*Golf Digest's* photo library seemed strangely incomplete), but that merely allowed my imagination to run riot. The farther north we drove, the more I salivated over the thought of confirming what I knew and discovering what I didn't.

In retrospect, I have to admit that I didn't like the 16th hole at Dornoch. A mundane, staircased, uphill par 4, its green was flat and featureless, and the elevated greensite offered scintillating views of a trailer park in the distance. Strangely, every great course I'd played in Scotland had one curiously bland, out-of-place or altogether bad hole that cooled my ardor. One would expect nearly great, second-echelon layouts like Gullane No. 1, North Berwick or the New Course at St. Andrews to stumble through the odd clunker now and again, but my favorite courses suffered as well. At Cruden Bay, as mentioned previously, the poor hole is the ninth. On the Old Course, it is also the ninth, a short and flat par 4 to a plain, undistinguished green shared with no other hole. (The green seems to live a charmed life, for nobody I know seems capable of getting near the hole with his second shot—but "supernatural powers" is not on the list of features that characterize great golf course architecture.) And at Dornoch, it is the 16th. Very curious.

I must dispassionately criticize Dornoch's 16th, because Royal Dornoch, on a calm November day, was otherwise a vision of earthly paradise. Perhaps the 16th at Dornoch exists to remind me that earthly pleasures cannot capture perfection.

What ingredients make a memorable round of golf? For me, either the setting or my score must be of the highest standard, and the other mustn't ruin it. At Royal Dornoch, par is 70, and on my first day there I shot 76. Good, but not otherworldly, especially as I played Dornoch's two par 5s from forward tees. In my Scottish Record, I noted my "birdie" at the ninth in apologetic parentheses.

The setting, on the other hand, was incomparable. In purely architectural terms, Dornoch was fantastic. The greens were large; most were subtly contoured, and many were crowned steeply at the sides, but they still seemed receptive and inviting. Then I missed one and endeavored to recover from a neck-high swale with gorse scratching at my ear. The greens seemed much smaller after that. That's how Dornoch works. Strategically speaking, it lulls the golfer to sleep. Dornoch is never penal, and average golfers will be buoyed by the absence of visible hazards like water, tall rough, tight gorse and high-walled bunkers. But every hole has an optimal angle of approach, often originating from the outer or inner corner of a dogleg, and finding these angles takes guile, imagination and a good golf swing. The most celebrated hole at Dornoch, the "Foxy" 14th, has no bunkers, no water, nothing quirky or bizarre. Just grass, most of it closely mown, and a few plateaued slopes. One would never need a rulebook to play it. And in its own way—like every other hole at Dornoch, including the 16th—its challenges work superbly.

Other courses have great holes, too, but none of them has the spellbinding tranquillity of Dornoch in early November. The Old Course is too popular, for most of the year a hive of frantic hurry-up-and-waiting. Golfers with more souvenirs than sense trample the beaten path into a pulp. In their wakes trail tut-tutting locals, looking at their watches and wondering why the Old Course isn't how it used to be. But Royal Dornoch remains how it has always been. Geography preserves the miracle of Dornoch: were it 100 miles to the south, it would be overrun, like St. Andrews in the summer, but even in a fast-shrinking world relatively few people seem to know about Dornoch. Still fewer investigate it, even though its gates are eternally open to member and commoner alike. Its staff treats golfers and non-golfers the same—with dignity and respect. Its land is shared between club and country; Royal Dornoch Golf Club owns only the land that encompasses holes seven through 11, at the far end of the course. Pedestrians, dog-walkers and cyclists can and do take polite advantage of the paths and open spaces of the back nine; during my visit, the passersby even outnumbered those golfers spaced few and far between across the linksland.

Royal Dornoch's accessibility appealed to me greatly. Exclusive clubs cannot possibly radiate the type of warmth that Dornoch radiates. Although I thought Cypress Point was truly wonderful when I played there, feelings of pride and alienation corrupted the experience: pride, because I was playing a course at which very few were allowed; alienation, because the club only welcomed my father and I on the strictest of terms. Dornoch eliminated these diminishing, self-defeating qualities, and the grass seemed greener, the sand brighter, the sea a richer shade of copper in consequence.

I reached the crest of the fairway on Dornoch's eighth hole, a par 4 that tumbles down a steep hillside to a green near the sea. The low-flying sun, peering through a veil of gray translucent cloud, sparkled on the still ocean. A breeze whistled softly across the gorse, tugging gently at the sleeves of my jacket. The dying embers of autumn flickered in the darkly proud gorse, in wispy fields of soft beige and muted green twice removed from the golfer's progress. The stillness, the ethereal peace of the moment, overwhelmed me. The earth itself reposed in contentment: miles of tiny, pimpled dunes beyond the eighth hole mirrored my goose bumps, beckoning me away from Royal Dornoch, away from golf along the arcing shoreline toward the sleepy hamlet of Embo. In the near-silence I stood: alone, yet not alone.

How COULD I possibly describe Royal Dornoch to Heather and her non-golfing family? They asked if I had enjoyed my day, and I said, "Yes, very much, thank you." At the same time, I felt sheepish. Dunrobin Castle was closed, so they had wandered around the grounds for a while, enjoyed a lengthy pub lunch, then returned to wander around the grounds some more until I finished. To their credit, they remained in good humor, although they did make me listen to Abba music the whole way home.

The next day we drove east instead of north. Heather's aunt and uncle lived in Elgin, one town south of Lossiemouth on the Moray Firth. Moray Golf Club, Lossiemouth, lacked Dornoch's magic. Sprinkled between its fairways were large, wooden poles that supported landing lights for a nearby military airbase; RAF Tornados screeched a few hundred feet over my head at regular intervals. Lossiemouth has one of the great finishing holes in Scotland, an uphill par 4 to an amphitheater green beneath an imposing clubhouse and the formidable gray stone wall guarding the town from the sea. But the rest of the course left me cold, literally and figuratively. A chill wind sliced through my windbreaker and turtleneck, tying my stomach in knots on the difficult holes, of which there were 18. I tacked into the wind to reach several greens.

Even Moray's scorecard bothered me. A ridiculous monstrosity in cardboard, it allocated four and a half of its eight panels to advertising:

> Graham Electrical — Domestic & Industrial Electrician — All types of work undertaken — Free quotations
>
> The Stotfield Hotel, Stotfield Road, Lossiemouth — Moray's Premier Golf Hotel — "A wedge to the green"

Johnstons of Elgin — Cashmere Visitor Centre — For Quality
Cashmere at Mill Prices — Visit Our Cashmere Exhibition
Centre — Audio Visual Presentation in Six Languages

Feeling a little under par! — we'll soon have you in the pink
and back on the green, if you book your holidays at Beaver
Travel. — 4 Commerce Street — Elgin, Moray

The scene improved that evening, or so I thought. Back in
Inverness, after Ian, Alison and Laura had retired to bed, Heather
and I sat cupped in each other arms on the living room sofa.
Smooching sweetly and passionately in the dim glow of the ceiling
light, I blurted out something that at that moment came naturally to
me: "I love you."

Heather sat up with a startled, Bambi-caught-in-the-headlights
look in her eyes. "You what?"

"Yes, I love you," I said, a little more timidly. "That's how I feel.
I hadn't thought about it in those terms before, but yes, I think I'm
in love with you."

"Oh, dear," she said. "I'm not in love with you, you know. Not
yet, anyway."

Uh-oh. Not good. Then I thought, Wait a minute. You're the guy
here. *You're* the one who's supposed to suffer phobias of physical and
emotional commitment. She still won't call you her boyfriend, for cry-
ing out loud—you're her "special friend." And yet *she* invited *you* up to
meet her parents. What is wrong with her? Or what is wrong with you?

Seething, confused and anxiety-stricken all at once, I mumbled a
trite "That's okay," and awkwardly grasped for a hug. The unspoken
question "Where do we go from here?" loomed ominously. We soon
drifted upstairs into our respective bedrooms. I needed to clear my
head, and I couldn't get out of Inverness fast enough.

I WAS VERY thankful to have my rental car reservation kick in the following morning. I sped north on my own, sitting in a right-side seat, cruising on the left side of the road, passing other cars in the right-hand lane. "Surreal" wasn't strong enough an adjective.

The course at Tain, on the south side of Dornoch Firth, was a disappointment. I'd expected better, but no layout could compensate for the blandness of Tain's terrain. Toward the start and finish of the course, only thin wire fences separated the fairways from out-of-bounds cattle pastures. The damp turf, tufty and spongy, and thick clusters of pine trees belied the nearness of the sea. Several holes nearer the turn were quite good, but the main redeeming innovation at Tain was the chart at the tee on the "Alps" 11th, a par 4 to a blind green. A three-by-three grid partitioned a diagram of the green, tic-tac-toe style; an "X" in one space indicated the current pin placement. A great idea, worthy of imitation at all courses with blind holes. Otherwise, Tain was tame. It could have at least let me post a decent score, but I played poorly as well.

I drove directly from Tain to Dornoch, seeking an antidote that afternoon. But in my second round at Royal Dornoch, I bore down upon the course, trying to have it on my terms — to actively create, not semi-passively enjoy. In wanting a score to at least match the setting, I primed myself for a steep fall.

I began well enough, with a bogey and five pars, but at the par-4 seventh I literally threw everything away. I blocked my drive weakly to the right, 10 yards short of an echelon of gorse bushes. Pressing, I attempted a risky recovery from rough with a 3-wood over the corner of the gorse — and failed. My ball plugged into the gorse. I had to take an unplayable lie and pitch out diagonally into the fairway, lying four. I raged inwardly, one loose swing away from spontaneous self-combustion. Then, from the middle of the fairway, 150 yards from the center of the green, I blocked another horrible, pitiful, weaselly shot to the right with a 7-iron. By the time it landed short of the bunkers in front of the green, I had jerked my club downward from the top of my follow-through and flung it forcefully into one of the legs on the stand of my golf bag. The leg bent backward like Joe Theisman's after Lawrence Taylor's infamous tackle on *Monday Night Football.* The shaft of my 7-iron snapped in two.

Elapsed time between start of swing and end of 7-iron: two seconds. That's how long it took me to regress from apparent golfer to momentary psychopath.

I've broken clubs in every conceivable setting. Georgia Class AAA High School State Championships, Dublin, Ga., Marist School, freshman year. Fifty-Ninth Annual New England Intercollegiate Fall Golf Championships, New Seabury, Mass., Harvard University, sophomore year. Intrasquad tournament qualifying at Harvard, Primrose Nine, The Country Club, junior year. Atlanta Junior Golf Association . . . I'd rather not talk about it. Semiformal and informal practice or vacation rounds, too many courses and dates to mention. And those are only the ones I've broken, not thrown—thrown for distance, for accuracy, for destructive impact. I've never hit anyone with a flying club, but I've come close. The explanation I give is that I care too much. I want so badly to do well, in all circumstances, that when I fail to achieve a minimum standard of competence, I snap. Invariably, a trip to the shaft repairman follows, and I travel through a shopworn cycle of horror, repentance, forgetfulness and backsliding for the umpteenth time.

The incident at Royal Dornoch horrified me more than most of my previous lapses. I poisoned paradise with a horrible tantrum while playing a round that should have meant nothing. Was score *that* important to me? Possibly. Had the twist in my relationship with Heather wound me up? Certainly. Could anything justify such a moment of stupidity? Definitely not. I put my head in my hands, donned the customary sackcloth and ashes and hoped—again—that this would be the last time I ever threw a golf club. So help me God.

I GATHERED MY thoughts during the back nine and in my Dornoch B&B that evening, where it dawned upon me that I was stuck in a morality play of my own writing: John Milton my muse, Royal Dornoch the main stage, my scorecards and I the *dramatis personae*. Act I, "Paradise Found," carried me from the Monadhliaths to Dornoch One on Monday. In Act II, "Paradise Lost," ill fortune and hubris corrupted me between Lossiemouth and Dornoch Two on Wednesday. I had two days and four rounds of golf to script Act III, which I hoped could be titled "Paradise Regained" after Dornoch Three on Friday. After Dornoch Three, I was supposed to return to Heather and her family. I desperately wanted to be in a good mood when I got there.

Brora was an ideal place to start searching for inner peace. Brora Golf Club is so relaxed, it extends still further the squatters' rights offered to non-golfers at Dornoch and St. Andrews: sheep and even cattle may safely graze in Brora's fairways as the local crofters herd them along the coast. To safeguard Brora's integrity as a golf course, the club erected a series of shin-high, electrically charged fences around its greens and greenside bunkers. Powerful enough to jolt animals into a hasty retreat, these fences impede the occasional pitch-and-run approach, but from a scoring standpoint one can hardly complain: the sheep systematically trim the fairways and eliminate the roughs. Brora doesn't need a greenkeeper so much as a rancher.

These curious fences were what drew me to Brora, but the golf course itself made me long to stay: I was shocked at how much I enjoyed it. Most of the turn-of-the-century, 6,110-yard layout can no longer challenge the best golfers, but it tested me just enough to allow me a sense of accomplishment when I did well. And Brora's four par 3s were a class apart: ranging in distance from the 125-yard 13th to the uphill, 201-yard 18th—a diabolical finishing hole reminiscent of the one at East Lake Golf Club in Atlanta, only better—each pointed in a different cardinal direction, adding welcome variety in all wind conditions to an already charismatic out-and-back layout. The short ninth, at the far end of the course, rolled delicately down to the beachside; from there, on a cold, calm, bright morning, Brora had an icy, arctic beauty to it. I could almost see the rolling, bluish hills beyond the course reflected in the shiny sea. Against Brora's par of 69, I shot 75—but honestly, I hardly cared.

My afternoon round, at Golspie, posed a question still unique in my golfing travels: how to begin? All entrances to the clubhouse were locked; both club and course looked deserted. I had called ahead, and Golspie was definitely open for play. But where was everyone? A peek under a sheltered awning of the clubhouse revealed what is known in remote regions of Scotland as the "Honesty Box." I plunked my green fee, all of £7 ($11), into the box, collected a scorecard-*cum*-course map and went on my merry, transcendentalist way. I couldn't understand how, on a sunny afternoon, Golspie's peculiar and intriguing mix of heathland, parkland and linksland holes could remain unpopulated. Not that I would ever complain about having a course like Golspie to myself.

I've always liked playing alone, especially on a quiet golf course. Golf is easily the sport most conducive to solitaire play. Unless leaderboards are involved, stroke play golf is an individual pursuit, a contest between man and nature. And on my own, I can compete as fiercely as I want without fear of reproach. When I too readily yield to the desire to score, I can be my own worst company, but rounds like those at Brora and Golspie restore a healthy, natural narcissism. Moreover, solitude breeds contentment. Alone, I don't risk annoyance from others' uncomfortably slow or embarrassingly bad play, disgust from others' horrible stories or boredom from forgettable ones, irritation at others' basic violations of etiquette. Nor do I risk appalling anyone with my intense disposition or the odd display of psychotic behavior. I don't have to get to know me, nor is anyone else compelled to try—so I can focus my energies on the golf course, my swing, or demystifying the vagaries of the game itself.

Good companionship enriches the golfing experience, but bad companionship can ruin it altogether. The ritual of courting playing partners as a solitary golfer makes a great variant of prisoner's dilemma. All else being equal, if I enjoy my own company, I will enjoy playing alone. By forming a group with unknown partners, I could enjoy my round much more, but I might enjoy it much less. Terrible partners might cause all forms of golf-related enjoyment to cease altogether. Safety, and guaranteed enjoyment, can be found only by playing alone.

These principles operated decisively during my round at Brora. I was thoroughly enjoying my solitude when I caught up with another single golfer on the tee of the par-3 13th hole. Half hoping that what worked at Cruden Bay would work at Brora, I asked to join him, eager to spiritually bond with what looked to be a salty, bearded veteran of the Highland links wars. Instead, he introduced himself as a native and resident of Virginia, and for the next six holes droned on in a tinny, nasal voice with a blow-by-blow recitation of events at his home club's recent member-guest tournament. Before long, I wanted the round to end. On the 17th tee I let him have the honor and then targeted the edge of the fairway farther from his ball.

Golspie posed no such problems. Its course wasn't as special as Brora's, but its atmosphere was. The only man I saw at Golspie wore apposite blue raingear and wellies; he and his dog, a scruffy white terrier, crossed my path on the 15th tee, heading toward the far end of the course. After putting out on the final hole, I sat on a bench outside the still-locked clubhouse, basking in the sunshine of a crisp day in the Highlands, and waited for man and dog to complete their circuit. They returned, and we exchanged greetings—two "hellos" and a bark. The effect was as if I'd pinched myself. I had begun wondering if Golspie Golf Club were a figment of my imagination.

BETWEEN MY ROUNDS at Brora and Golspie, I was involved in a car accident. I rolled to a stop at a crossroads behind an 18-wheeler, and as I idly asked myself what an 18-wheeler was doing at a small village crossroads, the truck began reversing very slowly. Its driver hadn't seen me sneak up behind him. I instinctively palmed the center of my steering wheel, again and again, but to no response. I cursed the car horn; I didn't know its triggers were two small buttons at four and eight o'clock on the wheel. I froze, my eyes bulging. The truck crunched into the front of my car in super-slow motion. To my relief, it jerked forward much more quickly, and I got out of my car as soon as it came to a halt.

Out of the truck clambered the driver, ashen-faced. He looked much younger and less grizzled than I'd anticipated. "I'm so, so sorry," he said mournfully. "I don't normally drive this lorry."

"I can tell." I smiled. "I don't normally drive on this side of the road."

We swapped contact information and surveyed the damage. Not surprisingly, the truck looked pristine. My bumper had survived intact, but my front license plate had cracked and squashed its plastic holder. Nothing major, but the sight wouldn't have impressed my car rental agency.

The driver's eyes brightened slightly. "I work at a place where we make number plates," he said. Then he frowned again. "But you don't sound like you're from around these parts. Where are you heading this evening?"

Not where you're going, I feared. "To a hotel in Wick, on the north coast," I said.

But the tension drained from his face. "My shop is in Wick. Where are you staying?" I told him. "Leave it to me, then. Park your car so I can get at the number plate, and I'll fix it up for you during the night. You'll never know there was a problem."

"Great," I said. "I'll just forget this ever happened, then. One question—can I keep the broken one?"

"Sure." He laughed. "I'll put it under the car."

He was as good as his word. The cracked license plate took pride of place on my Melville walls.

THE WORLD ENDS somewhere near the north coast of Scotland. Around such outposts as the sleepy town of Wick, where I stayed, and the sleepier village of Reay, where I golfed, do smart governments hide their dark secrets. A major nuclear reactor lies just over the horizon from Reay Golf Club, out of sight but never entirely out of mind. As I prepared to play from the tee of the "Vikings Grave" 15th, at the end of the course nearest the reactor, a loud siren pierced the air in short, sharp bursts. It stopped before I could yell "Chernobyl!" but if my firstborn child has three heads or five arms, I think I'll know why.

Still, I liked Reay's golf course, for the same reasons I liked Brora's. Reay wasn't as good, but it possessed one or two sublime holes and a barren, windswept beauty of its own. A pale, rocky gray, not the usual yellowy dun, tinged the bare spots alongside Reay's green turf. The sixth hole, a sweeping par 5 along the sandhills by the sea, greatly impressed the early golf professional and architect James Braid, and today the hole bears the nickname "Braid's Choice." Of Britain's northernmost links, I had expected nothing. The forlorn, back-of-beyond charm I discovered heartened me immensely. The lone gentleman in the clubhouse told me that a high-summer traffic jam at Reay is a 20 minutes' queue on the first tee. Were it located in suburban Ohio, Reay could charge $40 per six-hour round and do a roaring trade. But then it wouldn't be Reay, would it?

The drive from Reay to Dornoch took just over an hour. I took my time. I would not force any happy endings at Dornoch Three. When I arrived, I cheerily announced myself in the pro shop—"Me again!"—and paid for a burgundy sweatshirt along with my green fee. I resolved to dwell in happy cliché-land and play one hole at a time, take the rough with the smooth and stop to smell the, um, gorse bushes.

And it worked. I birdied the first hole and stayed calm. I double-bogeyed the second and breathed deeply. Such a lovely day, again, the hairs up on my neck with delight . . .

Par-bogey-par-par-bogey-birdie-par. Out in 37.

Why is golf so darn easy when you don't care what you're doing? I purged that thought from my head before I could start fuming about score again . . .

On the tee of the 147-yard 10th, I debated my club selection at length and ultimately decided upon my 7-iron. I couldn't find it in my bag—and then I remembered the seventh hole of Dornoch Two. Oops! Silly me. I punched a 6-iron under the wind instead . . .

Par-bogey-par-bogey-bogey-birdie . . .

Three birdies through 15 holes—I couldn't help myself. My bag felt lighter without the 7-iron. Come to think of it, Hogan didn't use a 7-iron either when he won the U.S. Open at Merion . . .

Par-bogey-par. Home in 38, round in 75. Five over.

Only on the drive back to Inverness did I tally my score. For one brief, shining interlude, despite my best efforts, Royal Dornoch had liberated me from score; in due time, I would welcome its return. But the vacation had been soothing. And Dornoch, divorced from score, was truly love at third sight.

Chapter 9

OLD FAITHFUL

❖❖❖

I WOULD HAVE gladly ended my northern trip after Dornoch Three, but to finish my article I still had to go to Nairn, east of Inverness, on Saturday morning. The course at Nairn brought me back down to earth. I know a number of worldly golfers who rate it very highly, but I think some of them, desperate to justify their long trips to Dornoch, let subconscious desires impair their judgment. Nairn demanded a lot of me: gorse straddled nearly every fairway, even those by the sea, and its greens were almost glassy, rolling even in November like velvety *Poa annua* in a California summer. I was glad I played it, and I can see why it hosted the Walker Cup (the amateur equivalent to the Ryder Cup) in 1999, for only Dornoch definitely bettered its architecture among courses in the Highlands. But it lacked a certain *je ne sais quoi* possessed by Brora in abundance. Nairn challenged me; Brora inspired me.

Back in St. Andrews, I got my 7-iron fixed at Auchterlonies, on the corner of Golf Place and North Street. I know I should have shopped around a bit, but the lore of Auchterlonies sucked me in. Willie, David and Tom Auchterlonie, three of six brothers born and bred in St. Andrews, founded the shop in 1895. Willie had won the Open in 1893 at Prestwick, using clubs he made himself, before retiring to concentrate on clubmaking. Laurie, the prodigal Auchterlonie, emigrated to Chicago and won the U.S. Open in 1902. The shop is now the largest of its kind in St. Andrews. Its prices aren't always the best, but who else can compete with a century of clubmaking tradition? Hundreds of times I had walked along North Street past Auchterlonies' museum-piece shop window, full of hickory-shafted cleeks and mashies and gutta-percha balls and antiquated clubmaking equipment. Very clever advertising, I thought, though perhaps not for those dim enough to believe that they still *used* the equipment in the window.

My relationship with Heather also needed mending. She felt pressured by my declaration on the sofa in Inverness, although she wouldn't admit as much. Confused, in love but not yet loved, I tried to please her more, to lavish her with more care and affection. I booked two expensive tickets—mine cost more than I could spare—in the stalls for us to see *The Phantom of the Opera* at the Edinburgh Playhouse. We went to Edinburgh early, as Heather wanted to buy a new black dress. I offered to shop with her, to help her pick it out if she liked. I thought I might earn brownie points for gallantry. We looked at one dress together before she banished me from her presence.

"It's not you," she said. "I just hate shopping."

"Are you sure?" I asked. Slightly miffed, I left and went to cool my heels for an hour in a bookshop on Princes Street. I started in the Sports section before drifting successively into Humor, Self-Help and Philosophy.

We had a thoroughly unromantic meal at McDonald's and went to the theater. To my chagrin, our seats were underneath the Circle. We couldn't see the chandelier when it swung out over the audience. Heather was underwhelmed.

"We're paying *how* much for these tickets?" she asked pointedly. I offered to pay for hers as well. Maybe bribery isn't the most effective relationship-building technique, but during the pandering stage of the relationship I was willing to try anything.

AMAZINGLY, A RESURGENCE of good weather swept through the British Isles in mid- to late November—this, shortly after a spell of renewed Dunhillesque conditions threatened to drive away all but the hardiest souls from golfing in St. Andrews until the new year. Temperatures above 10 degrees Celsius (50°F), relatively minimal winds and even substantial outbreaks of sunshine brought the locals to the linksland like lemmings to the sea, proof that just as the weather can be miserable at any time of year in Scotland, it can also be surprisingly tolerable.

By then, I had played eight rounds on the Old Course—one less than I had played on the New Course. That ratio was nowhere near what I'd expected before coming to St. Andrews (I'd imagined I'd play the Old more often than the New, Jubilee and Eden courses combined), but I had my reasons. For one, the Old could be a hassle. Often, I didn't want to put up with its slowish pace of play or the wide-eyed tourists I usually had to play with. I also preferred waiting a *maximum* of 30 minutes for a time on the New or Jubilee to hovering around Ye Olde Starter's Hut, possibly for two hours or more. The times I spent on the Old's practice putting green, going through the motions, keeping both ears attuned to the starter's crackly loudspeaker, always filled me with emotions I'd rather forget —boredom, anxiety, powerlessness over my destiny. If made to wait too long before starting, I would inevitably go hungry during the back nine somewhere; when queuing, one cannot leave the area around the starter's hut or the practice green, and I never bought a sandwich beforehand to cover my bases. The possibility always existed that my queuing might come to nothing—especially on busy days in winter, when the days became shorter and the available tee times fewer. When waiting as a single to play the Old, I was always one string of unbroken foursomes away from deep depression.

The other reason I preferred the New? For a long time, the Old Course drove me crazy. I don't think the Old induces tepidness in any of its visitors; it is possible to wax extremely hot and cold about it during the same visit. But on the whole I think golfers pass through three stages of experience when first exposed to the Old Course: I call it the "Good Course, Bad Course" theory.

I.

Once the supreme moment of first-tee horror is out of the way, your first trip around the Old Course becomes almost exactly that: a *trip*. Dazed by historical musings on themes of Old Tom Morris circa 1860 and Fat Jack Nicklaus circa 1970, or by bunkers with names and stories of their own (Who was "Kruger"? And why is "Mrs. Kruger" two bunkers over?), you glide around the first 16 holes in a narcotic sort of ecstasy: the odd par or two gives you irrational amounts of pleasure, while tanglings with the gorse and four-putts for eights barely flicker on your personal Richter scale of disaster.

A school of thought in modern golf course architecture, advanced by Pete Dye and some of his disciples, holds that a golfer remembers the one great shot he hits in a round and forgets everything else. Nowhere is this concept validated more fully than on the Old Course: a birdie for the first-timer on any hole on the oldest course in golf is the stuff of bragging rights for years to come.

Maybe you feel let down by its comparative incomprehensibility, next to other Scottish courses you've played. But surely you'd been warned to expect that, the first time around? You also notice the width of every fairway, each one merging with another on its left, and the enormity of every green. You think you could be scoring much better than you actually are, and the thought occurs to you that maybe the Old Course is so well-liked because it's so easy. The course record is 62, after all (Curtis Strange, 1987 Dunhill Cup), and there are no fewer than 10 par 4s on the medal card measuring less than 400 yards—seven of those less than 360. Not one forced carry in the lot, and nearly always 40 yards of fairway to aim at— you can envision yourself tearing the Old Course to pieces, and who wouldn't like that? Then you come to 17 and 18, and the last 25 minutes of your round blend into one serendipitous Kodak moment, no matter what your score.

These feelings are intoxicating. But in due time euphoria gives way to a nasty hangover. Maybe it takes you only one round, maybe three or four, but soon enough you pass into the second stage of Old Course consciousness.

II.

Suddenly it dawns on you: good Lord, there are bunkers out there. Lots of 'em. Ones you can't see. You'd check your yardage book again to try and figure out where they are, but you're tired of being harangued for slow play by your companions so you surrender to the vagaries of fate. And sure enough, your next shot sees you shaking your head, holding a lob wedge, trying to excavate your ball from a trap the size of a nickel 170 yards from the green to a spot in the fairway 168 yards from the green.

You *can't* play far enough left on some holes. Nearly all of the Old's serious trouble—what gorse and out-of-bounds it has—lurks on the right. You can find the best angles of approach to the greens from the right side of most of the fairways, but prudence dictates caution: for most golfers the advantages of flirting with disaster are minimal, so the optimal line of play is well down the left. Alas, safety isn't so easily grasped. On the sixth, a blind driving hole bending slightly to the right, your best line starts at a tower on the Leuchars RAF base, fully 10 degrees to the left of where your brain tells you the hole is. On the 14th, a long par 5 dominated by a massive bunker known simply as "Hell," playing safe to leave yourself a good line into the green turns a straight hole into a double dogleg up to 40 yards longer. At this point, you start running against the "shortest distance between two points" logic you've used throughout your golfing life. Even if you can convince yourself to aim far enough left, your body may well deduce that something is amiss and tilt you back into a wicked slice, wind unassisted.

Then you have the 12th hole. On the medal card, it weighs in at a sprightly 316 yards, and from the elevated tee it looks as if an uninterrupted carpet of fairway welcomes you to the putting surface. Your rookie playing partner unsheathes his driver, and you think about telling him of the nasty collecting bunkers hidden behind knolls in the middle of the fairway, 175 and 220 yards away—bunkers that would have served their country well at Passchendaele and the Somme. You nearly mention that the central tier of the tabletop green is no more than six paces deep, and how you've taken consecutive sixes on the hole in your last two rounds. But you think better of it. Better to let him figure it out for himself, you think. Then he pops up his drive between the bunkers and skulls a wedge to 15 feet, and you start to think that if what you don't know can't hurt you, maybe you should stop getting intimate with the Old Course and take up lawn bowling or tossing the caber.

Or perhaps the New Course—a *proper* Scottish layout—is itself a sufficient remedy. Many have said that were the New located elsewhere, were greenkeepers to dawdle over it and develop it into a marquee attraction of its own, many championships and fewer spectator grandstands (pointing toward the Old) would have graced its turf. It certainly feels more like the golf course on which you grew up than the Old does. Each hole has its own fairway and, with two exceptions (Nos. 3 and 15), its own green, and most of its hazards are clearly visible. The selection of holes offers variety between long and short, tight and open, dogleg left and dogleg right, and you couldn't justly call any of its shots unfair. Shots of subtlety and drama linger in the memory: my favorites are the approach at the par-4 11th, a short iron to a green softly framed by dunes to the rear and right, and the tee shot on the par-3 13th, where two bunkers pose a Scylla-and-Charybdis menace similar to that of the Old's 11th but at a more accessible maximum of 157 yards.

After two or three rounds on each of the Old and the New, you may well objectively conclude, heresy or not, that the New is the better golf course. You figure that with marginally better maintenance, the New Course could vault well up the rankings of the great courses in Scotland. As for the Old Arse . . . you can understand what possessed Bobby Jones, having turned in 46 shots and staring at a putt for his second consecutive double bogey to start the back, to pick up his ball and quit his third round of the 1921 Open.

III.

But Jones came full circle later in life. Of the Old Course he ultimately concluded, "The more you study it the more you love it, and the more you love it the more you study it." It loved him back, bestowing upon him an Open title in 1927 and the British Amateur leg of his Grand Slam in 1930. "Study" is perhaps too scholarly a word for most of us; apart from the occasional pause beside the 17th or 18th, I was happy enough to play the course, not view it as another lecture hall. But the Old Course certainly grows on you: round by round you absorb its intricacies, gradually learning where the bunkers and the vital contours are. And sooner or later, you find yourself playing left and creating doglegs because you want to, not because you've been told to, an important collaboration between pride and intellect that can yield decisive results on your scorecard.

It's important not to do *too* well in your first rounds on the Old Course, lest you lose that masochistic zest for the challenge of discovery, but I suspect that this stage of experience usually dawns when skill for the first time begins to combine with luck and brings some of your first-stage scoring fantasies to reality. I remember how I felt as a little boy when for the first time I put a jigsaw puzzle together with no help from my parents. I felt similar innocent feelings of accomplishment on the 12th hole of the Old shortly after I finally pulled out my 2-iron on the tee instead of my driver. I steered a shot into the open space well right of the bunkers but very much still on the golf course—and discovered the shot I had left, to a pin on the right side of the green, was much easier than the one I would have had from the same distance in the middle of the fairway!

This sensation wasn't unique. Nearly every time I played the Old Course, no matter how badly, I discovered at least one new angle of attack, often by accident but occasionally through experimentation. From day to day, the possibilities for discovery changed: ever-altering wind conditions added new wrinkles to each shot's execution, and each minor adjustment in pin position brought different subtleties of the terrain into play. Because its greens are larger and have more interesting pin positions than any in the world, the Old Course *always* makes you think hard about where you want to place each and every shot. If you want to shoot a good number on the Old, a good swing isn't nearly enough.

The more I think about it, the more strongly I feel that the Old Course should not be ranked against its peers. Normally I'm perfectly happy to compose Top 100 course lists, or engage in petty, scholastic debates about the merits of Cypress Point vs. Pebble Beach, Pine Valley vs. Augusta National, or Royal Dornoch vs. Cruden Bay; they don't necessarily get me anywhere, but they can illuminate the strengths of one course and the weaknesses of another. However, the Old Course asks questions that no other courses ask, and it asks them in an unrefined and blessedly unique style that will, for a variety of reasons, never be duplicated.

Whenever I try to compare it to something else, I inevitably fall back on the phrase ". . . but it's the *Old Course.*" The Old Course is its own and only yardstick. Within the realm of Scottish links golf, Royal Dornoch and Cruden Bay are more aesthetically pleasing than the Old Course . . . but it's the *Old Course,* and as such its historical beauty stirs the soul like no natural beauty the others may have.

Did I ever enjoy a day on the Old Course quite as much as my Dornoch Three experience? Possibly not . . . but it's the *Old Course,* and a great day on the Old is packed with deep, multifaceted meaning that no other course can match. Which is the better short par 4: the third at Cruden Bay or the third on the Old Course? Every Socratic dialogue I've ever tried to hold along these lines about the Old Course has broken down. Well, not *every* dialogue; I can unequivocally say that I like the Old Course better than the Jubilee Course, and Stonehaven, and Tain. But once you raise the bar to a certain height, these questions become unanswerable, no matter how much you try to study them.

Having said this, I fervently believe that every golfer should spend a great deal of time and energy pondering one subjective question about the Old Course. Objectively, very few golfers will deny that the Old Course possesses greatness of *some* form or fashion. But what kind of greatness is it? Or, if you prefer, *why* is the Old Course considered to be such a formidable pillar of golfing greatness? Is it because St. Andrews is the primeval Home of Golf, and the Old Course a testimony to how it was in the beginning, is now and ever should be? Is it because anyone can play there, because golf was always played by the common man and because of the way the townspeople mingle with tourists and students to give St. Andrews such a glorious atmosphere? Is it because of what people do and have done on the Old Course, the "Great Man" theory of history embodied in the achievements of Open champions past, present and future? These three possible answers—biological, sociological, historical—are all good ones. Having examined the Old Course thoroughly, one can also respond in strictly architectural terms: Is it because every shot you'll ever face on the Old Course demands a unique mix of intelligence, foresight, confidence and execution? Personally, I'd say *all* these answers are correct. But because discovery of this last point is so intensely individual and only laboriously achieved, it brings with it a meaning that transcends the easily identifiable truths of the other three.

I WOULD PLAY the Old Course 28 times during my year in Scotland, and I truly loved playing it, especially once I moved beyond the grumpiness and frustration. Even the most mundane rounds taught me something about the course, and usually something about myself. I remember once cracking a big drive off the tee of the par-4 sixth hole and from 60 yards deciding to use a putter for my second shot—half because I thought I could get as close to the hole with a putt as with a bump-and-run or lofted wedge, half simply because the putt was there to be attempted. I hit the putt 20 yards beyond the hole, all the way to the back fringe, and grinned impishly, having let score for once take a backseat to a childish escapade. A moment like that didn't mean much by itself, but the cumulative effects of it and others like it did help me become less uptight, less stiffly logical about golf in general.

I never fully unraveled all of the Old's mysteries. But at least I gave myself a sporting chance; golfers who jump off a bus, play the Old Course once and never see it again haven't. Nor have professionals who play the course a few times every few years when the Open or the Alfred Dunhill Cup comes to town. I'm convinced that if the pros came to St. Andrews for a month at a time instead of a week, the record score on the Old Course would be in the 50s. For a great player who knows the Old Course intimately, isn't afraid of its ghosts, and gets a spot of decent weather and a lucky bounce or two, the Old Course can be *easy*. When Tiger Woods won the 2000 Open, in four days of idyllic conditions, he shot a tournament record total of 19-under-par 269. Even given the pressures of a major championship, I can't imagine that by his standards this total would be any better than average for him if he knew the course well.

Unless the next Tiger Woods is raised in St. Andrews, my idealized scenario will never unfold: professional golfers don't have time enough on the job to get to know the Old Course well. But for those of us amateurs who do, great things can happen.

On a beautiful Tuesday afternoon in November, I was paired by the Old Course starter with a serious-looking Scotsman in his thirties named David. We introduced ourselves to one another; he said he belonged to the New Golf Club, one of six or seven other formal clubs calling the St. Andrews linksland home along with the R&A. (The New Club's clubhouse is one of the buildings to the right of the Old Course's 18th fairway.) I asked him his handicap: "One," he answered.

I smiled. That's the kind of companionship I like, I thought. "Fancy a game, then?" I asked.

"Sure," he said, warming to my cocky challenge.

No money at stake, no strokes asked for or given—just straight-up match play, although I putted everything into the hole as usual. Both of us competed fiercely for competition's sake, no other incentives needed. My kind of match.

My game rose to the occasion. I turned in 36: three bogeys, three pars, and birdies at holes three, eight and nine. I parred the 10th, to stay at even par—and went two holes behind. David had begun with eight pars and then birdied the ninth and 10th. I'd never played a better match: each of us inspired the other to play his best golf. Neither of us dared make a mistake for fear of being left in the other's wake.

On the par-3 11th, two legendary bunkers guard the raised green: "Hill," off to the left, and "Strath," off to the right, roughly halfway along the long, slender green shared with the seventh hole. The dark and deep Strath Bunker rivals the Road Bunker for sheer nastiness; many a golfer desperate to save bogey from its clutches has played his second shot at the 11th directly away from the flag. With the pin tucked awkwardly behind Strath Bunker, David played first and safely found the back part of the green, leaving himself a lengthy, curving downhill putt. I played second—and blinked first. I choked, pure and simple, and skanked a 5-iron into *Shell* Bunker, fully 40 yards short of the green. Shell Bunker is massive, but it is only supposed to affect play on the seventh hole, where both downwind drives and upwind approaches can find it. Yet there I was, facing not just any long bunker shot, but a long bunker shot up a near-vertical slope, with the left edge of Strath Bunker directly between me and the pin. I took out my 9-iron, opened its face and played the shot like a regulation explosion with my sand wedge, putting the ball back in my stance and aiming just to the left of Strath Bunker. I swung, and splashed into the sand beautifully: the ball pitched into the front bank, hopped up onto the green and spun hard to the right. It stopped six feet from the hole—nothing less than a miracle. I willed my putt for par into the hole; David, possibly shell-shocked, three-putted. I was back to one down. Game on!

At my nemesis, the 12th, I had learned my lesson: I played safely to the right again with a 2-iron. My 9-iron approach pitched gently on the tabletop and stopped, and I made my 10-foot putt for birdie to level the match. David and I were now both one under par.

I had broken 80 on the Old Course only once before. Never mind that: *I had only ever broken par for 18 holes once before.*

I parred the 13th, but David hit a fine approach to 20 feet and drained his putt to get back to two under and, more importantly, back to one up. Our dialogue had ground to a halt. I hadn't fancied my chances at the start of our match—not at match play, and not against a Scot with a handicap five shots better than mine. But now I smelled blood, and I desperately wanted to win. I knew he did, too. This was sport at a level I'd never experienced before. Between us, we'd made six birdies in the last six holes.

Trying to control my emotions, I played the 14th, 15th and 16th cautiously but solidly: on each green in regulation, two putts for par every time. David bogeyed the 14th hole, undone by the contour in front of its green; he matched my pars at 15 and 16, so with two holes to play, we both stood at one under par, the match again all square. On the Road Hole I pounded a drive down the left side of the fairway and played conservatively with my second, finishing just short of the green. (Never had I been more thankful to see the flagstick on the front half of the 17th green.) David's drive was better, but his second was worse, finding rough just short of the Road on the right, and he could only pitch to 15 feet. I rolled a great lag putt from off the green to within 12 inches of the hole and breathed a fierce sigh of relief. I needed one par for 71. David's par putt grazed the edge of the hole and stayed out. One up with one to play— "dormie one," in match play parlance. I couldn't lose.

Lady Luck then picked a fine time to desert me: I drove smartly down the middle on the last, but my ball came to rest on Grannie Clark's Wynd, one foot short of grassy salvation. As at the Road Hole, local rules dictate that a ball resting on the Wynd must be played as it lies. I gritted my teeth and swung hard, chipping the bottom of my 8-iron as I struck through the ball into the concrete. But the contact was poor and my ball ballooned into the air, dropping short of the green into the Valley of Sin. Up ahead, David played a bold approach shot over the flagstick; it stopped beside its pitch mark, no more than 10 feet from the hole. I strode up to the green, gathering my thoughts one final time. My heart pounding furiously, I withdrew my putter from my bag and tossed the bag aside. I had never been more nervous on a golf course. I studied the line intently. What more could I do?

I aimed two and a half feet to the right of the hole, drew back the putter-head and popped into the ball with a wristy stroke: up the hill it climbed, over spike marks it bobbled. For a moment I thought it might go in . . . but it stopped short. Six inches short. *Yes!* Seventy-one: one under par. David could still tie me, but his putt never threatened the hole. He ruefully crinkled his nose, then bit his lower lip and scratched his head. We shook hands. David limped away to the New Club, while I walked over to the concrete steps leading from the green to the R&A clubhouse and sat down to collect my breath, and my wits.

Even now, I cannot believe everything that happened that day. I shiver just thinking about it. *I broke par on the Old Course. I beat a very good Scot on his own course, at his own game. Nah. . . .* But I did. After striving in vain to properly love the Old Course for what felt like years, it turned around and blessed me with an afternoon of golfing joy greater than nearly anything I could ever imagine. And for someone of my modest abilities, even if I thought the Old Course was anything less than a great, great golf course, that afternoon will be reason enough for me to think of it as a wonderful place for the rest of my days.

Chapter 10

WEATHER-BEATEN

·❖··❖··❖·

WHAT DO YOU do after you've broken par on the Old
Course for the first time? You try to break it for the second time.

Greedy guy that I was, I phoned in an entry to the daily Old
Course tee time ballot shortly after returning to Melville from my
71. Old Course tee times are like gold dust, and the St. Andrews
Links Trust allots them to four different groups: private clubs in St.
Andrews, like the R&A; tour operators and corporate hospitality
types who can guarantee visitors tee times, for a price; members of
the general public both willing and able to book up to a year in advance; and those lucky enough to win times through the ballot. For
town residents like me, the ballot was the standard route to playing
the Old Course. If there were fewer entries than tee times available,
as sometimes happened in the winter, everybody won, but sometimes as few as one in five applications were successful. You never
knew your odds; you only knew if you'd won.

On this occasion, Scott Campbell, Martin Parry and I entered the ballot as a threesome and won a time, for 9:30 in the morning. Perfect, I thought. I wouldn't be missing any classes; I should be back to Melville before 1:30, in time to grab lunch. I really liked playing with Scott and Martin, and my game was "on song," as the Brits like to say. What could go wrong?

When I woke up the following morning and looked outside, the scene answered my question for me. Rain pelted down at 45-degree angles. A howling wind rattled my window frames. The sky vacillated between slate gray and charcoal. Even by Scottish standards, it looked pretty miserable.

After breakfast, Martin and Scott shook their heads as we stared through the double glazing of the Melville foyer. The weather had improved—very slightly. I had my golf clubs and raingear with me. They didn't.

"I dunno," said Scott. "I don't like it."

"Yeah," said Martin. "I've got class at ten o'clock, anyway." He smiled mischievously.

I pleaded, with them and with the heavens. "C'mon, guys . . . I don't think the really heavy stuff is coming down for quite a while."

"You been watching *Caddyshack* again?" asked Martin.

"Hey—I've never seen lightning in Scotland. Have you?" I was grasping at straws.

"Darren, I'm sorry, but I really don't think today was meant for golf." Scott's opinion resonated like thunder. "No way am I going to get caught out there right now."

"Me neither," said Martin. "Thanks anyway—we'll get back out there again soon." He patted me on the back in sympathy.

The two of them left, and I stood alone, disconsolate. I grunted, and I fidgeted, and I huffed, and I sighed . . . and then I said, What the heck. Might as well give it a go myself.

I opened my umbrella and began my long walk into town. I hadn't yet learned that umbrellas are dead weight in a Scottish downpour. Either your waterproofs work or you get wet; the wind sees to that. I cut a solitary figure, rain dripping all over me, trudging along what might have been a tributary of the Eden Estuary were it not actually a tributary of North Street. I took the speedy route to the first tee, cutting through a corner of the town, and as my spikes clicked in syncopation with the raindrops on the pavement, I became aware that several older Scottish gentlemen in brown macs were laughing at me, even pointing at me and my clubs. I politely laughed back, now resolute. I marched straight across the empty 18th fairway from Grannie Clark's Wynd to the starter's hut, where a clearly incredulous white-haired gentleman told me, "Son, you need to have your head looked at."

I smiled wanly at the starter and flashed him a look that said, Listen, I know I'm stark raving bonkers, but just humor me here, will you? "Is the course open for play or not?" I asked.

"Yes, you may go ahead."

"Does the Old Course ever close for rain?"

"No, not really." He smirked. "People don't normally come out here on days like this."

"And a Merry Christmas to you, too," I stammered. I was the butt of all St. Andrews hilarity, and I knew it.

On the other hand, I now had the Old Course to myself. This realization enthralled me: on some courses you might expect to enjoy solitude, but never before had I thought I might ever be the only man at Mecca. I didn't care that I might have been alone for a reason. I struck a surprisingly solid drive down the first fairway, and the thought occurred to me, as it often does when I am possessed by such lunacy, that I had it right and everyone else had it wrong. I was almost livid with self-righteousness: you make a tee time in St. Andrews, I thought, and you keep it. At least until the grounds crew starts rolling out tarpaulins.

I smiled a toothy smile as I walked down that first fairway. The puddles only seemed to mimic the vast, rolling, comforting sea; seagulls dipped and swayed in the wind, dodging the raindrops. Flecks of silver popped over the horizon, brightening the sky. Away from the world's condemning gaze, I breathed deeply and closed my eyes. I felt very, very happy.

One dumped shot in Swilcan Burn and two double bogeys later, my smile had given way to a shiver. I hadn't dressed warmly enough —only three layers of clothing, no thick gloves, no winter hat. I had given up on my baseball-style cap because when I leaned over the ball, water ran down to the point of the cap's bill and dripped maddeningly around my ball. (As if the weather weren't bad enough on its own, the random drop-dripping proved that I couldn't keep my head still.) With the cap in my bag, my hair fused into thick, soggy strands that flopped across my forehead like renegade windshield wipers. Instinctively, I reached up to whisk them out of the way, which momentarily helped my hair—and permanently ruined my golf glove. I might as well have coated it and my grips with Vaseline. Not that any of this would have stopped me. I would have contentedly shot a three-digit number to claim hegemony over the birthplace of golf, if only for a day. I didn't fear score, but I did fear pneumonia. As I putted out on the second green, I decided enough was enough.

Still, I had the last laugh—not the course, not the townspeople, not the starter, not my erstwhile playing partners. From the second green I walked across the 16th green to the 17th tee. As long as I was in the area, and heading back home, the least I could do was attempt to play the Road Hole on my way. Despite tricky winds and my Teflon golf glove, I somehow managed to finesse two drivers around the corner of the hotel to within range of a bump-and-run (or, to be more accurate, a slip-and-splash) to the front pin placement. Then, magic: for my third I squeaked a wedge shot into the front face of the green, and it ground its way up the hill to a halt six inches from the hole. I removed the flag and tapped in for my par four, and as I restored the pin to its proper place, my huge grin of half an hour earlier returned to my face. I had just recorded one of the greatest pars in the history of Western Civilization, and it served millions of golf fans right if they were huddled in front of their warm fires and electric heaters and not outside with me to see it.

THE NEXT TIME I played the Old Course, I played it off artificial turf. The Old Course closed for essential maintenance between November 20 and December 1. When it reopened, and continuing until the end of March, the starter gave golfers small, rectangular, green mats with their scorecards and instructed that all shots from the fairway more than 40 yards from the green were to be played off them. The Links Trust first instituted this policy in the winter of 1994–95, hoping to minimize divot damage done to the course and to help prepare it for the Open the following summer. The plan worked so well, the Links Trust decided to go back to the mats again the following winter, and the one after that, and the one after that. Its official position is that a new decision regarding the use of mats will be made every autumn, but I suspect golfers in years to come will continue to count "matting" among the Old Course's less desirable traditions.

I hated the mats. It's one thing to surrender your rights as a golfer for an Open, quite another to do so for a tourist season in which you'll have only a small cameo. I could understand the stance of the Links Trust; it says the use of mats prevents the taking of 150,000 divots each winter, which is great news, although I'm curious as to who does the counting. (What do 150,000 divots look like? How does one define "divot"?) But playing off a piece of green plastic with a frilly top and dimensions of roughly 6 by 15 inches is no more similar to golf than a home run derby is to baseball. The worst aspect of the mat was its inch of thickness: on every shot I felt as if I had a hanging lie, and I didn't dare sole my club on the mat for fear of jostling it on my takeaway. The mat had very little mass, and a slightly misplaced waggle could cause the ball to topple off— usually, it seemed, halfway through my downswing. The mats weren't maddening enough to make me stop playing the Old Course, but I was sorely tempted to imitate those students who put their mats on the ground next to the ball, so that from a distance it looked like they were being used, and then scythed divots from the earth normally.

During the winter, the keepers of the Old Course shifted the pin on the 11th hole 45 degrees to the left of its usual green, to a tiny target bracketed front and back by depressions. Only a towering, Nicklaus-style 4-iron could hope to hit this temporary green and hold it, and shots falling short and to the left could ricochet off the Old Course's one and only tree, a small and sickly-looking birch. The revised 11th was an affront to golf: how could anyone take one of the world's great par 3s and turn it into something so un-linkslike, so unworthy of its surroundings? At least the change led directly to another more pleasant alteration: the winter tee on the 12th shortened the hole by nearly 100 yards. Even a weak hitter like me could hope to drive the green on the revised 12th with a moderate tailwind. In late January, I came to the 12th at even par, straight from a chip-in birdie on the 11th, and snaked a powerful drive onto the green within three feet of the hole. I tapped in for a two and asked my playing partners, "You didn't see a sign changing this to a par 3, did you?" I claimed my first Old Course eagle, but my comeuppance arrived in due course: from two under par with six holes to play, I slumped to a five-over 77.

The Old Course always remains open during the winter months, but the other main St. Andrews courses operate just like the medieval three-field system of farming: one of the New, Jubilee and Eden courses always lies fallow from December to March, allowing essential repairs to be made. The New, my favorite of the three, closed during my year in St. Andrews; I felt cheated until I discovered the joys of the Bronze Course, the wintertime reincarnation of the Jubilee. I quickly realized that revenge for my opening round of 100 was a dish best served cold. The defanged Jubilee played to only 5,800 yards and a par of 69, and even its evil 15th green migrated from its lofty perch to a temporary green in the valley beneath it, which is where my better approach shots usually came to rest anyway. In three rounds on the Bronze I shot 74, 72 and 73. And I thoroughly enjoyed myself, although I couldn't claim any credit for these numbers.

"So where'd you play today?" Scott Campbell asked me once that winter. He'd heard my clubs rustling in the hallway between our rooms and popped out to say hello.

"The Bronze," I answered.

Scott gestured as if to spit on the carpet. "Like that counts," he said in his clipped Kirkcaldy accent.

Scott was normally an exceedingly mild-mannered and friendly guy, so I assumed he was joking. "Oh, come on," I said, smiling. "Anyway, I played really well . . ."

"But it was *only* the Bronze."

". . . and I shot 73."

"But it was *only* the Bronze!"

Now I was confused. "What's up with you?" I asked.

"The Bronze isn't real golf, and you know it. No way am I letting you brag about anything you've done there."

"Well, say what you like," I scoffed. "But I'd rather shoot in the low 70s on the Bronze than in the low 90s on the Jube."

WITH THE EXCEPTION of the gorse and the putting surfaces, the linksland turns brown in winter. The healthy green patches of grass disappear, and the yellowy hues that give the linksland fairways their autumnal richness fade to a bleak, sickly beige. On some days, thin, ice-like layers of turf crunched under my feet like shredded wheat. Golf by the sea in the winter makes you ill. Socks and sweaters don't come thick enough to combat the cold. A Scotsman I played with remarked, "The thing I'd like to ask the scientists is where all of the liquid in your head comes from in winter." It poured out of my nose too quickly for tissues to soak it all up, and I'm sure new diseases mutated into being within the petri dish of my golf towel. And my fingers! Rule number one of winter golf: thinned shots are *evil*. Trust me. Do *not* under any circumstances contact the ball below the center of your clubface in the winter. Sparks will fly up the shaft straight into your hands, which will immediately feel like casualties of a rare bone disease. Gestapo jailers would have been proud to pack so much pain into one lash.

To enjoy golf in the winter, it helps to be of hardy stock. Although I craved golf after a week of inactivity, my enthusiasm quickly waned when I played. But the longer I rested, the less I remembered winter golf's tortures. The Scots must know this natural cycle intimately, and yet the demand for golf in St. Andrews never seems to diminish; if anything, it seemed to grow in the winter. On a dim, raw weekday afternoon in January, Martin and I timidly walked down to the starter's hut at the Eden, half dreading the weather but expecting to breeze around an empty course. The walk-up queues were an hour long. Stuff that, we thought, and crossed over to the Bronze—but the wait there was even longer. I wondered aloud if the tourists and students were really so bad that the locals would come out in force in any conditions just to enjoy St. Andrews golf on their own terms, not those of their visitors. But upon reflection I think the townspeople play in the winter because golf in St. Andrews is a year-round passion. If you're from St. Andrews, you play golf or you get bored quickly. Winter doesn't change that.

Winter reinforced one of the lessons Scottish golf kept trying to teach me: to enjoy myself, I couldn't take the game too seriously. One wintry weekend my former *Golf Digest* colleague John Huggan invited me to his hometown of Dunbar, along the coast from North Berwick, for the Dunbar Golf Club annual dinner. *Golf Digest* photographer Dom Furore also flew over from the States, and we had a grand time in the true Scottish tradition, singing and carousing into the night. Dom and I rented kilts especially for the occasion, and if you can't have fun among a throng of crusty, kilt-wearing Scots, you're taking life much too seriously. At one in the morning, Dom and John nominated me for the role of designated driver, but I couldn't operate a stick shift, so we had to walk for a mile through Dunbar town center to get back to his house—in subfreezing conditions, and bare-legged, of course. At one dimly lit street corner a clutch of loitering teenaged girls spotted us and started wolf-whistling. John strode on purposefully, rakishly cocked his head and greeted them with a reserved "Ladies" and a wink. I've never wanted to be Scottish more than at that very moment.

We were due on the tee at Dunbar at eight o'clock the next morning. Frost carpeted the course when we arrived, so we waited. Drowsy and aching, I shivered at the thought of three-plus hours outdoors. We reached the first green and discovered that the greens had been recently aerated. Rather than get agitated, I chuckled and relaxed. Why worry about score when score was impossible? The sun shone brightly, and I drifted pleasantly from hole to hole, glancing often at the shimmering sea. I wouldn't dare offer an opinion about the course at Dunbar; in such conditions, any course would have seemed a cruel joke. But I laughed serenely all the same. And on the par-4 17th something really funny happened: out of the rough to the left of the fairway I hit a 9-iron that landed in an aeration hole six feet to the left of the flag, jumped hard right, hit the center of the pin and plunged into the hole for an eagle two. I playfully tossed my club in the air and thought, I'm getting good at this cold-weather malarkey. I knew I was a loon, but I also make a pretty good penguin.

Chapter 11

GAMES THESE PEOPLE PLAYED

❖ ❖ ❖

BETWEEN THE START of December and the middle of
February, I played golf only six times. I had other things to do.

Back in October, Scott had approached me with a hangdog look
and an offer I couldn't refuse. His beloved Raith Rovers Football
Club, having won the Scottish League Cup the previous season,
had qualified for the UEFA Cup, a pan-European competition involving some of the best clubs in the world. Tiny Raith struggled
past opposition from the Faroe Islands and Iceland in two preliminary rounds to join 63 other clubs in the first round proper, where
a random draw paired Raith against Germany's biggest club, Bayern Munich. Scott was ecstatic: his boys had come of age. I compared Raith to a small college team reaching the NCAA basketball
tournament for the first time, oblivious of its lowly seeding, ready
to conquer Arizona, Duke and Kentucky in turn. Bayern's two
world-class strikers, Jürgen Klinsmann and Jean-Pierre Papin, cost

much more than Raith's entire squad. But did Scott care? Of course not.

Scott forlornly offered me his ticket to Raith vs. Bayern, for he had to attend a mandatory overnight field study for his geology degree that day. My heart went out to him, but I gladly took his place. Nick Price once said that living in America makes him homesick for the sports he grew up playing, like cricket, rugby and soccer: "They do have soccer," he said, "but it's not quite like watching Aston Villa play Manchester United." For me, the chance to see the likes of Aston Villa and Manchester United on a regular basis was one of the major attractions of living abroad. I'd followed European soccer intently ever since I went to Germany on a high school exchange trip during the 1990 World Cup. (My host student partied in his local discotheque every night while his father and I stayed home, glued to the tube.) And at Harvard I'd watched many live English games on Saturday and Sunday mornings at an Irish pub in Cambridge. But I had never seen a proper match in person. Scotland was a great place to see one: Simon Kuper, in *Football Against the Enemy,* says the Scots watch more soccer matches in person per capita than anyone in Europe outside Albania. Some parts of Scotland prefer rugby or shinty (a sort of full-body-contact field hockey), but in general, whereas the Scots *play* golf, they *follow* soccer.

The match, relocated from Raith's ramshackle ground to Hibernian FC's Easter Road stadium in Edinburgh, was barely competitive. Bayern won, 2–0; Klinsmann scored in the sixth minute to quickly kill off the game as a contest. But the atmosphere! Even before the opening whistle blew, the Raith fans rollicked back and forth and around like whitewater rafts on the Colorado River. Throughout the match they chanted:

COME ON YE RAITH!

COME ON YE RAITH!

And they sang (to the tune of "Winter Wonderland"):

THERE'S ONLY ONE JIMMY NICHOL

ONLY ONE JIMMY NICHOL

WALKING ALONG

SINGING A SONG

WALKING IN A ROVERS WONDERLAND

They taunted their local rivals:

ARE YOU WATCHING

ARE YOU WATCHING

ARE YOU WATCHING, DUMFERMLINE?

ARE YOU WATCHING, DUMFERMLINE?

And during a spell of Raith's territorial dominance in the first half, one man screamed at Bayern,

YOU'RE WORSE THAN THISTLE!

in reference to Partick Thistle, another club languishing near the bottom of the Scottish Premier League standings.

British soccer team names used to seem archaic to me, redolent of an age long forgotten. American sports nicknames connote ferocity, power or grace, whereas British soccer clubs are named for plants (Partick Thistle, Nottingham Forest), nomads (Bolton Wanderers, Wolverhampton Wanderers) and days of the week (Sheffield Wednesday). Even "Manchester United" is an oxymoron: half of England's third-largest city prefers Manchester City. But the quaint nicknames belie a fierce parochialism. Nearly everyone in Britain who cares about soccer supports one club, from cradle to grave, and venomously dislikes all others. Why other fans *must* call Aberdeen supporters "sheep-shaggers" I don't know, but at least fans channel their spite into the chants and songs these days. The big "Old Firm" matchup between Scotland's two largest clubs, Glasgow Celtic and Glasgow Rangers, used to be a holy war waiting to happen. One 1975 match inspired two attempted murders, two cleaver attacks, one ax attack, nine stabbings and 35 common assaults. The rivalry has cleaned itself up considerably; still, for sport-related passion, even Auburn-Alabama football and Kentucky-Louisville basketball are nowhere near the likes of Celtic-Rangers.

After Christmas I traveled to London, stayed in a youth hostel and attended four English Premiership games in four days. I'd read Nick Hornby's *Fever Pitch,* a must-read for anyone with a season ticket to anything, and duly fell for Hornby's club, Arsenal, even though it lost 3–1 at home to a dour Wimbledon team captained by Vinnie Jones (lately of the movie *Lock, Stock and Two Smoking Barrels*). The seats at Highbury, Arsenal's 38,000-seat stadium, encroached within two or three yards of the pitch on all four sides; American football stadiums don't give fans such immediate and intimate attention. At Highbury I also learned that different clubs sang the same tunes: for Arsenal, there was "ONLY ONE DENNIS BERGKAMP." Two nights later, on New Year's Day, I heard fans of Tottenham Hotspur sing "ARE YOU WATCHING, ARSENAL?" as they drubbed league-leading Manchester United, 4–1. Another popular one was "STAND UP IF YOU HATE [ARSE-NAL, or TOTT-NAM, or CHEL-SEA, or MAN U, etc.]" to the tune of "Go West" by the Pet Shop Boys.

The intensity addicted me. A roaring, frenzied crowd at Highbury is the polar opposite of a quiet afternoon at Dornoch or Brora, but

I savored both equally, if differently. I never felt remotely threatened at any of the games I attended; British soccer violence gets disproportionately bad press in America. (Excepting high-profile contests involving English teams abroad, at which the nation's reactionary hooligans take their racist roadshow to extremes that have nothing whatsoever to do with sport, British soccer matches in general are nowadays just as safe to attend as American college football games.) The only people whose safety I feared for during my trip belonged to an honest-to-God marching band from Wilmington, Delaware, which entered the field to perform during halftime of the West London "derby"* between Queens Park Rangers and Chelsea. Halftime at an English soccer match is supposed to be the calm eye of a fierce hurricane of action, and at the very least I expected a pitch invasion from irritated fans. To my surprise, everyone enthusiastically applauded the band's performance. But a mustachioed middle-aged gentleman to my right spoke for the entire crowd, and encapsulated the essence of British soccer, when at the end of the show he put down his beer, clapped, and smiled as he bellowed, "Aaaaaaaaay! Now, fuck off and bring the players back!"

BEFORE GOING TO London, I went to Inverness again to spend Christmas with Heather and her family. It was a disaster: too many relatives I didn't know, too little time to work through our increasingly patchy relationship, too much strange food served at Christmas lunch. Little things gnawed at me. I wasn't homesick for America, which felt less and less like home the more I lived in St. Andrews. But Inverness felt disdainfully foreign. So, for the first time, did Heather.

On the bus ride to Inverness I tried to explain to Heather why I

---

*A local rivalry. (Incidentally, the word in Britain is pronounced DAHR-bee.)

watched so much soccer on the Melville communal television, why I found Raith vs. Bayern so enthralling. I quoted passages of *Fever Pitch* to her. The real question, I asked, was why people allowed themselves to be manipulated by the writers of soap and sitcom scripts. Plot twists on the back nine of the Masters on Sunday or in the Super Bowl aren't manufactured to titillate, but they so often do.

I freely admitted that I used soccer and golf to escape from the world's demands. I said, "For me, when all else fails, there's sport."

Heather looked downcast. She said, "I would have hoped you'd rely on something more meaningful." The bus rumbled on; we sat in silence.

Heather still wouldn't commit to a formal boyfriend-girlfriend relationship, but the steady pressure she subconsciously exerted drove me to distraction. On Christmas Eve I declined to attend church services with the family, using my denominational leanings as an excuse to remain behind at their house and mope. (Needless to say, this didn't exactly endear me to anyone.) On Christmas morning I gave Heather a card that said "To My Special Friend" on the front, a subtle dig at her excessive caution. The following night I stayed up until four in the morning, writing Heather a letter I felt I needed to write. I shudder to think of the sappy garbage that flowed from my poisoned pen that night—young lovesickness is not a pretty sight. But the letter got my points across. I slipped it in an envelope under the door to Heather's room, and by the time I'd woken up the next morning, she knew we needed to talk.

We discussed things at length that night after everyone had gone to bed: Heather, calm and measured; me, frustrated and anxious. I was a mess, but toward the end of our conversation I didn't care what I was. We were finished anyway, I thought. I still liked her a lot, but if she wanted to sit on the fence, there wasn't much I could do to make her come down. So I gave up. And I asked to end our talk prematurely: the weekly NFL highlights were about to come on television, and if my hometown Falcons had defeated the 49ers, we'd be in the playoffs.

IN JANUARY IT SNOWED. The Old Course shimmered in its blanket of white for several days, its mounding muted as drifts gathered in the dales and bunkers. Snow nearly hid Road Bunker: ice and snow encrusted its edges and highlighted the indentations in its sod wall. The flagsticks remained on each green, standing proudly, the flags flapping defiantly in the breeze. By the end of the second day, a snowman stood in the 18th fairway, 60 yards from the green, facing the town. A long branch jutted triangularly to the ground from its midriff—even Frosty, it seemed, wanted to learn how to play the Old Course bump-and-run. That afternoon I walked partway across the half-hidden Grannie Clark's Wynd and looked up to the R&A clubhouse and beyond, the evenness of the white fairway contrasting sharply against a starkly blue-gray sky. A chill ran through my spine —the Old Course seemed haunted. Its spirit would remain troubled, I felt, until the veil of snow lifted and golf could begin again.

Melville remained as animated as ever. I learned how to play European-rules eight-ball (your opponent plays until he misses twice when you commit a foul) on the battered pool table in the upstairs common room. Students congregated in the lower common room to play and watch table tennis. The more intense players kept personal paddles in their mail cubbyholes along the hall foyer; the unscrupulous would "borrow" these paddles at a moment's notice and occasionally break them, flipping them in disgust after a bad shot against the white-painted walls or the cigarette-stained, brown- or green-cushioned chairs.

Much of Melville's camaraderie centered upon team sport. Shanty Town FC's good league form continued; my goalkeeping improved markedly, and halfway through the season we were all but assured promotion to the top division of the St. Andrews Sunday League. We even attracted several female supporters. At least once a match I turned beet-red in my goalmouth when they sang:

SHANTY'S FULL OF SEX GODS
SHANTY'S FULL OF SEX GODS
LA-LA LA LA (HEY!)
LA-LA LA LA (HEY!)

I blame myself for our exit from the League Cup, though. At 1–1 in extra time, I came out to the edge of my area to claim a high cross and got an elbow in the face for my troubles. Blood dripped from my nose down the front of my jersey, but I refused to be substituted—I badly wanted to be the hero of a penalty shoot-out. Two minutes from the end of the match, an opposing forward chipped the ball over me from 25 yards for the winner; I'm sure I would have made the save had I not been so woozy. My injury proved minor, which was very lucky. Had I broken a bone and been unable to play golf for any length of time, I couldn't have forgiven myself.

Melville also sent a team to the university's intramural basketball tournament. Ten Scots attempting to play basketball is transcendent comedy. American eight-year-olds have more skill. The Scots hurled the ball at the rim from all angles, sans arc, on those few occasions they dribbled into position for a shot. Their idea of defense was slide-tackling. I volunteered to referee several games not involving Melville, and on one occasion one of the point guards took an age to cross the half-court line, so I whistled for a 10-second violation. All 10 players on the floor turned to me, not understanding what I'd called. I smiled inwardly.

First-semester exams loomed on the calendar at the end of January, and I found an unlikely study aid in the Melville common room: televised cricket. An élite troop of posh Melville Englishmen spent as many hours as possible during England's tour of South Africa in front of the screen as the cameras honed in on the live "action" (using the term loosely) in its near-entirety, which for cricket is a near-eternity. Slightly exaggerating my American accent to emphasize the legitimacy of my ignorance, I asked my English colleagues questions about the strange spectacle unfolding on the screen. "Test-match cricket," the longer form of the game, was akin to a form of baseball in which: each team bats in succession twice until everyone gets out or injured; runs are scored by getting to each base, not just to home plate; the strike zone is the size of a keyhole, but one called strike and you're out; pitchers ("bowlers") alternate after every six deliveries; only the catcher ("wicketkeeper") gets to wear gloves; long foul balls in any direction are just as good as home runs; great hitters ("batsmen") can score hundreds of runs and bat for hours without getting out; and the five-day time limit often expires before a match has been won, with a draw resulting no matter what the score. (The shorter form of the game, "limited-overs" or "one-day cricket," has each side face a set number of deliveries, takes only eight hours to finish and usually produces a winner and a loser.)

Cricket-watching and studying for exams were made for one another. Every match day I would take my notebooks and study guides up to the common room, where I'd plop myself in a comfy chair and scan my notes intently until I heard noise from the television:

shouted appeals of "HOWAAZAT?" to the umpire, claiming an out ("wicket"); cries of "Catch It!" when a ball looped in the air; or applause from the crowd as a ball raced beyond the boundary rope, along the ground for four runs or over the rope on the fly for six. I would quickly absorb the magnitude of the moment and then resume studying without skipping a beat. During the first test match I watched, England's Michael Atherton scored 185 runs against South Africa in his team's second innings (an "innings" ends after all 11 players have batted), battling bravely for 11 hours over two days and turning certain defeat into a historic draw. At the same time, I cruised through 30 pages of notes from my European Union class and pronounced myself ready for the exam. Men notoriously bad at multitasking should take up cricket-watching *immediately*—they'll feel much better about themselves.

Not content with figuring out and learning to enjoy cricket, I challenged myself to learn several other games invented by the British and exported to the far corners of the Commonwealth. I didn't take to rugby; even its devotees are hard put to explain why the referee has blown his whistle, and relative to American football, rugby overly accents punting and goal-kicking at the expense of strategy. On the other hand, I quite liked snooker, a form of billiards played with small balls on a 12-by-6 table that accentuates good safety and positional play in addition to precision potting. Pot one of 15 red balls worth one point, and you earn the right to shoot at a color worth between two (yellow) and seven (black) points. I find snooker infinitely more difficult to play well than pool, but the best professionals can pocket red-color-red-color-red-color at will, sometimes scoring over 100 points in one visit to the table. And the British love televised snooker: 18.4 million people watched the post-midnight conclusion of the 1985 World Snooker Championship Final, a two-day, best-of-35-frames(!) contest that came down to the final ball of the final frame.

I liked soccer, cricket and snooker on merit, but I liked them more because they were different. I couldn't relearn baseball or basketball from square one, but everywhere in Britain I looked, my eyes were opened by new players, new rules, new types of competition, new everything. I didn't know what I would do when summer came— Americans don't *do* soccer, and most don't know cricket and snooker exist—but I vowed to enjoy everything to the fullest while I had the chance.

MY GROWING FASCINATION with British sport had one important, unintended consequence. Toward the end of January, I trekked from Melville to the other end of St. Andrews to talk to Heather. I had written her another letter in the interim, softening my demands for affection while still decrying how I felt I had to "finagle a kiss" every time we met. (She teased me about that phrase unmercifully in the weeks to come, and rightly so. I could be *so* cheesy and unpoetic around Heather. While sitting together on my bed in my mood-lit Melville room one night back in October, she had asked about our relationship: "What do you think?" My response, as I leaned over to kiss her for the first time, came straight from the Michael Bolton school of lyricism. "Let's not think," I said.)

Heather welcomed me up to her room, and we sat on her bed to talk. I told her, "I'd rather have you in my life than not in my life. I'll take you however I can have you." She nodded, somewhat nonplussed, but she seemed happy with my decision and declaration. I'd gone a long way with her to get right back where I'd started. But there was a difference: now, I figured, I had soccer, cricket and snooker to keep me interested when she wasn't interested in me.

In retrospect, I can see what a dunce I was. Heather had her quirks (the "special friends" thing *still* drives me crazy when I think about it), but my behavior was generally far worse than hers. I didn't really know why she put up with me. I'd quoted the lyrics of "Mystery," one of my favorite Indigo Girls songs, to Heather early on in our relationship:

Maybe that's all that we need is to meet in the middle of impossibility
Standing at opposite poles, equal partners in a mystery

It really was a mystery to me how such a bonnie Scottish lass (and a non-golfer at that) could fall for a sport-crazed, testosterone-driven American like me.

Still, at the end of January she came to Melville and watched the Super Bowl with me—live, after midnight. We had American-style apple pie and Pringles potato chips for snacks. She fell asleep during halftime. I called it progress.

Chapter 12

PRIDES AND PREJUDICES

❖ ❖ ❖

EVEN THE BENIGN pursuits I took up in Scotland were competitive. In late autumn I had joined the Tayport Instrumental Band, an ensemble recommended to me by friends in the university's music department. I played the euphonium, a sonorous horn similar in sound to a trombone and in appearance to a small tuba. Although I'd played to an All-State standard in high school, I gave it up when I went to college, a decision I'd regretted often. But as with nearly everything else in my life, Scotland gave me a chance to start afresh.

The ensemble in Tayport, two villages north of St. Andrews, was a musical revelation. It performed annually in the Scottish Brass Band Championships. My year, we competed in the second of the event's five divisions, hoping to gain promotion to the top flight and from there to plot an assault the following year on the British Championships held in London's Royal Albert Hall in the spring. Every band in each division played the same "test piece" on competition day, one after the other, and a panel of experts awarded points for technique and musicianship. Our division played an inspired piece called *Spectrum*, written by the British composer Gilbert Vinter in 1968, shortly before his death. A creepy work using the colors of the rainbow to define and describe its seven sections, ranging in intensity from fiery "Red" to moody "Blue," *Spectrum* lasted 12 minutes and was by far the most difficult piece I'd ever played. By the time we reached the festival hall in Stirling on competition day, repeated rehearsal of *Spectrum* had driven me to the pinnacle of my musical prowess. We choked on the day and finished last of the 12 bands in our division, but I didn't much mind. I thought I'd played pretty well, all things considered, and I was thrilled to have taken part in the competition at all.

I could write many chapters about the time I spent in Tayport. When I saw the movie *Brassed Off* (1996, Pete Postlethwaite, Ewan MacGregor, Tara Fitzgerald), about a brass band in a depressed Yorkshire coal-mining town, I recognized every character from my ensemble: brilliant talents with erratic personalities; boisterous young lads and lasses, at whom our conductor barked constantly; middle-aged lifers who'd never known any other leisure. We played Christmas concerts in the Tayport Town Hall and on the cold streets of Dundee and St. Andrews, raising funds; we sight-read reams of legendary test pieces and brass favorites, to stay musically sharp; I challenged a blue-collar local for the role of euphonium soloist, and narrowly lost; after rehearsal, we frequented one of two equally dodgy Tayport pubs en masse, where large men with tattooed biceps threw darts and everyone else downed pints of lager and shandy with smooth efficiency. I fanned away the cigarette smoke, drank blackcurrant cordial and water, and ate packets of potato chips with surreal flavors like Hickory-Smoked Ham and Prawn Cocktail. I enjoyed every minute of it.

If I was lucky, I hitched a ride back to St. Andrews with two female students, one of whom dated a French horn player, a Dundee osteopath in his thirties with a car. If not, I walked up the road from the band hall and waited up to 30 minutes in a dank shelter for a bus. The band's music and musicianship thrilled me, but Scotland can't be much more depressing than Tayport at night in winter when waiting for a bus. How many different shades of dark are there? Sporadic pale orange street lighting glowed like nuclear waste, more disturbing than illuminating. Unused clothes lines crisscrossed outside grimy stone houses. Rickety door frames of corner shops and newsagents rattled in the wind. Tough-eyed teenage boys in black jackets and black jeans huffed past at regular intervals; I kept my instrument and rucksack within touching distance at all times. When the double-decker bus arrived, I stayed downstairs. What was there to see?

Tayport's troubles sometimes rubbed off on St. Andrews. Heather told me that in her third year in St. Andrews, the local council tried to implement a free bicycle-usage scheme, with designated parking areas and green-painted bicycles with no locks. The scheme lasted a week. Townies from Tayport and Dundee drove to St. Andrews at night with moving vans.

During my year, the small St. Andrews cinema unwisely showed *Braveheart* for six weeks on its initial release in the autumn and again for three weeks in the winter at the height of Scotland's participation in the Five Nations rugby tournament. I thought this quite funny, but that was before I heard that drunken youths, both from St.

Andrews and from the tougher towns to the north, began pretend-
ing they were William Wallace and attacked any students looking
or sounding overtly English in the dead of night. A subculture of
English students known as "yahs" existed within the university. The
typical yah talked with a posh accent (the Scots think they say "yah"
instead of "yes" or "yeah"), wore threadbare cricket sweaters and
faded red jeans, turned his shirt collars annoyingly upward, and
wouldn't have been at St. Andrews at all if he'd been accepted at
Oxford or Cambridge. Most of the non-English students despised
the yahs on principle, and the coexistence of yahs, non-yah students,
local Scots and tourists always lent a frisson of class tension to the
genteel St. Andrews atmosphere. Over 20 yahs, and one unfortunate
American with yah-like qualities, were allegedly injured before the
attacks ceased. I was appalled, but then I'd never looked beyond St.
Andrews's reputation as a haven of golfing tranquillity and purity. I
had to remember that St. Andrews is part of Scotland and as such
bears many of her character flaws, including an overbearing but
undersophisticated sense of nationalism.

CLASS TENSIONS OCCASIONALLY surfaced around the golf
courses, especially between crotchety locals and those they perceived
to be rich-kid, bad-boy students. Certain starters at the Old and
New/Jubilee booths showed much less patience with students than
with locals or even tourists. One of them (the same one who had
laughed at me in the rain at the Old Course) once put a foursome of
Japanese tourists off the first tee of the New Course between groups
of a University Golf Club match, accusing the St. Andrews captain
of not promptly submitting his order of play. "If you're not ready to
go," he said curtly, "I'll find someone who is." Many of my friends

and I were treated equally brusquely by the Links Trust office staff when inquiring about season ticket information or tee times on the Eden and Strathtyrum courses. The staffers and starters suppressed their hostility toward us, but I definitely detected it; maybe they treated others equally poorly, but I suspect not. We students had no leverage with which to change the situation, but I felt that for £90 I couldn't expect a full year of great golf *and* great service. So I swallowed my pride and accepted whatever stupidity came my way.

Not everyone in the University Golf Club submitted to authority so easily. Several years previously, the Scottish Universities Championship had been held at Lossiemouth, and one of the St. Andrews players was party to an incident involving the brother of a well-known Scottish club professional. He hit a driver and an 8-iron to eight feet at Lossiemouth's difficult closing hole in particularly impressive circumstances: the temperature was minus-6 degrees Celsius (about 21°F), it was 11:00 at night, he was *very* drunk, and he was stark-naked save for his golf shoes, socks and a winter bobble hat. (Gives new meaning to the phrase "having a bare lie.") Extracurricular frolicking dominated that entire week, including among other things a drunken fight between two golfers staged —unbeknownst to them—in front of the secretary of the Scottish Golf Union. Needless to say, the Scottish Universities Championship will not be returning to Lossiemouth any time soon.

I had joined the St. Andrews University Golf Club during Overseas Orientation Weekend. The use of the word "Club" instead of "Team" was significant, for the organization differed from my Harvard golf team in several important aspects. First of all, any student who wished to join the University Golf Club could do so. Operating like the R&A, the New Club and all the other golf clubs of

St. Andrews, it processed official Scottish Golf Union handicaps, wrote letters of recommendation for those wishing to play at private clubs, and governed itself through elections and an Annual General Meeting like a proper British club. It didn't have its own building, but the St. Andrews Golf Club, across from the Old Course's 18th green, let us convene in its bar and sitting room on Wednesday evenings. On occasion one or two of us snuck upstairs to the club's snooker room, but mostly we sat eight to a table, fraternizing and listening to the week's orders of business as announced by the secretary, in a brightly wood-paneled room among awards, trophies and grainy black-and-white photographs that had nothing to do with us. (We had a notice board in the Student Union for the posting of handicaps and announcements about upcoming golfing and social events.) At the beginning of the year everyone who wanted to participate in a weekly "sweep" anted up £5, and the golfers posting the lowest gross and net scores every Wednesday on any of the Old, New, Jubilee or Eden courses each won £5. On the very first official Wednesday, I carded a New Course 77 on a windswept afternoon and won the low gross award. Not only did I win my money back, but I had taken an important first step toward playing an active role in the University Golf Club's first team, just as I had at Harvard.

Or so I thought. In reality, some of the best student-golfers in Scotland go to St. Andrews, and I had little chance of competing with the best of them. Ben Pile, the consensus best golfer on the team, had a two handicap at the start of the season. No sweat, I initially thought: I can compete with him. My USGA handicap index had once been as low as 2.4. But before winter ended, Ben posted a 64 on the New and a 66 on the Old in informal play. I hadn't realized how different the American and British handicapping systems are. In America, you weight your scores according to course and slope ratings and then average the best 10 of your most recent 20 scores. The USGA system emphasizes a golfer's *potential*. In Britain, only tournament scores are used, and they're weighted according to "Standard Scratch Score," a less golfer-friendly measurement (in my experience) than course rating and slope. Relatively speaking, the British system emphasizes a golfer's *ability*. For certain types of golfers, the two systems can produce similar handicaps, but I would imagine my American 2.4 was worth only a British 5 or 6. Not good enough.

For most of the season I drifted along the outer fringes of the first team as it vied with Stirling University, as it always does, for top honors in Scotland. Stirling had recently dominated St. Andrews, thanks in no small measure to a big Scottish amateur named Gordon Sherry, once touted as a potential challenger to Tiger Woods. But Sherry had recently graduated, and in quick succession our own crop of talent claimed the Scottish winter league championship and both the individual and team titles at the Scottish Universities Championship. I badly wanted to be part of the latter, an orgy of golf held during spring break over nine rounds in five days on the No. 2 course at Gullane, but I wasn't even considered for selection.

Which brings me to the second salient point about the title of the St. Andrews University Golf *Club:* it wasn't run like any golf *team* I'd ever heard of. On the Harvard team—an informal outfit, by NCAA Division I standards—we had organized practice sessions every weekday afternoon. Our coach monitored each player's progress and impartially picked a team for each tournament. Even given the seasonal limitations of New England golf, our schedule became very hectic for six weeks at a time, and the shared level of intensity during these periods forged close friendships among many team members.

The St. Andrews club was nothing like this. Nothing like the NCAA exists in Britain: university sports are very loosely regulated, and students are left to organize their teams themselves with no "adult" involvement whatsoever. (To ensure that I remained NCAA-eligible upon my return from St. Andrews, I filled out a variety of forms and met with Harvard's NCAA compliance officer on several occasions. To join the St. Andrews University Golf Club, I turned up at the first meeting.) Our club secretary, treasurer and first- and second-team captains made every important decision, from match scheduling to team selection. With no full-time, independent administrators operating on its behalf, the club's organization inevitably suffered. Randomly parceled-out invitations at the eleventh hour seemed the norm rather than the exception. One Friday night, I happened to be passing by the club notice board in the Student Union when the first-team captain strolled by and asked me if I wouldn't mind doing him a favor—that's how I was selected for my first-ever first-team match. I participated in various home club matches during the year, all of which involved panicky early-morning phone calls to sleeping team members as the captain scrambled to field a full team. Not once were my team's final pairings submitted before our first designated tee time. The aforementioned incident of the crotchety starter, my captain and the Japanese tourists became more and more explicable as the season went on.

Furthermore, when the inmates run the asylum, team selection often comes down to who knows whom—especially early in the year, before the club officers know the abilities of the club's newcomers. Our first-team captain—a yah, it should be said—almost always picked himself and several of his mates no matter how poorly they were playing, leaving a surplus of qualified players to fight over what few places remained. One Wednesday I played the Old Course with one of the captain's mates, and on the back nine he suffered from one of the severest bouts of the shanks I've ever seen, but come the winter league match that weekend his name appeared on the team sheet in the Student Union, and mine didn't. (When I plaintively queried the captain the following Wednesday, he muttered something about "going with experience.") The social nature of the club also affected the selection process: attendance at the Wednesday meeting was a primary requirement for match selection. A high tolerance for alcohol consumption didn't hurt your chances, either. The old boys' network and the road to membership in the R&A started every Wednesday evening, and if that meant the strongest possible team wasn't chosen from match to match, so be it.

At the start of the academic year, Martin Parry had no connections, the wrong accent and definitely the wrong haircut. He opted to play along with the system, though, and by the end of the spring he seemed well on his way to the first-team prominence his ability deserved. I, on the other hand, had only one year to stake my claims, and I had no desire to surrender my social life to an interminable sequence of hopeful politicking. My colleagues were mostly a fun bunch of guys, but I hated being so conscious of the fine line between hanging out with them and worming my way into their good graces.

My one salvation was the length of our schedule. We played so many first- and second-team matches that even supporting-cast members like me received some choice table scraps. February was an ideal month to receive them. An unfortunately high proportion of matches in other months were sloughed off to the Strathtyrum Course, by far the newest and least formidable of the five 18-hole courses in St. Andrews. But with the St. Andrews calendar otherwise bare in February, the Links Trust could allocate courses worthy of the occasion to a number of good matches, and with the weather passable, we could just about enjoy them.

Not that the weather really mattered. Nearly every head-to-head match involving the University Golf Club was contested at match play. Team match play in a formalized setting allowed me to compete fiercely *and* relieved me of all score-related pressure—a winning combination I wish I'd discovered far earlier. In one intrasquad match in the autumn I rallied from four down on the back nine of the New Course, getting up and down for pars in true Ballesteros style from a succession of increasingly unlikely locations within 100 yards of the hole, to halve a match I had no business halving. I computed my scorecard afterward and realized I'd shot level bogeys (45) going out and one under par (34) coming back. I highly doubt I could have rallied so strongly in a competitive situation under strict stroke play conditions.

My best day with the University Golf Club, though, came in February. Somehow I had gained selection to the first team for a 36-hole match against the Scottish Universities Golfing Society, an amalgamation of alumni from university golf clubs around the country. (I think my teetotaling ways for once stood me in good stead with my superiors.) The format matched that of a Friday or Saturday at the Ryder Cup: foursomes in the morning, four-ball in the afternoon. On a dreary but dry day I won both my matches; my partner carried me in the morning, although I drained a 20-foot birdie putt at the last to clinch a 2-up victory, and in the afternoon we both played well and cruised to win 4&3. Best of all, both teams were feted in the R&A clubhouse with free food and drinks before and after the afternoon matches. The general public is allowed into the clubhouse only on the national holiday of St. Andrew's Day (November 30) or upon written application; women are allowed in the clubhouse only on St. Andrew's Day, period. Heather and I had visited the building together on November 30, and I marveled at the Open Championship trophy (the Claret Jug) and the Walker Cup (at the R&A thanks to Europe's victory in the most recent competition). But although Heather absorbed the history well enough, the year-round prohibition on women visitors miffed her, and I didn't enjoy my brief tour as much as I might have. To later be welcomed in after the match, to eat even a no-frills meal upstairs in one of the club's dining rooms, to stroll through the vast library and peruse its contents, to briefly spy upon Old Course golfers from the upper balcony and, best of all, to sip tea while lounging behind the imposing windows of the aptly named Big Room, surrounded by oaken lockers and massive paintings with vaguely recognizable names and faces—I felt so *included*. It's much easier to rail against the Establishment from the outside than it is from within the walls of the building that stands for everything honorable about golf. By the end of the post-match tea, I felt royal . . . and quite a bit more ancient in thought and deed than I had in the morning.

Still, even as I played that day, I wore or displayed the standard issue Harvard golf team sweatshirt, golf bag, towel and umbrella. My first team loyalties lay elsewhere. I longed to depart the St. Andrews University Golf Club's oligarchy, however benevolent it may have been, for the Harvard team's meritocracy, where score reigned supreme. The thought of relocating from the Old Course to

The Country Club hardly depressed me, either. Of course, I had to pay around $30,000 a year for my "membership" to the latter, and only 1/200th of that to play the former. I decided to remain in St. Andrews until summertime, after all. As the comedian Steven Wright once said, "You can't have everything—where would you put it?"

Chapter 13

HOW THE OTHER HALF PLAYS

❖ ❖ ❖

ON THE LAST day of February, I took a pad of paper and
a pair of thumbtacks with me to the Student Union. Earnest students jockeyed past me as I leaned against the University Golf Club's
message board and scrawled the following advertisement:

> INTERESTED IN PLAYING MUIRFIELD ON 7 MARCH? I
> HAVE A TEE TIME AND NO PARTNERS! RING 467093 AND
> ASK FOR DARREN — OR MEET ME AT THIS WEDNESDAY'S
> MEETING.

I posted the announcement next to the first-team fixture list,
sighed deeply and shook my head in disbelief. This isn't right, I
thought. Tee times at the top-rated course in the world are like gold
dust, and I have one but might not be able to use it!

Season after season, scores of Americans—celebrities and PGA
professionals among them—try to scissor through Muirfield's red
tape without having made the proper arrangements and are turned

away from its gates. Posh voices on the telephone tell them that Muirfield is too busy to accommodate them. They then play next door at Gullane, and when they reach the seventh tee of the No. 1 course, atop Gullane Hill, they gaze across a sea of dunes to Muirfield's expansive pastures and see empty fairways. They wonder: why is Muirfield so arrogant, so full of itself? How can such a snobbish, stuck-up, men-only institution call itself "The Honourable Company of Edinburgh Golfers" when the course is miles away from Edinburgh and the club treats its visitors so dishonorably?

Scottish golf has *always* been for the masses, not the classes. James II's pronouncement in the Scottish Parliament of 1457, "Golfe be utterly cryit doune, and nocht usit," is often quoted for its incongruity: James forbade the playing of golf because it interfered with archery practice. But the social context of the remark is revealing; archers were the *Untermenschen* of the warrior class, deemed unfit to associate with knights and chivalric noblemen. The implication is that the lower classes were passionately playing golf long before Mary Queen of Scots "found out what dormie meant and invented the back nine," to quote Dan Jenkins. Five and a half centuries later, little has changed: many courses of real quality, especially in more remote areas of the country, offer membership to virtually anyone living locally who can afford the membership dues. In America, golf is open to anyone who is willing to stand in line for three hours and take twice again as long to finish 18 dust-ridden, trash-infested, tire-track-blighted holes that nobody could enjoy while fully sober. When I visited Brora, its annual dues were only £100 ($150); Royal Dornoch's were only £170 ($255). And of course, at St. Andrews the price is only £90, although my season ticket gave me golfing privileges only, not membership in a club.

When perceived interlopers transgress this natural order, the Scots instinctively cry foul. While settling down in the Cruden Bay clubhouse bar after my hole-in-one, one of my playing partners told me of a friend for whom membership at Gleneagles was a lifetime ambition. (The Kings and Queens courses at the Gleneagles Hotel complex are among the finest three or four inland layouts in Scotland.) He was a two-handicapper and a devoted golfer, but he also worked as a window cleaner. Try as he might, his applications for membership were continually turned down on the grounds that the club was full and that the waiting list was being properly maintained. Then one day he read in the paper that the application of Stephen Hendry—an occasional golfer from Edinburgh who happened to be a six-time world snooker champion—had been rushed through ahead of his.

"Ach, my friend was distraught," the storyteller said.

"Aye, too right," added my other playing partner. "That's just not on, is it?"

"What's Hendry's handicap?" the storyteller asked rhetorically. "Sixteen? Eighteen?"

The other nodded. "To let someone like that into your club, instead of a golfer . . ."

He clucked his tongue twice; both men shook their heads and lapsed into a momentary, memorial silence. They looked bereaved.

I could have told them that in America, where "private" means *private,* golf clubs always operate like this. Members nominate new members, usually people like themselves; geographical proximity doesn't matter. Nobody writes to Augusta National, even years in advance, asking for tee times and expecting to get them. Nobody writes to the likes of Augusta Country Club, either. That's just not how things are done. Within this context, Muirfield's attitude seems liberal: The Honourable Company allocates tee times to unaccompanied visitors on Tuesdays, Thursdays and Fridays throughout the year. Anyone with a modicum of courtesy, patience and advance planning can expect to procure a time. In any event, as a private club, surely Muirfield is within its rights to demand blood oaths from prospective visitors, should it wish. The Honourable Company is the oldest formal golf club in the world—older than even the Royal & Ancient. Why should Muirfield feel obliged to conform to an unwritten standard of behavior at odds with its own instincts?

WHILE I WAS still in America, plotting my future Scottish adventures, I viewed Muirfield as a pleasant puzzle to crack and gladly jumped through its hoops. In August I wrote to the secretary of The Honourable Company, Group Captain J.A. Prideaux (ex-RAF officers seem to run all of the posh clubs in Britain), played my *Golf Digest* card and asked him if it might be possible to twinkletoe into a foursome in September. I wound up playing Gullane and North Berwick instead, of course, but the letter I received from Captain Prideaux thrilled me nonetheless. I felt queasy just opening it; the last letter to make me tremble like that said "Harvard-Radcliffe Colleges, Office of Admissions" on the front. The plain envelope and stationery bore no street address, only "The Honourable Company of Edinburgh Golfers, Muirfield, Gullane, East Lothian" in a classical, italicized red typeface. I nearly framed the letter before I came to my senses, and I pored over the enclosed sheet on club policies like an archaeologist studying Sanskrit runes.

For some reason I waited until December to write again, asking for a time in May; again the good officer rebuffed me, but he also wrote to suggest that a game in late February or March could be arranged. We hemmed and hawed before agreeing upon March 7. Excellent, I thought. Problem solved. But there was a catch: The Honourable Company doesn't allow singles. Twosomes and foursomes are strongly preferred. I booked my time as a twosome; I wasn't worried. I had a tee time at *Muirfield*. How tough could it be to find a partner?

I asked Scott Campbell first: he was busy. I asked Martin Parry: he was broke. I asked John Huggan: he said neither he nor any of his friends would pay £57 ($90) to play at Muirfield when they knew club members and could play it for free. I broadened my search to others in Melville: one friend had a dissertation to finish, another was morally opposed to paying £57 for *any* round of golf. I began to panic. If The Honourable Company accepted visitors at all, why wouldn't it accept them in odd-numbered increments?

I didn't know what to expect from my advertisement in the Student Union. But within two days three acquaintances rang up to say they were interested. Now I faced a new dilemma: do I turn two of them down? Or do I contact Muirfield yet again and ask to modify my initial request for a twosome? What if The Honourable Company determined I was a troublemaker and told me to sod off? But I couldn't face turning away my comrades, either, so I plucked up the courage to phone the secretary's secretary, a lady named Ms. Elizabeth Mustard, who was in charge of visitor bookings. She was extremely un-Muirfield-like: not only did she happily make the change for us, but she also seemed genuinely interested in my life at the university, chatting with me well after proper conventions had been observed. As I hung up, I feared for her job.

• • •

COMETH THE HOUR, cometh the golf. Stuart, Philip, Calum and I donned jacket and tie, as mandated by The Honourable Company, and drove to Muirfield in a gray drizzle. In morning rush-hour traffic, the trip took two hours. We waited, motionless, on the Forth Road Bridge for 10 minutes, listening to the trendy music and breakfast-time chat on BBC Radio One, and when we finally eased forward a catalogue of roadworks kept us from making up lost time. I wouldn't have called this optimal preparation for my dream round, but the delays merely whetted my appetite as we drew nearer and nearer. My companions likewise gushed at the prospect of Muirfield. Only Stuart among us had played the course before, but typical of him, he was so hungover at the time that he now remembered no more than the sketchy details of four or five holes.

Muirfield did not advertise its existence loudly. It hid off a small, tree-lined side street at the eastern edge of Gullane town. We missed the entrance our first time around and had to double back. Very few sights stir the soul like the first glimpse of a well-hidden, highly regarded golf course; when I focused through a copse of trees and first saw flecks of dun peep through the darkness, my thumping heart told me exactly where I was. We swung around into the rear parking area, gathered our clubs and duffel bags, and strode to the main clubhouse entrance, which faces the 18th green. I turned around and scanned the horizon: not a golfer in sight.

A smiling Ms. Mustard greeted us as we peered at the plaques and drawings on the walls as if in a museum. She then escorted us to the deserted men's locker room and bade us farewell. If I had any doubts about male preeminence at Muirfield, the locker room dispelled them. The room's gentle mustiness and dark wood paneling weren't exceptional, but the huge façade of curtainless windows opening up to the 18th green, barely 40 yards away, certainly was. Naked bodies of overripe businessmen must waddle around in the changing rooms after post-round showers, and I didn't notice any window-tinting. As a men's club, I suppose, why would The Honourable Company even pretend about caring to bare? Me, if I'm putting to win a match on the final green, I don't need those sorts of distractions.

We put on our raingear and made our way outside, where a gray-haired steward instructed us to proceed to the 10th tee. This confused me: while I could see 10 or 11 holes from where I stood, I could just make out two or three distant golfers within my range of vision. The steward explained: a twosome was making its way up the 14th or 15th hole and would presently be beginning again on the front nine, so it was best for us to keep well out of their way. How ludicrous! Great golf courses are designed to be encountered in first-to-climactic-last fashion. I don't mind first opening to the middle of a newspaper, but you don't start with Act III when reading *Hamlet* for the first time. And why should we have to play the grand 17th and 18th holes halfway through our round just so two members might not be hypothetically inconvenienced by four outsiders they weren't likely to catch anyway? I'd been naïve enough to think that once I actually won a tee time, most of my troubles with The Honourable Company's haughty behavior were over.

It occurred to me that had I been friends with a member, accompanied by someone who would welcome me into his home as readily as his golf club, I wouldn't have felt the object of so much antipathy. Those who don't have to toil for hours to procure a tee time, and who then have red carpets fully rolled out for them when they do, are more likely to unreservedly enjoy days at courses like

Muirfield (or Pine Valley, etc.) than peasants like me. Furthermore, the people in charge of ranking the greatness of courses like Muirfield almost unanimously fit this description. Are rankings such as *Golf Digest*'s "100 Greatest in America" and *Golf Magazine*'s "100 Greatest Courses in the World" unduly colored by the many panelists chosen at least partly for their access to élite courses with effete atmospheres in which they feel most comfortable?

IN MUIRFIELD'S CASE, the answer is no. And yes, perhaps. The course was undoubtedly great, filled with variety, splendor and magnificence. To continue my composers analogy, if Cruden Bay is Mahler, Muirfield is definitely Mozart. Muirfield was the only course I played in Scotland that batted a perfect 18 for 18—no hole was markedly inferior to any other. I was amazed at the degrees of subtlety we encountered. The massive hollows of Dornoch, the craters and rolling mounds of the Old Course, and certainly the towering sandhills of Cruden Bay had no place at Muirfield. The terrain leaned in various directions without ever falling over, giving the course an intimacy that even first-time visitors like me could readily appreciate. What's more, Muirfield had neither hidden bunkers nor blind approaches. Herbert Warren Wind called this absence of "capricious terrain" Muirfield's greatest quality (his opinion is hardly unique), and as such I could easily understand why scores of golfers, especially foreigners, who can't readily adapt to links golf are thoroughly captivated by Muirfield.

Muirfield is also traditionally among the best-conditioned courses in Britain, which probably helps. The story is told of the fastidious Colonel Evans-Lombe, a prior club secretary, who accosted members and their visitors seen to replace their divots with the grain of the grass pointing in the wrong direction. The greens were perfectly maintained for us, even in early March. I had to stroke my putts, not hit them, and I could only imagine how greasy the surfaces must get by August.

After 12 holes, I was still only two over par. At the 11th, my second, I'd rolled in a sweet, curling 20-footer for birdie, and I cruised through Muirfield's famous finale with fewer nerves than I had any right to expect. In a weird way, I think my playing companions probably had something to do with this. Stuart, Philip and Calum were all decidedly "yah"-ish, and two of them were officers in the University Golf Club. They weren't the first three people with whom I would have chosen to spend a day at Muirfield; I highly doubt they shared any of my high-society angst, because I heard many "best-ever" references even before we turned to the front nine. At times it felt like I was one against three, but the slight discomfiture they caused me actually distracted me from the physical and historical presence of the golf course and helped me concentrate on my swing. Even though I bogeyed five of my last six holes, I was still thoroughly pleased with my score of 77, seven over the members' par. I have always shared Mr. Wind's belief that one cannot fully appreciate a great golf course unless one's swing is in reasonable order. This was not a problem for me at Muirfield.

But for everything that Muirfield had in its favor, something still didn't quite seem right. Muirfield, though well segregated from civilization, was strangely removed from the panoramic ocean views and Gothic beauty of many other Scottish links, and I prefer courses with more drama and more scenery. (For what it's worth, I'm not temperamentally inclined to like Mozart, either.) I was prepared for that, but I couldn't expect that my first impressions of Muirfield in

February would be less favorable than those of Gullane No. 1 in September; and if any two courses can be fairly compared they are these two, situated on the same stretch of linksland and designed in the same style. Granted, Gullane was my first Scottish links experience, and mid-September is far kinder to most golf courses than early March; in the clear light of day Muirfield is undoubtedly better, but I don't think the difference in quality is anywhere near as marked as many might have you believe. Maybe Muirfield was *too* perfect for me, a series of 18 robotically good golf holes where the whole somehow became less than the sum of the parts. Whatever it was, Muirfield lacked a tiny element of charisma—not much, but enough to prevent me from embracing its charms as warmly as I'd expected. It was a great course, but it wasn't *that* great.

I've tried to make that judgment on architectural merit alone, but ultimately anyone who plays Muirfield also has to decide what to make of The Honourable Company. Some visitors will revel in the rarity of the Muirfield experience, but I couldn't help asking myself why Muirfield can't just wallow comfortably and openly in its history, like St. Andrews. In the last 30 years alone, Muirfield has hosted three unusually electric Opens. Two of them fell into Nick Faldo's lap when Paul Azinger (1987) and John Cook (1992) stumbled over the last several holes; the third, in 1972, finishes a close runner-up behind the 1986 Masters on the list of golf tournaments I most wish I'd seen in person. Jack Nicklaus, Tony Jacklin and Lee Trevino staged a memorable Sunday duel that wasn't resolved until Trevino chipped in for *par* on the 71st hole, after which a dumbfounded Jacklin three-putted from 15 feet and handed Trevino the title. At most golf courses with Muirfield's history, you wouldn't talk about anything else, but because of The Honourable Company you barely mention it at all. Muirfield could feel timeless if it wanted to; instead it feels like an anachronism, which is a shame, really.

Nevertheless, I lobbied fiercely with my playing partners for a second round after lunch, costing only £20 more. I failed, but in retrospect this proved a worthwhile decision, for the Muirfield luncheon had to be savored in its own right. A jacket-and-tie affair, we had to book it with our tee time, but even at £14 per head it offered incredible value. Help-yourself buffets don't come any better: we each got one bowl of soup, one plateful of main course and one bowlful of dessert. For our own sake, these limits were necessary. I stacked so much gourmet food onto my main-course plate, I could have played Jenga with it. During the meal, a Muirfield member mysteriously turned from his companions to us and said, "Best thing about Muirfield is the meal, eh?" We nodded. How could I ever face another Melville meal again?

From the dining room we retired into the adjacent library for coffee. We had the room to ourselves; sitting at the table closest to the windows, we talked about the course and golf in general, and gazed outside at what had become a gloriously sunny day. Muirfield, showcased in full uniform, glistened in the sunshine; we stared again from within at the final green and wondered why it seemed so much smaller from the fairway than it does from the clubhouse or on television. Eventually I paused, looked at our group and quietly said, "You know, I could almost get used to this." As critical as I'd been before and during my round, at that moment I felt accepting of everything to do with Muirfield. The person who had played next door at Gullane in September couldn't have sat in the Muirfield library and felt so composed, so peaceful, so unbothered.

And then I broke into a grin. "Too bad we're stuck with the Old Course," I said.

We laughed.

AFTER MUIRFIELD, THE weather faded to black and I didn't play golf for several weeks. Melville life carried on as usual; much vehement debate centered upon our dining hall menu. A rumor made the rounds that the Melville staff were spending only 49p (80 cents) per person per meal. I, Scott and the Shanty Town gang debated this fact at length, but it seemed at once too detailed and too true-to-life to deny: at every meal, the kitchen offered only one starter, one main course and one dessert—and each student could choose only two of the three. Chalky, graying potatoes were our staple. On separate occasions I was accosted by prowling Melville sub-wardens for using too much ketchup, too much salt and too many napkins. I was once threatened with revocation of my "napkin privilege." Melville offered 19 meals a week as part of my room-and-board package, but I soon learned to hoard my pennies for fish and chips at Joe's on Market Street and properly baked potatoes at JT's on South Street.

By the end of March I craved the haute cuisine of Taco Bell and Waffle House. So I fled to the States, and Heather came with me. In the St. Andrews University calendar, spring break was two weeks long—which seemed outrageously lengthy, considering that I hardly had anything to take a break from. But the British do love their time off. On top of the eight public holidays interspersed throughout the year, most workers receive an annual vacation allowance of at least four to five weeks. None of my Scottish friends believed me when I told them that many Americans weren't half as lucky.

Two weeks of vacation allowed enough time for me to show Heather around Boston and Atlanta, introduce her to my family, catch a Sweet Sixteen game at the Georgia Dome in the NCAA men's basketball tournament, and return to Scotland for another far-flung golfing expedition. Heather and I had a great time together, but when we returned to Glasgow, we temporarily went our separate ways. She bused directly to see her family in Inverness, where I would meet up with her again in due course. First, though, I rented a car and drove north to the whistle-stop village of Luss. I can't sleep on airplanes, but my overnight flight and subsequent jet lag didn't curb my anticipation at all. I had four days of quality golf coming up, and the first of them, at Loch Lomond Golf Club, promised an even more rarefied experience than the one I had at Muirfield.

LOCH LOMOND IS an American golf club that happens to be in Scotland. The people who run it would almost certainly contest that notion, but to me it certainly felt like one, and its golf course, an inland layout with no linksland characteristics, looked and played an awful lot like one. An outspoken former colleague of mine once called Loch Lomond Golf Club "one of many modern complexes springing up all over the British Isles that would be right at home in Orlando," to my mind a pretty damning indictment. The most compelling evidence for the prosecution is that visitors are not allowed at Loch Lomond except as guests of a member. I know of several other, older clubs in Britain (such as Swinley Forest outside London, and Rye on the English Channel) at which this is the stated policy, but most of them don't really mean it; with a well-written and suitably groveling letter to the club secretary, you can usually weasel your way on. Unfortunately, at Loch Lomond, the gates are truly barred if you don't have the right references.

On principle, this policy should have disgusted me; but without it, I wouldn't have had any reason to feel as triumphant as I did during my drive north from Glasgow. The banner of journalism can be pretty handy sometimes, I thought. Loch Lomond Golf Club had opened for play less than two years earlier, and everyone there was keen for the world to know how good their course really was. So I'd written to the Lyle Anderson Company, the Arizona-based golf real estate developer that owns and operates Loch Lomond, and asked to come and play it. I explained that I worked for *Golf Digest,* that I was based in St. Andrews and that I'd like to write about the club in my running column on the *Golf Digest* web site. All of this was true. But when Lyle Anderson sent a fax to Melville telling me my application was granted, I felt just as giddy as I had when I'd skipped out of my interview with Harvard's history department head a year earlier. The letterhead on the fax began, "LOCH LOMOND GOLF CLUB, SCOTLAND," and continued with an address ending with "Scottsdale, AZ 85258." If they wanted to emphasize Scotland over Scottsdale like that, I felt perfectly entitled to talk about writing an article when I only *really* wanted to play the golf course.

Loch Lomond rolled out every bit of red carpet it could find for me. I wheeled around the lengthy entrance drive and parked my car next to Rossdhu House, a pillared Georgian mansion undergoing conversion to Loch Lomond's guesthouse-*cum*-clubhouse. I had hardly opened my car door when Donald Macdonald, the club's director of member services, arrived to welcome me to the club and to apologize for the construction site. We strolled through the vast entrance hall and into the club's main restaurant for tea and biscuits, and after I'd finished, Macdonald answered my questions about the club with great tact and warmth.

The course at Loch Lomond was originally planned as the centerpiece of an upscale golf resort to rival Scotland's two established luxury hotel and golf facilities, the inland retreat of Gleneagles and the seaside complex at Turnberry. But when the project went bankrupt in the recession years of the early 1990s, the Lyle Anderson Company took over, and through Anderson's vision the Loch Lomond seems to have morphed into what could only be called a "second club" club. "To become a member here," Macdonald explained, "you have to already be a member of a club elsewhere and hold a valid handicap. At the moment, we're trying to restrict the annual number of rounds to no more than 16,000, especially in the first few years as the course and its surroundings mature." That figure translates to an average of 11 foursomes a day—not a lot. Of course, the current (as of 2001) joining fees are £20,000 ($30,000) for U.K. residents and £8,000 ($12,000) for overseas residents, price tags that are bound to keep the club's limits under control.

The evolution of Loch Lomond did interest me. And by American standards, Loch Lomond is and will undoubtedly continue to be a success, both as a real estate venture and as a golfing paradise. But in Scotland? Overseas ownership? A "Director of Member Services"? Golf in the United States had a similar scare in 1992, when Pebble Beach seemed set for privatization under Japanese ownership. It didn't happen, but true to form, we Yanks seem to have co-opted the idea ourselves and gone one better. Say what you will about the tyranny of The Honourable Company, Muirfield isn't *that* far removed from the mainstream Scottish golf experience. Loch Lomond, on the other hand, had the duo of Jay Morrish and Tom

Weiskopf build an American-style golf course with flashy contours and receptive greens. At the time of my visit, the club even used U.S. Senior PGA Tour–style black-and-yellow checkered flags on its flagsticks, a visually jarring choice I hadn't seen anywhere else in Britain. It's sadly typical to see that the club has given its holes titles like Shi G'Arten, Sherrif's Mount, Glen Fruin and Dun Na Bruich, as if they belonged to a course dating back hundreds of years. Traditions can only evolve over time, I thought; the faux-Gaelic hole nicknames at Loch Lomond seemed little more than a cheap public-relations gimmick.

BY THE TIME I was escorted to the practice range, and noticed that the club's omnipresent stewards had tidied the range balls into neat pyramids next to each bag stand, I was prepared to dislike Loch Lomond's golf course. That prospect didn't bother me much. I would have been happy to play 18 holes, tick off another "been there, seen it, played it" on my running record of Top 100 courses in Britain and the world, and move on to the next of my four days of spring-break golfing fun. I was ready to fall asleep, too; by the time I reached the first tee, I knew I was in Scotland, my eyes told me I was still in America and my body clock thought I must be in Japan.

Physically, my front nine was a disaster. I became more and more zombie-like as it wore on, and my golf swing threatened to utterly desert me before a rush of adrenaline woke me up. Fortunately, Macdonald had paired me with Charlie Green, the former British Amateur champion and Walker Cup captain who at the time worked for Loch Lomond in a representative capacity. Charlie wasn't playing much better than I was; he seemed a shadow of his former self, but I must have really caught him on an off day, for friends tell me that he still plays off scratch and regularly shoots his age. Still, Charlie told me a number of funny stories about his amateur exploits, so I remained in good humor even while repeatedly snapping my drives into the woods, a fault that does not go unpunished at Loch Lomond. (I quickly realized that for all the Old Course's merits, it puts almost no premium on accurate driving. Sure, preferred lines of approach are there to be found, but the Old Course never intimidated me with narrow fairways and flanking rows of conifers, and I'm afraid my long game suffered as a result.)

The setting did much to keep me going. Weiskopf once said that Loch Lomond offered him "the finest piece of land I'll ever work with." That may be an old golf course architects' chestnut (Gary Player, for example, has said something similar at the grand opening of *many* of his courses), but he and Morrish used the land to produce as photogenic a golf course as one could ever hope to see. To the west, the panorama rolled across the grassy highlands to patches of evergreens and mountain streams; more dramatically, to the east the loch itself lapped against the bonnie, bonnie banks of five holes, with Ben Lomond and other perpetually snowcapped peaks gently looming in the distance. On another day, I might have failed to appreciate Loch Lomond's appearance. Normally "business golf" frustrates me—it makes me maintain a veneer of calmness and dignity and drains the lifeblood of competitiveness from me. But my partner and my fatigue mellowed me out, and the surrounding beauty entranced me as it might not have otherwise.

Slowly but surely, I also came to appreciate the mastery of Loch Lomond's design. Morrish and Weiskopf didn't try to build an imitation links, nor even a classic-looking inland course in the mold of great English layouts like Sunningdale or Ganton; their product has very modern features, in terms both of hazards employed and of strategic decisions forced upon the golfer. The 14th hole, named "Tom and Jay's Chance," best exemplifies such modernity. Even from the back tees, it measures only 345 yards along the conservative, dogleg-right line: a simple long-iron or fairway wood leaves but a pitch, albeit over a bunker fronted by a stream to a green sloping away and to the right of the line of approach. Or one can take the "Chance" and try to carry the stream, and the bog short of it, on a direct line to the hole: the reward is a putt for eagle or a flip wedge into an unguarded green and an uphill slope; the price of failure is a stroke-and-distance penalty. From the marked sprinkler heads on each of the four tees, the carry is either 169, 204, 244 or 256 yards. It's a great match play hole, the kind of hole that television loves to showcase on a closely fought Sunday afternoon.

Speaking of which, Loch Lomond has cannily chosen to air the European Tour event it hosts on the BBC instead of a satellite channel like Sky Sports, gambling immediate profits against maximum exposure. If that's the idea, it seems to be working: in *Golf World (UK)*'s latest biennial ranking of courses in Britain and Ireland, Loch Lomond has risen to number three. Given the competition, that rating is *absurdly* high; that said, Loch Lomond will one day be a great Ryder Cup venue. I don't doubt that it will eventually get one, such is its clout already on the European Tour—and when it does, it will do the event proud.

THE HIGHEST PRAISE I can give Loch Lomond is that I shot 48 on the front nine and still enjoyed myself nearly as much as on the back nine, where I was 11 strokes better. My "second wind" was a typhoon: having not recorded a single par through seven holes, I notched seven pars and a birdie the rest of the way. So I was in a buoyant mood when I retired to interview a few additional staff members and pick up a quick sandwich—which, in early April, was all that could be had by way of catering. The remodeling of Rossdhu House had stripped its innards virtually bare in spots, and while I could change my shoes in front of a pristine ground-floor locker, to use the bathroom I had to forage outside through masonry and mud to a port-o-cabin out back.

Apart from that, everything at Loch Lomond seemed to be falling nicely into place. The club had hired Colin Campbell, fresh from seven years at Oakmont and a previous spell at Turnberry, as its resident professional. The strikingly (some might say jarringly) white sand in the bunkers was settling, and the grass in April was a richer green than what one normally finds on many Scottish courses even in high summer. And, as might be expected, plans were already under way for a second 18, which has now been completely routed by Jack Nicklaus but still is not scheduled to open for several years, at least. As we said good-bye, Director Macdonald gave me a press pack of material on Loch Lomond, its 24 pages of printed material containing all sorts of press releases, glossy brochures and a yardage book. I happily kept the last, but everything else seemed superfluous. Piddling layouts in Myrtle Beach may need that kind of publicity help, but a course like Loch Lomond does not.

As I drove away from Loch Lomond, I thought back to my experiences at Muirfield. I realized that all the two clubs really had in common with one another were the "Keep Out" signs, but that alone united them against the overwhelming majority of their peers. The exclusivity really should have bothered me, for it represented much of what I hated about golf outside Scotland. St. Andrews isn't élitist, it isn't closed-minded, and you don't need deep pockets to experience it and appreciate it. But the more I thought about it, the less annoyed I became. Most people feel that the game of golf is better off for the existence of Muirfield and Loch Lomond, and if they opened their doors to anyone and everyone, well, they wouldn't be Muirfield and Loch Lomond, would they? This conclusion made me smile. For the first time, I understood that *my* closed-mindedness almost kept me from enjoying either of them.

Long after I returned to St. Andrews, I still possessed both my season pass for the Old Course *and* memories of two fun rounds of golf on courses fit for royalty. I know I prefer the constancy and catholicity of the former, but that doesn't mean I couldn't enjoy myself during the latter. I'm glad that all courses aren't Muirfield or Loch Lomond, and more importantly I'm glad that very few places in Scotland seem to want to become them. But although Scotland is a tiny country, I guess it might just be large enough to support a couple of Loch Lomonds and even a Muirfield or two. Golf in Scotland probably works because everything is taken in moderation, including moderation. If so, it uses two pretty fair exceptions to prove the universal rule.

Chapter 14

SMOOTH SAILING

⬧⬧⬧

FROM LUSS AND Loch Lomond, I immediately drove north to Tarbet, then west to Inverary, southwest to Lochgilphead, south to Kennacraig and beyond. Mountains, rivers, oceans, forests, road signs . . . everything faded into a bleary blur. The second stage of research on my *Golf Digest* article on "hidden gems" began unsteadily—I'd wasted my second wind on the second nine at Loch Lomond. No matter how stunning the scenery, driving for three and a half hours on zero sleep in the previous 30 hours is not my idea of fun, but that's exactly what my self-imposed itinerary demanded. At Campbeltown, on the Kintyre Peninsula, I turned west, steadied myself along three final miles of rippled farmland and crashed—not literally, thankfully—almost immediately into my bed-and-breakfast room in Machrihanish. I zonked out for what seemed like weeks. (While asleep I missed the best soccer match of the season, Liverpool's last-second, 4–3 victory over

Premiership title contenders Newcastle United. I'm still bitter about this.)

I think even connoisseurs are subtly intimidated by Machrihanish, the El Dorado of Scottish links golf. Its name (pronounced Mahk-ree-AHN-ish, with a slight rolling of the "r" and the merest hint of an "h" sound before the third syllable) tangles the American tongue. Its location, near the end of a narrow finger of land so near (by air) and yet so far (by land) from mainstream civilization, confounds trip-making, defying attempts to link it to any reasonable Scottish tour itinerary. Despite its growing reputation as a great golf course, few photographs of it exist, and it takes a giant leap of faith to visit Machrihanish on anecdotal evidence alone. The rickety skeleton of what was once a grand hotel, white paint chipping from its walls, stands forlornly next to the Machrihanish clubhouse. Now subdivided into cheap apartments, its diminished existence testifies to the difficulties of selling tourists on Machrihanish.

But this is one-half of the paradox of Machrihanish: the legions who *don't* come make it special for the stragglers who do. Its monastic setting magnifies the greatness of its golf course; on the Mull of Kintyre an American can begin to experience great Scottish golf as the Scots themselves do, because Machrihanish has never been pressured by the dark forces of international tourism. This leaves writers like me on the horns of a selfish dilemma: how can I rave about Machrihanish's peaceful setting without fearing for its future? And yet, the town and the region desperately need tourism to survive. The local economy is depressed, and depressing: farmers live in perpetual recession, the whiskey distilleries that haven't closed are struggling, a ferry link between Campbeltown and Northern Ireland closed for want of interest, and NATO closed the air base adjoining the far end of the golf course for want of Cold War enemies. Only golf and the natives' outward cheery optimism separate Machrihanish and Kintyre from the utter bleakness of a Yorkshire coal-mining town. But if battalions of tourists were to come, the very fabric of life that makes Machrihanish what it is would be irreparably torn.

If I can't even begin to reconcile the facts of Machrihanish life, I *can* talk about its golf course. It begins as majestically as Pebble Beach ends, from a promontory jutting into the sea, with a tee shot over a corner of the ocean. That's the theory, anyway, but while the opening hole at Machrihanish may still be the game's greatest, I felt somewhat let down. The aesthetics seemed all wrong; try as I might, I could never squeeze the ocean and the fairway into a single good camera shot. The hole appears to be guarded by a waste bunker, not by the Atlantic Ocean. The tide rarely comes far enough in to pose a watery hazard, so even topped drives can be salvaged and played back to the fairway from the rocky clutter on the smoothly packed sand of the beach. It still packs a strategic punch, but if the water level ever rose to the top of the beach, the first hole at Machrihanish would be truly world-class. (This is why it tops my small list of golf holes that could be significantly improved by global warming.)

Machrihanish finished with two substandard holes: the 17th plays along an ugly line of out-of-bounds stakes to a featureless green, and the 18th is an open, drive-and-pitch par 4 to a huge green lacking subtlety. But Machrihanish also possessed a staggering repertoire of memorable holes; at each of the first eight holes I glimpsed a different vision of links nirvana. All of the greens were large and receptive, but not a single one was easily puttable (the second green was particularly wild), and woe betide the golfer who misses one on the wrong side. The back nine had its moments, but the front nine lingered longer in the memory, zigzagging in and out of the dunes by the sea. Grand, sweeping vistas and images were numerous. I liked the long, thin third green, nestled between multiple humps and bunkers, and the green at the short fourth hole, its vertical front wall dumping short shots into a vat of a bunker. In profile, the seventh hole looked like an upside-down letter "V"; just to the right of its apex sat an unkempt hollow that looked like the pit on Tatooine into which Jabba the Hut wanted to throw the good guys in *Return of the Jedi,* its fringe flapping ominously in the wind. Sadly, the green-keeping staff grassed it over after I first visited it (the wind was spilling sand over its edges, threatening the fairway grass), but while it existed, it perfectly symbolized Machrihanish: wild, natural, un-relenting, out-of-the-way.

I played Machrihanish on the sort of day when you can see the wind. It looked like an expertly wielded scimitar, a silver blur that pierced me from every direction. In the morning, the par-3 15th played at 158 yards from the members' tee. I chose a driver and aimed 45 degrees to the left of the flag. I didn't know what to do at the next hole, another par 3 in the same direction; it was 62 yards longer and had no fairway to speak of. The afternoon was slightly kinder, but both rounds highlighted a quirk of the traditional out-and-back links layout: both Jekyll and Hyde can live on the same course in the same day. On the front nine I hit the ball like John Daly—I lacked only control. On the back nine I felt like Clark Kent —and couldn't do much about it. My Scottish Record tells me that in nearly a third of the 18-hole rounds I completed during my year in Scotland, I shot at least four shots better on one nine than the other—thanks mostly to the wind. I did well not to extend that streak to my afternoon round: after a 40-47-87 in the morning (par = 35-35-70), I birdied two holes on the back nine to salvage a 40-41-81.

One of those birdies came at the last hole, and as I walked off its green I somehow knew I would come back to Machrihanish, again and again. During my year in Scotland, I never made it to the Ayrshire coast and the great links of Troon, Prestwick, Turnberry and Western Gailes—they always seemed excessively distant, especially after my experiences at Muirfield. They demanded many things of me: travel time, money, deference to rules and regulations I couldn't be bothered about. Physically, St. Andrews is twice as far away from Machrihanish as it is from these Ayrshire courses, but culturally it never felt that way.

I'D HEARD OF MACHRIHANISH. I didn't know what I might find there, yet I expected to find something. But I had no preconceptions whatsoever about The Machrie Hotel and Golf Links, on the rocky island of Islay (pronounced EYE-luh), because I only vaguely knew it existed. What I discovered blew me away.

Islay, principally famed (I'm told) for its pungent, peaty single-malt whiskeys, is a ferry ride away from Kennacraig, at the top of Kintyre. I didn't give myself much time to explore it, because to get on and off Islay in the same day, I had to debark at Port Ellen on the south coast and then embark at Port Askaig on the north coast six hours later. Ferry travel isn't for anyone in a hurry: no matter how thick and frothy the wake behind your boat, you never seem to make any headway. I stared at the isle of Gigha until my eyes hurt, its milky beauty for once projected against a pale blue sky as we crept past it. I ducked below deck for a while, and when I reemerged,

Islay's craggy hills enveloped my boat in all directions and Port Ellen speckled in the sunshine.

Machrie is near Port Ellen. I rushed through its creaking club-house and greeted someone I assumed to be the proprietor, and he apologized for the disheveled state of the building. He explained that the club was under new ownership, and it would be pumping money into the renovation and expansion of the adjacent hotel. Talk about a hard sell, I thought. No time to chat, though—I rushed outside, hoisted my bag over my shoulder and hustled to the first tee by myself. On my way I passed two women wrapped in pastels and deep in conversation, tugging their trolleys and wandering slowly toward the forward tee. I whisked past them before I froze in hor-ror: I can't just waltz in front of them, I thought. I turned around and apologized.

"No problem, son," one of the women said. "We've already played once this morning. We're in no hurry."

"Thank you," I replied.

"Have you played here before?" she asked.

"No, I haven't."

"Ah. Well . . . good luck!" Her eyes twinkled.

The first hole was only 299 yards long from the members' tee; I cracked a good drive up the fairway without much thought. When I reached my ball, a zebra-striped directional pole sat on a hogsback 50 yards in front of me. I started pacing ahead to see the hidden green. Glancing back to the tee, I saw that the two ladies had already hit, albeit weakly and sideways, and had begun walking. I broke into a jog. At the top of the hogsback I spied a small green sloping fiercely away to the back and left sides. I trotted back to my ball, try-ing to ponder my shot selection. Lob? Pitch-and-run? Bump-and-run? Putt? The ladies marched on relentlessly and hit again, creeping up behind me. I chose my pitching wedge and stood over my ball, still not knowing what shot I was going to hit. I opted for the lob-and-pitch-and-bump, the in-between shot we all choose when not thinking clearly. I chunked it, and my ball landed just on the crest of the mound and trickled forward. I wiped the perspiration from my forehead. This wasn't easy.

At the next hole, an "L"-shaped par 5 with the shorter side connecting the tee to the fairway, I overcut the corner and landed just out of bounds. I grimaced and reloaded quickly. The third, another short par 4 near the sea, blocked my path with another mound and another directional pole—the green, though, twisted beneath the dunes differently. The fourth was longer and uphill—but still blind. More mounds, more striped poles (What is this, I asked myself, a barbershop convention?), more confused pacing as I tried to play intelligent golf. From the ladies I heard laughter, and divot-taking, and footsteps.

On the fifth tee I finally waved the white flag and let the ladies play through. The lippy one smiled at me knowingly. I could barely look her in the eye: does a *real* man surrender his on-course position so meekly? To two com*plete* hackers . . . to two middle-aged *wo-men*? I bit off each chauvinistic syllable in my mind. But then I realized: they played speedily and laughed their way past me because they were content with their golfing selves, large warts and all, and with a pretty golf course on a sunny day. I, on the other hand, played under self-imposed time pressure (I had plenty of time to finish comfortably and catch my ferry), and as usual I tried too hard to do everything without gaining anything. So I gathered my composure—*again*, I frowned inwardly—and promised to enjoy myself.

As I left the ladies to waddle efficiently into the distance, I resolved to "play the poles": on every future blind shot, I would assume the middle of the green was just beyond each mound with a directional pole on it. I'm not really good enough to play otherwise, I told myself with a chuckle. My pushes and pulls would have just as much chance of getting close to the pin as my pure shots.

Very quickly, Machrie changed from a threatening nightmare-in-waiting to a friendly mountaineering expedition. Sand dunes billowed like puffy cumulus clouds with unrestrained abandon. A quite extraordinary specimen, 40 feet tall, reclined 60 yards directly in front of the seventh tee, just where I thought the fairway should start—normally when golfers talk of "forced carries" they speak in terms of length, not height. From the side the 17th hole, called "Ifrinn" (Gaelic for "Hell"), looked like an average two-week graph of the Nasdaq stock index. I pinballed back and forth between the dunes, and I couldn't help noticing that the layout appeared to purposefully use most of them. I yearned for more time on Islay, to analyze whether Machrie really was designed as well as it seemed, to distinguish between blind greens and landing areas and learn how to truly play golf by feel and memory. And also, how to play golf well: yard for yard, at 6,226 yards from the tips Machrie must be the toughest Scottish course west of Carnoustie.

Whereas Machrihanish staggered to an uninspiring finish, Machrie's 358-yard finishing hole towered uphill and to the left to another wonderfully hidden target. Into the wind, it played about 490. I crunched a drive and forced myself to approach the green with my least favorite club, a Titleist DT 3-wood I keep in my bag for no good reason. I don't like it, it doesn't like me, we aren't suited for each other, and I'd get a quickie divorce if another 3-wood fell into my lap. But just this once I puckered a shot off the sweet spot, and it rode the wind, soared above the dunes and curled softly over the striped pole and onto the green. I knew it was good; my uphill march to find out *how* good filled me with an expectant tension that is one of golf's neatest sensations. I crested the hill and received my answer: four feet. I rolled in the putt and thought about retiring to Islay—immediately.

HAD MY RENTAL car been a Ferrari instead of a Ford, that afternoon and evening I would have lived the pinnacle of adult male fantasy. The narrow, hedge-lined streets plunging down to the cove of Port Askaig were lovely, and the gently winding roads from Kennacraig to Inverness were lip-smackingly delectable. I've never had so much fun with power steering; the coastal panoramas of Argyll, near Inveraray on the A83, segued into the heaths beneath the jagged Cairngorms along Loch Ness on the rarely traveled B862. The latter was a lane and a half wide, with ample soft shoulders and periodic paved passing places, and utterly bereft of humanity. No villages, road signs, other cars, places for highway patrolmen to hide . . . nothing. Just speed and centrifugal force.

I spent the final Friday and Saturday nights of spring break with Heather and her family. We all got on famously, and I couldn't remember why Inverness had ever seemed inhibiting. Heather and I made plans to visit Turkey together at the start of summer. We even began to talk about what might happen after that.

We would drive back to St. Andrews together, but first I had one more course to visit. Boat of Garten, tucked in the Cairngorms an hour south of Inverness, was much quainter and quirkier than polished inland courses like Loch Lomond. Laid out over hilly and mostly bumpy ground, it began with a boring, flat par 3, continued with a fabulous, twisting and moguled par 4, and progressed through 16 more holes of similarly uneven quality. Although the good holes definitely shaded the indifferent holes, Boat of Garten had one sublimely good bad hole: the 307-yard 15th hole looked genuinely smooth from the tee, but a hidden depression chopped the legs out from beneath most of the fairway beyond the 150-yard marker, and I was told that the smart locals played the hole with two 7-irons. Above all, Boat of Garten was fun. I wouldn't recommend it to everyone, but I rate it quite highly among Scotland's inland courses, behind only Loch Lomond and one or two courses at Gleneagles. Whether or not this faint praise damns Boat of Garten I leave to the reader.

On the par-3 16th hole at Boat of Garten, I pulled my tee shot to the left of the green and found my first bunker of the day. I used to be quite a good sand player (several of my Harvard teammates called me "bunker boy"), but good bunker play is largely immaterial in links golf and I couldn't be sure if I still was. The one goal of Scottish bunker play is escape; even when you record an up-and-down, technique matters little. Most bunkers leave little room for maneuver, and nearly all are revetted with deep faces. The sand curls up only slightly to the faces, so the golfer has to create most of his own loft, and the sand itself is densely packed just below the surface. Your only realistic shot 8 times out of 10 is a steep-angled gouge lacking any preplanned finesse. If you manage to find the green and drain a 20-footer, great. If you somehow massage a shot to tap-in range, either you're very lucky or Old Tom Morris would tell you the bunker wasn't deep enough.

Boat of Garten was different. As I prepared to play my shot on the 16th, a strangely familiar sensation washed over me. I paused to analyze the shot and to think about proper technique for 30 seconds, and for the first time in months I felt as if I could expect to make par from a bunker without executing an above average shot. I had an abundance of green to work with, my lie was reasonably plush, and even though the ball sat slightly above my feet, I'd hit the shot hundreds of times before back home. Sure enough, I splashed out to four feet and made the putt.

The USGA rule book defines bunkers as "hazards." It affords no such special status to ankle-deep bluegrass, knee-deep fescues, sticky kikuyu, gorse, ice plant or other deadly, ball-eating flora. This apparent contradiction used to irritate me every year around the time of the U.S. Open, during which hundreds of golfers would scream at their occasional errant shots to "Get in the bunker!", from where they could save par half the time, and to not stick in the rough, from where they would make double bogey half the time. Each successive year, television commentators noted how they'd never seen better-conditioned sand at a major championship. The competitors would splash out to within a foot of the hole two times out of three, and I found myself wanting to spearhead the charge to make bunkers "hazardous," as the rules imply they should be, by leaving them unraked as at Pine Valley or by dumping into them truckloads of pebbles, rocks and broken glass.

Scotland made me think otherwise. Only the very best golfers in Scotland ever regard bunkers as anything less than one-stroke penalties. Unfortunately, instead of distributing bunker skill along a continuum, what linksland bunkers produce is a class of players who can escape in one shot and a trail of hackers and weak-wristed players in their wake who might take two or three shots to escape or, worse, might never escape without resorting to the rulebook or the more common "hand wedge." Around the greens, good players can judiciously choose their escape routes, but no matter how delicate the splashout, score is determined much more often by the quality of the resulting chip and putt. Scottish fairway bunkers neutralize a good player's skills even more. Who cares if you can pick a ball cleanly from an iffy lie with a 3-iron, a talent that elevates the professional over the weekend player as much as any other, when players of all skill levels can only hope to advance the ball 30 yards from 7 fairway bunkers out of 10?

The irony is that the good Scottish links courses in general (and the Old Course in particular) are otherwise extremely cagey, especially from the fairway within 50 yards of the green. Links golf generally allows superior skill and imagination to succeed in a variety of different ways. Scottish bunkers, though, only prove the better golfer negatively; I think even Seve Ballesteros at his peak would agree that he who stays out of them will do better than he who goes in them. I'm not saying that it should be the other way around, as it so often can be on the American tour. Bunkers are one of the strongest weapons in a golf course architect's arsenal, and their placement should dictate strategic play. And for all the evils lurking beneath the revetted bunker face, I marvel at the aesthetics of the face itself—layer by layer of sod stacked like bricks in the wall of a one-room schoolhouse. If only its lessons weren't so unpleasant.

THE BEST THING about deep pot bunkers may well be their tendency to speed up the average hacker—revetted faces block many skulls and shanks otherwise headed for the fescues and the gorse.

That said, not long after spring break, I played the par-4 seventh hole on the Old Course and ballooned a 5-iron approach shot into the wind that dropped gently into, and some four feet away from the face of, Shell Bunker. Had I hit the shot five yards farther, I could have used a putter for my third; had it fallen five feet shorter, I would have faced a relatively straightforward long bunker shot. (Shell Bunker, which is gargantuan by St. Andrews standards, offers some leeway.) Instead, I was just far enough away from the bunker face to risk a forward escape without being assured of success — and at five over par through six holes, I hardly relished the thought of playing out sideways or backward.

My first attempt at getting out hit the top of the face and clattered down at my feet. My second attempt did the same thing. So did my third attempt. And my fourth. And my fifth. And my sixth. My seventh at least did me the favor of cushioning into the face and stopping directly at the base of the revetment, leaving me no choice but to play out sideways. Otherwise, I might still be in the sand, tunneling to Australia as Shell Bunker slowly evolved into a journey to the center of the earth.

I chipped up and two-putted for a 13. And if I hadn't played the Old Course so many times already, or if I had plunked down £60 for the privilege of being so comprehensively humiliated, I probably would have broken down and cried. (I came close as it was.) I know that people have been trying to get out of Shell Bunker with varying degrees of success for centuries, and deep down I knew in this instance that it had tested my course management abilities and found them wanting. I could have played out sideways the first time; I should have the second time, and every time thereafter. And the long bunker shot I hit out of Shell Bunker to the 11th green had kick-started my Old Course 71 in November, so I can hardly complain. But at the time I thought about Shell Bunker the way Bill Murray thought about the gopher in *Caddyshack:* Give me a little plastic explosive and a detonator, and nobody will ever have to worry about Shell Bunker again.

Chapter 15

ALLISS IN WONDERLAND

❖··❖··❖

FEW GREENS IN all of golf are more dastardly than the one on the 14th hole of the Old Course. Shape a green on a lush American course into a plateau no more than 25 paces deep, and it would be tough enough to approach. Give it the firmness of coastal Scotland, slope it from front to back, bury a hippopotamus on the front-right and park a speed bump on the top of the swale at center stage, and you have the ingredients of psychological torture. You can't even see the tabletop itself: even in the absence of physical barriers, the approach feels nearly blind. There are many nefarious contours on the Old Course, but I found these to be among the most difficult—you have to play either the bump-and-run or the lofted pitch with *total* confidence to achieve a satisfactory result. The green complex at Augusta National's 14th hole very closely mirrors its difficulties. I'd love to say I came up with that comparison myself, but I must confess that Peter Alliss made it first.

I'd never heard the plush grounds of Augusta compared to anything like linksland before my year in Scotland, but then again, never before that April had I followed a major championship entirely through the eyes and ears of the British Broadcasting Corporation. The experience unnerved me, especially at first. Whether they consciously realize it or not, for most Americans CBS *is* the Masters. If CBS ever so slightly tweaks the leaderboard graphics, the camera positions at each hole, the commercials for Cadillac and The Travelers, or the lineup of voices in each tower, we notice the difference, for the Masters is golf's most compelling spectacle. To miss a year is like missing an episode of your favorite nighttime drama series; friends can help out with plot details, but you don't watch the Masters just for the plot. I obsessed about the Masters and Augusta National more than most—but how could I not? I lived in Georgia, and my adolescence was graced with the Nicklaus/Norman/Kite/ Ballesteros soap opera of 1986, the Larry Mize chip-in of 1987, the Sandy Lyle fairway bunker shot of 1988, the Scott Hoch lip-out of 1989, the Faldo playoff repeat of 1990 and the Woosnam-Watson-Olazabal duel of 1991. (I didn't learn the Masters could be dull until I went to college.)

British television in general is a strange amalgamation of disparate entities. "Terrestrial" television as I knew it, to distinguish it from the wide variety of British and European satellite programming available to those willing to pay for it, consisted of four channels (a fifth has since been created). Two of them are BBC1 and BBC2, both of which are in effect paid for by taxpayers' money and can flow smoothly—without commercials. Every household in Britain is supposed to pay around £100 ($160) a year for a "television license." Fines for avoiding this payment can exceed £1,000, but the

former seems a small price to pay for commercial-free movies and
(better still) sports coverage. Nevertheless, BBC programmers have
their foibles; they scheduled the first half of the crucial European
soccer championship playoff match between Holland and Ireland
for BBC1 and the second half for BBC2. Very annoying, especially
for anyone looking to videotape the match.

At number three on the dial is the local ITV (Independent Television) channel. Wales and Northern Ireland have one each,
Scotland has three (along with most of Scotland north of the Glas-
gow-Edinburgh belt, St. Andrews receives the "Grampian" ITV
channel) and England has 10. Each of these local branches functions
much like an affiliate of one of the large American networks, sharing
a core base of news and feature programming with the mother station while at the same time producing shows of more regional interest, including a "local" newscast of sorts. ITV wins most of its
ratings wars with the BBC; *Who Wants to Be a Millionaire?* was first
an ITV production before ABC copied it. That said, I rarely watched
ITV because it dumbed down most of its programming beyond belief, and it scheduled 40-minute newscasts every night at 10:00, even
when its feature films began at nine. (The least logical line in television history: "You will be able to see the second half of the film after the news.")

The ITV network stations are commercial channels, and as such
they share a common bond with Channel Four, whose lively "alter-
native" programming style belies its matter-of-fact title. Channel
Four owned the rights to the best of American television: *NYPD
Blue, The Larry Sanders Show, Seinfeld* and Heather's two favorite
shows: *Friends* and *ER*. (It has recently acquired HBO shows like
Sex in the City and *The Sopranos* as well; after Britain's 9:00 P.M.

"watershed," terrestrial channels may air R-rated language and nudity.) Every Wednesday night at nine Heather and I watched *ER* with her flatmates, but in America we dared not watch *ER* together since the British cycle of "new" episodes is usually six months to a year behind the American one. Channel Four featured some appallingly poor programming as well, but it more than compensated by showing live American sports after midnight on Wednesdays and highlights of the NFL and the NBA during the week.

For general sports coverage, though, only Rupert Murdoch's Sky Sports conglomerate of satellite channels seriously challenged the BBC. Murdoch's financial muscle gives Sky an unparalleled breadth of coverage. When it comes to golf, Sky holds the exclusive rights to the U.S. PGA Tour, most of the European Tour, the U.S. Open, the USPGA Championship (to distinguish it from the Volvo PGA Championship, which is referred to in Britain as "the PGA" and is one of the few rights the BBC retains) and the Ryder Cup. Murdoch's money talks, and the BBC, so long golf's protector and voice in Britain, retains just a few scattered European events, the Masters and the Open Championship. Even the latter would surely flee to Sky but for legislative intervention. Satellite television has not taken off in Britain the way cable has in the States—less than 10 percent of the British public subscribes to a satellite or cable service, and the House of Commons has shrewdly determined it would be politically suspect not to guarantee coverage of events like the World Cup, the FA Cup Final (something like the Super Bowl of English soccer), the Wimbledon finals, the Olympics and the Open Championship to the widest possible audience. (Shockingly, and frustratingly, the Ryder Cup is not on this list.)

The BBC, however, retains the patent on beautiful methods of sportscasting. The British still believe that men entrusted with microphones must keep the English language sacred; while the best American sportscasters rely upon emotion and delivery, British commentators use these qualities more as ingredients to flavor their powers of description. (Stylistically, John Madden is very "American," while Bob Costas is much more "British.") The Brits typically know how to deliver a good line, how to make you look at something in a new light and, importantly, when to use what the late Henry Longhurst called "brilliant flashes of silence" and let the drama of the game speak for itself. They also know when to criticize someone for making a mistake, and how to correctly and decisively deliver such criticisms without flinching. Sometimes they even get to work without color commentary: the BBC regularly employs one-man commentary dynamos for its most-watched sports program, the Saturday night *Match of the Day* soccer roundup show.

The BBC has an announcer named Barry Davies who manages to sound intelligent and professional about everything from the World Cup Final to Wimbledon to figure skating to the annual Oxford-Cambridge Boat Race. He doesn't need ex-athletes alongside him, and he doesn't need coy catchphrases or Maddenesque exclamations to help him get his points across. When listening to Davies, I became quite certain that the three-man American announcing booth holds two people too many. Then there's Alan Green, a Belfast-born wordsmith specializing in radio soccer who also covers the Open and the Ryder Cup for BBC Radio Five Live. (Golf on radio? Don't ask.) Green curries favor from nobody, and the British love him for it. No American broadcaster would dream of saying to the nation things like

And there goes Beckham, racing down the right—he tries the cross . . . oh. That is *dreadful*. He should be ashamed of himself. Simply appalling for someone of his class.

Or even better:

There he goes up the left . . . and Barmby hits that pass with his usual inaccuracy. He's having a *wretched* game today—absolutely wretched.

Or my favorite:

This match is thoroughly miserable—turn off your radios now, folks. How much longer do I have to sit here in the cold and watch this?

I'D ALWAYS WANTED to be a sportscaster. Great broadcasters can make great sporting moments come to life in a way great writers cannot; no prose has ever tingled my spine the way Al Michaels at Lake Placid, Verne Lundquist at the 1986 Masters or Skip Caray at the 1992 National League Championship Series have. (I don't think the sound bites "Do you believe in miracles? YES!" or "Maybe . . . YES SIR!" or "BRAVES WIN! BRAVES WIN! BRAVES WIN!" will *ever* get old.) In the world of make-believe I fashioned on the practice putting green of my adolescence, the putts I repeatedly made to win the Masters wouldn't have been the same without the voices of Lundquist and Ben Wright echoing in my head. I could think of no vocation more noble than to make other people feel the way men like these made me feel, and in my teenage years I began commentating, to myself or out loud, on just about everything. My middle brother's rec league basketball games always sounded something like "And there's blue number 13 on the dribble-drive, kicking it out to number 52—and the shot is blocked by green 24!" My plastic table hockey game relived countless Stanley Cup championship series between my little brother's Edmonton Oilers and my Philadelphia Flyers. I remember calling one memorable computer basketball game between Duke and Georgia Tech into a dictaphone. Rounds of golf I played by myself usually degenerated into story lines like "And with his closest challengers already in the clubhouse, Kilfara knows that if he can only play the last six holes in one over par, he will become the new U.S. Open champion." I often worked the role of on-course commentator into my preshot routine.

Somehow I missed the signs for WHRB, Harvard Radio Broadcasting, at the activities fair during my first week as a freshman. I signed up for the sports department of the student newspaper, the *Harvard Crimson,* almost before I realized what I'd done. But I parlayed my subsequent position as a beat writer for the men's hockey team into an occasional commentary role, and I knew the full-time play-by-play position would be waiting for me when I returned from Scotland. So in St. Andrews I listened to men like Davies and Green with particular interest. I fantasized about marrying their styles to those of my favorite hockey commentators back home, the New Jersey Devils' Mike Emrick and the Chicago Blackhawks' Pat Foley. In November I even rented a television set and VCR from one of the local electronics companies on a six-month contract. This arrangement had many benefits, not the least of which was the guarantee that I'd be able to watch—and videotape—every second of the Masters come April.

Ironically, my year in Scotland saw CBS cover the Masters for the first time in nearly 30 years without a British accent behind a microphone, dating back to the first time Henry Longhurst said, "Ah, well, there it is," to an American audience. The BBC had both sides of the ocean covered, though: BBC golf's two mainstays, the talkative Peter Alliss and the amiable Scotsman Alex Hay, joined forces for the year with the homespun, twangy Texas wisdom of Dave Marr.* Alliss, Hay and Marr's rainbow of contrasting styles filled my ears with joy; their stylish candor added rich meaning to the job title "color commentator." Not since the CBS heyday of Pat Summerall, Ken Venturi and the dueling Ben Wright and Gary McCord had I related so well to a golf broadcasting ensemble.

(Bizarrely, Heather's Glaswegian grandmother had irrationally disliked Alex Hay for years. I discovered this at Christmas in Inverness after opening her present to me: a sleeve of Titleist Professional 100 golf balls, my favorite. She told me she didn't know anything about golf, but she'd gone to a pro shop and asked the clerk, "What is the Rolls-Royce of golf balls?" We began chatting about golf, and I mentioned something I'd heard Hay say on television. "Oooh, that Alex Hay!" she said. "Don't get me started!" I didn't. Since she never watched golf on television, I'm afraid that what Hay did to incur her wrath may never be known.)

Methods of producing a golf telecast are as varied as the networks that show golf on television. Frank Chirkinian, the producer and director of CBS golf for nearly 40 years, always preferred to station a voice and a pair of eyes in towers at each of several holes. ABC, in the days when it could call upon the skills of Marr, Jim McKay and Jack Whitaker, clustered its core of commentators in one booth near the 18th green while Bob Rosburg and Judy Rankin perfected the art of relaying club, lie and length information and analysis back to the booth from the trenches. NBC always combined the CBS men-in-towers and ABC on-course commentators approaches, but not until the 1990s and the arrival of Roger Maltbie did the network

*Marr died in 1998; golf is far poorer for his absence.

find a roving reporter worthy of the description. Nevertheless, the famously pessimistic Rosburg will always be my king of on-course commentary. Around my golfing peers during high school and college, imitations of any ABC commentator talking to Rosburg offered surefire comedy:

"Rossi, how does it look?"

"He's got *no shot*, [Brent/Jack/Jim/Roger/Mike]."

"But Rossi, he's in the middle of the fairway."

"[Brent/Jack/Jim/Roger/Mike], if he gets the ball anywhere within 30 feet of the hole, it'll be one heck of a golf shot."

"Rossi, you just said he's got a sand wedge from 120 yards. What's the lie like?"

"Oh, it's sitting very cleanly. But it's an *impossible* golf shot."

The BBC has on-course reporters, but it uses them sparingly; the studio commentators rely mainly upon their own devices to keep things fresh and interesting. At the Masters, Alliss, Hay and Marr sat in a broadcast center, away from the golf course itself, and took turns describing the action with two in the booth at a time. They passed around the lead commentary role like a hot potato, using lots of eye contact and signaling to make sure lines weren't stepped upon. Some leeway was allowed: if Alliss was in the middle of a rousing story when the camera switched from golfer X at the 15th to golfer Y at the 17th, he could keep going, but mostly he segued to Marr or Hay concurrently with the director's switch in focus. This flexibility played to Alliss's strengths.

I talked to both Alliss and Marr as they prepared to commentate on one of the few European Tour events remaining in the BBC's once-mighty empire. They were in Oxfordshire; I sat on a Melville corridor floor, propped against the wall, talking on a communal phone. I tried to put my journalistic game face on, but my admiration for my subjects made it very difficult to interrogate them properly. Marr had just flown into England from the States, and I asked him if it was tricky to make the transatlantic switch between networks and tours. "It's a little harder," he said. "I have to try to familiarize myself with players I don't normally get to see a lot. And after working with NBC and then arriving over here, I really have to try to turn myself on and work on the little things. But you're still talking golf, so in that sense it's not that different."

There is no "correct" way to do golf on television: as Alliss told me, the differences between styles "are just enough to keep things interesting," both for the viewer and men like Alliss continuously traveling between networks. But Marr had ample experience from his time with the three significantly different philosophies of ABC, NBC and the BBC, and I was inclined to listen when he said he liked the BBC's way of working: "You're on your schedule for 35 or 40 minutes here, and within that period of time you're trying to develop some sort of story. Back home, you tend to be limited to 15 or 30 seconds and can't really give more than a few lines—which may be a good thing, I don't know. I hope we're not boring anybody to tears!"

"You have to be much more aware of things in the States," said Alliss. "You can't sort of wax lyrical when in 10 or 15 seconds you might be going to a commercial break." In some sports, commentators crave such breaks, but both Marr and Alliss seemed to feel restricted by them, which is a credit to their creativity (men with ideas can fill time quickly) and integrity (who wants to interview sponsors or endorse products ad nauseam?).

Alliss loves to talk about golf—and anything else. Ironically, he credited practice and repetition for the stylistic spontaneity he has cultivated for himself in his years of broadcast experience. He does call himself "a great radio listener," and he admitted to me that he borrows the occasional nugget from one of the many talk shows he listens to. Mostly, though, Alliss's delivery is loose and unpredictable; he knows his boundaries, but within those limits he might stretch the golf lexicon in any direction, except the dull one. "I'm not a statistician," he said, "and I think American viewers tend to want more stats—who won how much money, or whatever. I really need to be *alongside* one who is a statistician. I'll see some kids licking their ice cream, or a dog peeing on a tree, something like that, and find it infinitely more interesting."

Alliss also has a knack for salvaging lost causes. One year, during a leaden day at the World Match Play Championships at Wentworth, near London, a golfer launched a ball high into the air from the 17th tee. The director cut to the view of a cameraman perched high above the golf course on a fire-truck crane, but said cameraman failed to track the white ball against the gray sky. Indeed, the camera wobbled around uncertainly, as though its operator were tentatively scanning the skies for enemy Messerschmitts. Having observed the golfer's body language on his follow-through, Alliss knew which way the ball was heading: "I believe that one is probably over on the left side," he said, trying to coach his colleague as inconspicuously as he could.

The cameraman began to pan to his left—toward the right side of the fairway. "No, I mean the golfer's left," said Alliss tersely. The hapless cameraman pulled out to as wide a shot as he could manage and rotated the camera very slowly—still in the wrong direction.

"Okay, to *your* right," urged Alliss, his coaching losing any semblance of subtlety. Finally the cameraman stopped and switched directions, panning to his right . . . at an elderly snail's pace. Five seconds of silence elapsed, and the ball still didn't appear. In the background, Alliss muttered, "Dear God, by the time he gets there, Gauguin could've painted it!"

Early in my chat with Alliss, I let slip that I was in St. Andrews. I quickly learned that Alliss talks the way he broadcasts. In rich, plummy tones he queried me about the local wind direction and velocity, and from there launched into a one-sided analysis of the brutal spring weather we'd both experienced so far. Some American critics pan Alliss for his wordiness, but even his casual soliloquies are so brilliantly crafted that I rarely care how long they take to finish. Occasionally he does cross the fine line between lazy eloquence and unfocused rambling, sometimes even hijacking the drama by talking over it, but he could hardly cut such a Falstaffian figure otherwise. As Alliss himself said to me, "I'm a bit mad, anyway."

OUR CONVERSATIONS TOOK place shortly after the Masters, which that year proved a dramatic touchstone by which to compare the approaches of the BBC and CBS. Greg Norman's epic collapse and Nick Faldo's triumph are now part of golfing folklore. From a broadcasting point of view, Norman's performance demanded strong commentary—words of condemnation, words of sympathy. Marr's description of the tournament to me was succinct: "I feel like I've seen a lot of golf in my time, from Arnold [Palmer]'s collapse at Olympic [in the '66 Open] on down, but I don't think I've seen anything quite like that."

The BBC has never had its own cameras or an extensive production team in Augusta; CBS handles the pictures and graphics for everyone, an arrangement that fosters tension in certain quarters. Of the BBC's difficulties, Alliss lamented, "I think we always used to have a better working partnership with ABC when we both covered the U.S. Open than we now do with CBS. Not to be uncharitable, but they [CBS] tend to consider only the home consumption, even though they are providing the 'world feed,' as it were. If Chirkinian wants to do whatever, it will happen almost instantaneously, with very little warning. He does tend to do it his way, and the attitude seems to be one of 'They can come along on our coattails if they like.'"

From a technical standpoint, everything was fine by me until Saturday evening. The powers that be at Augusta National believe you can have too much of a good thing, for the club allows only the USA Network and CBS between them to schedule a total of 10 and a half hours of live coverage of the Masters from Thursday through Sunday. (By way of comparison, the BBC shows nearly that much of the Open Championship in one day.) The BBC began its Saturday coverage of the Masters at 8:00 P.M. (3:00 P.M. Augusta time), half an hour before CBS, but not much happened. The CBS cameras were still inactive, and viewers and broadcasters alike were mostly reduced to scoreboard-watching. Steve Rider, the BBC host in charge of marshaling Alliss, Hay and Marr, apologized repeatedly for the "inconsistent shape of the coverage" and once sarcastically thanked CBS for "a positive glut of live golf action" that lasted 90 seconds. Then, when CBS finally revved into action, captions such as "Voice of Sean McDonough" and "Voice of Ben Crenshaw" appeared at the bottom of the screen. Alliss once retaliated cleverly ("Nice imitation I do, eh?"), but the obvious lack of synchronism frustrated me.

To compensate for such glitches, the broadcast trio remained in rare form throughout. Alliss began the Thursday telecast by comparing Augusta's 13th fairway to "the old banked racing track at Brooklands which sadly is no more," and from that promising start he roared through a weekend of the wonderfully bizarre. By way of example, I hereby nominate Peter Alliss's Top 5 utterances of the week:

5. Sunday, as Greg Norman peers from his ball through a gauntlet of trees well to the left of the eighth green: "Now, what do you think here . . . What would Sergeant Bilko do? Would he go through the middle, would he play out to the right?"

4. Friday, after Phil Mickelson delicately weights a flop shot to the eighth hole from left of the green: "Landed as softly as a vicar's handshake."

3. Saturday, while watching David Frost recheck his yardage book after his approach shot to the 10th green landed well long and bounded even longer: "All the struggling, all the pain, all the notes, all the photographs, all the writing down, and . . . 50 yards too far."

2. Thursday, as the gentleman in plus fours and—on this day—a tie addresses a shot on the 16th tee: "Now, the Great Gatsby, or Payne Stewart as he's known, in his new line of fine wear . . . [Stewart swings, then apropos of nothing:] purveyors of fine clothes for the gentry. [Stewart's ball lands to the right of the green.] Now, that's in the wrong spot. You get down in two from there, I'll give you a coconut."

1. Sunday, as Norman heads for the watercooler behind the 15th tee: "Just have a swig . . . I think if things go wrong, he might have something a bit stronger tonight."

HEATHER CAME OVER on Friday night to watch with me. She liked the pretty pictures of azaleas, magnolias and other greenery.

She sniggered at Alliss's commentary, less for its innate humor than because she'd heard the British comedian Rory Bremner's political impersonation of Alliss ("Ooop . . . ahhh . . . there's the Tory party wobbling over to the left . . . falling back to the right . . . wandering around in circles, unable to complete a proper sentence. . . ."). But she couldn't adjust to the camera cuts—those sudden juxtapositions of blue sky and a wobbly white thing from the tranquillity of the fairways and trees. And she only related at all to the golfers she'd heard of, for better or worse: "Faldo," she said, "he's the one with all the ex wives, right?" I watched on Saturday and Sunday without her.

On Sunday, Norman began with a six-shot lead over Faldo; Faldo shot 67 and won by five. Anyone who watches the Masters enough should know not to go left on eight, short on nine, left on 10, at the pin on 12; I sat in stunned silence as one of the best golfers in the world made each of these mistakes within the space of 60 minutes. Thank goodness, Alliss, Hay and Marr were paid to keep from becoming as tongue-tied as I was. I later learned that CBS largely pussyfooted around the historical ramifications of the collapse until Verne Lundquist finally chimed in with a strong commentary after Norman found the water at 16. Human nature wants to throw life rafts to drowning men, but impartial commentary demands condemnation of the bad as much as praise for the good. And none of the BBC announcers shirked his duties:

- Alliss, after Norman's three-putt bogey at 11: "This is where the game of golf, silly old pedestrian game that it is, can be distressingly cruel."

- Marr, during the back nine: "This might be a career killer if Greg doesn't win here today . . . I think we might be seeing the destruction of a guy."

- Hay, after the splashdown on 16: "We really are witnessing one of the saddest tales in the history of championship golf, and even Faldo is suffering with the man."

- Even Frank Nobilo, in the studio with Steve Rider following his final-round 69, after the shot on 16: "He's bleeding. He's honestly bleeding."

The mixture of gravity, empathy and awe with which the broadcast team discussed Norman's disintegration felt entirely appropriate. It was as if they were talking about the untimely death of a pop icon—and in a sense they were, for Norman's star has been in eclipse ever since that remarkable April afternoon, just as Marr had predicted. Too, under the circumstances, Alliss, Hay and Marr could have overlooked Faldo's magnificence, but Faldo's "home" network paid him due credit without ever getting rancorously patriotic. The BBC played like Faldo right to the very end, and as the final credits rolled, I felt enormous compassion for Norman, but also pangs of sympathy for myself. I didn't know when next I'd have the chance to watch a major championship on the BBC.

Chapter 16

THE CHOKE ARTIST

❖ ❖ ❖

ALTHOUGH I LIKED to think my academic year was no more than a glorified golf vacation subsidized in part by *Golf Digest* and Harvard's department of financial aid, every so often I did have to attend class, write essays and sit exams. Two classes a semester wasn't much, and my senior thesis never got off the ground; the British Golf Museum was dedicated to tourism and as such had no collection of golf books for me to research, and the R&A wasn't keen to give me unlimited access to its library. (Granted, I didn't ask very forcefully.) Perhaps because I had so little to do, I actively applied myself to academic life for the first time since high school. It helped that I enjoyed my classes (European Union and Britain in the Era of the Great War in the first semester, European Security and The Hundred Years' War in the second) and really liked my professors, who gave great lectures, led every discussion group and graded all of my work. My grades, between 15 and 16 on the university's 20-point scale, were roughly the equivalent of a B to B-plus average back home. I scored better at Harvard, but I learned more at St. Andrews.

Visitors like me have sought knowledge and enlightenment in St. Andrews for centuries. The local church was an important player in Scottish ecclesiastical affairs over a thousand years ago, a leading voice of Christianity in the British Isles even before St. Andrews became "St. Andrews." (In the Dark Ages the town was called Kilrimont, literally, "church of the king's mount.") The university dates back to the 15th century and was a hotbed of theological discord during the Protestant Reformation. Its library is the oldest in Scotland. Compared to these weighty matters, golf seems a pointless pursuit.

Golf and academic research usually make stranger bedfellows than honesty and politics. A clubmaking company wants a hot new gimmick that will sell more golf clubs, so it hires a few engineers to cook something up in the name of science. After extended experimentation and in-house testing, the company presents a spokesman to unveil its product: a kidney-shaped shaft, a cavity-fronted iron, maybe a Jupiter-size driver. No matter what the product, the spokesman and a flurry of press releases cite the legitimacy of the engineers' research to promise more distance, greater accuracy, softer feel, more spin . . . everything but a better sex life. If each successive sales campaign told the truth, we'd all be hitting the ball 400 yards by now. Reality, as defined by the USGA's and the R&A's independent club testers, suggests that advances in club- and ball-making technology aren't as dramatic as you might think.

New clubs *can* significantly help the average golfer for a variety of reasons. For example, golfers with slice swings will generally perform better with an offset club (whose face is set slightly behind the shaft relative to the point of impact) than with one using face progression (where the opposite is true). But new club X usually provides only short-term improvement to the average golfer, and then only because it brings him a clean slate of experience—erasing the history of bad shots he might have had with club X-minus-one. He wants to believe in club X. He trusts it. He swings freely. The ball flies straight and far, and for several glorious, flickering moments in his golf career he overachieves. Soon, though, he hits a bad shot with that same club, beginning a process that will probably end in the purchase of club X-plus-one.

Why do our psyches act so strangely? The secret to playing better golf, if it exists, almost certainly lies in the answer to that question, not in any product purchases. Wouldn't it be nice to have a detailed scientific explanation for why some people get the yips, or can't make left-to-right putts, or have mental blocks against using their drivers? Maybe some of these diseases might one day have cures. I know the truth is out there somewhere, and that researchers *are* trying to find it. I know this because I met one of them in mid-April, at a Wednesday meeting of the St. Andrews University Golf Club, and volunteered to become his guinea pig.

ROBIN JACKSON STOOD on a wooden chair in the middle of the St. Andrews Golf Club sitting room and made a startling announcement: "Would anyone like to make some money?" My stomach perked up. I hadn't eaten out in a while.

"I'm looking for a few golfers willing to take part in an experiment for the psychology department," he said. "You'll have the chance to win up to six pounds if you do well enough." I'm still with you, I thought.

He continued: "The experiment has to do with why people perform worse than normal in situations of high importance—what is colloquially referred to as 'choking.'"

Sign me up, I thought. I'll tell you anything you need to know!

Robin's announcement caused quite a commotion, but after he finished I managed to corner him at my end of one of the long sitting room tables. Robin had 50 spaces available on his sign-up sheet—it was empty, since he'd come to the University Golf Club first. "Good man," I said conspiratorially. I explained to him what I was doing in St. Andrews and asked him to tell me a little bit about himself.

Robin had started playing golf at home in England when he was nine years old and was "absolutely mad keen on the game" until he was 16. "I'm no longer golf-obsessive," he said, "but I still play off a 10 handicap and I like the game a lot." I gathered he had matriculated at St. Andrews because of its upstanding university, not its golf courses, although by his reckoning Robin knew every bunker on the Old Course from firsthand experience. He was working toward his Ph.D. in psychology, specializing in sports psychology, subspecializing in sports involving "self-paced skills" (when you initiate the primary action, as opposed to sports like soccer where you react to the movement of teammates, opponents and the ball), and sub-subspecializing in golf. He hoped to present a paper on the choking project in October to the Association for the Advancement of Applied Sports Psychology in Virginia.

"Any chance you'll be ready to show it to Greg Norman sooner than that?" I asked.

He groaned. I signed his sheet and arranged to meet him in the lobby of the psychology department the following Tuesday morning at 11:15. "Remember to bring your putter," he said, "and, if you like, a ball of your choice."

ROBIN GREETED ME slightly before the appointed time. "You're the only doctor I know who shows up for his appointments early," I said. For where I was, I couldn't believe how giddy I'd become. I hadn't taken a science class since high school, mainly because in-class experiments never promised as much fun as this one did.

Robin led me to his "laboratory," a rectangular, thinly carpeted room perhaps 15 feet wide. To the floor he had securely affixed a large white bedsheet. Upon it he had drawn a long grid of squares each measuring six inches across; at the far end of the room he had superimposed on top of this grid a series of five concentric circles, the innermost of which was 12 inches wide and blacked out to look like a bottomless golf hole. The other rings were labeled like a beginner's archery target, from a "1" at the outside to a "4" at the ring closest to the bull's-eye. Robin's foldaway desk and chair were positioned against the wall to the left of the floor markings by the bull's-eye. Only stacks of papers cluttered the desk, at least from what I could see.

"No bells, whistles or caged rats?" I asked.

"Nope."

"No electric-shock treatments?"

Robin laughed and began to outline the format of his experiment. "I'm going to have you stand right here," he said, pointing to the near end of the grid, about 10 feet away from the bull's-eye. "I'm going to have you attempt a total of 80 putts with your putter there."

I glanced at my thin, double-sided blade—an old model, popular in many quarters of the golfing world, called a Bullseye. This time I rolled my eyes before Robin could.

He continued: "The first 20 putts will be a chance for you to warm up—hopefully you'll get a feel for the speed of the surface and the conditions of the experiment. The second 20 putts will establish your baseline score: you get five points for each putt that touches any part of the bull's-eye area when it rolls to a complete stop, four points for a putt that finishes in or touches the ring next to the bull's-eye, and so on. Putts that miss the ring altogether are worth no points."

I squinted at Robin. The ring's diameter was five feet. "Does that happen?" I asked. "Do people really miss the whole thing?"

He smiled and ignored the question. "Your third group of 20 putts will also be scored and totaled, but before you begin, you'll be required to choose a brief swing thought of sorts, which you will then audibly say to yourself before you hit each putt." I nodded—I liked where this was going. "Finally," he said, "in your last group of 20 putts, we'll see how your nerves hold up when putting for money. If you do well relative to a group of players in your handicap bracket that have gone before you, you can win up to six pounds. Regardless, you'll win at least one pound, just for showing up."

"Great—let's get going," I said. I took a ball out of my pocket and dropped it on the carpet, hockeying it with my putter onto the bedsheet and into the center of Robin's grid.

"Right," he said. "Your 20 warm-up putts begin now."

I took two short practice swings, settled over the ball and tapped it forward. It rocketed through the blackened bull's-eye area and nearly banged into the far wall of the room. Zero points. I held my hand over my eyes. "I'm glad that one didn't count!" I said.

Robin had his own putter with him, and he used it to knock my ball back to my feet. "Take your time," he said.

My second putt also flashed well past the hole, barely clinging to the one-point outer ring. I felt like I was putting down to the hood ornament on a car from one of its windshield wipers—the floor seemed virtually frictionless. Like most golfers, I'd putted on artificial turf before: on the plush green carpet of the hallway outside my childhood bedroom; along the length of the smooth Persian rug in the living room to the leg of the coffee table at its top left-hand corner; on the creaky hardwood floors of the dorm room I shared with Joel, my Harvard teammate; from one *Golf Digest* staffer's office to another. But I'd never been methodical, or even mathematical, about it as Robin's experiment demanded.

Still, within six or eight strokes, I started to get a feel for the speed of the bedsheet. During my second group of 20 putts, Robin announced the score of each putt and recorded it on a homemade scoresheet; by the halfway point of this second stage, I figured out where most of the key bumps in the carpet were. If I aimed a putt six inches to the right of my target and tapped it at just the right speed, the ball veered gently to the left and a tiny crease backstopping the rear-left portion of the bull's-eye held it up to give me five points. I didn't always succeed, but I did well enough to briefly channel my obsession about score into a new outlet.

Whether or not this scientific configuration properly tested my putting ability or the effects of pressure situations upon golfers, I don't know. But the skill being measured was at least connected to my ability to strike a ball with my putter in a specific direction with a specific amount of force, so all in all I'd say Robin's experiment was as good as he could make it. If we'd left the lab setting and moved to a real green with real holes, Robin would have had to deal with variables like spike marks and wind. It would have been even more difficult for him to construct an experiment capable of measuring the vaguer effects of pressure upon the full swing. He later told me that he would love to experiment on tourists coming to play the Old Course for the first time ("That's a perfect pressure situation, that first tee shot," he said) if such a project were at all logistically feasible.

As it is, the individuality of the average golfer greatly handicaps the scientific study of psychical golf phenomena. "To generalize from a group study of 50 people to one individual is very difficult," Robin told me. "And you get big discrepancies between individuals even within that group of 50. That's why teasing it apart is so difficult." Which means we'll probably have a vaccination for cancer before a medical cure for the yips.

You have to start somewhere, though. Robin later confirmed to me that his experiment has, in fact, "determined to a degree that the use of visual or verbal task-relevant stimuli can achieve greater results than task-irrelevant stimuli in building one's concentration structure." Or, in layman's terms, "Swing thoughts work." Before I began my third set of 20 putts, Robin reminded me that I needed to choose an appropriate keyword or phrase. He also told me that it needed to be short enough to work without siphoning my powers of concentration away from the task at hand. I thought about what had and had not been working for me during the experiment and settled upon "Hands forward, accelerate through." I asked Robin if that would do, and he said, "Yeah, that's great. Be sure to say it before you hit each putt. And say it loud enough for me to hear it on the other side of the room."

I positioned my ball, hunched over and said, "Hands for—" My voice cracked. Flushing with embarrassment, I backed away and started again.

"Hands forward, accelerate through." I knocked my putt forward —three points, not bad.

"Hands forward, accelerate through." Bull's-eye, five points.

"Hands forward, accelerate through." Four points. I began to feel self-conscious. I envisioned golfers all over the Old Course muttering to themselves as they stood over their putts, their tee shots, everywhere. My mind wandered to this image . . .

"Hands forward, accelerate through," I said again, but my hands didn't go forward. I weakly tapped my next putt with the heel of my blade, and the ball barely reached the one-point zone. Extended concentration came to me no more easily in the lab than it did on the golf course.

I refocused myself: "Hands forward, accelerate through." Another bull's-eye.

"Hands forward, accelerate through"—four points. As I progressed, the spoken swing thoughts became musical, the pitch rising and crescendoing to "forward" and falling and quieting to the word "through." "Hands forward, accelerate through": a Gregorian chant to quiet my mind on the golf course.

Robin totaled the scores of my third set of 20 putts; he didn't announce my total to me, but he did say I'd done slightly better in my third set than I had when setting my baseline score in the second set. This corroborated his original hypothesis that, in his words, "verbalizing a swing thought, or visually concentrating on the dimple pattern on the ball or the texture of the ground behind the ball, before each shot keeps everything simple and stops you from thinking about other things." (I didn't tell him about my brief mind-wandering.) My stimulus was "task-relevant" because it related to the act of striking a golf ball. Robin had assigned a control group of 10 golfers to use task-irrelevant stimuli such as "Red, green, yellow, blue" before hitting each of their putts, but they failed to perform statistically better as a whole than they did when taking their baseline measurements. "There seems to be a positive element to the task-relevant stimuli," said Robin. "Not only does it keep you from doing something negative, it reinforces the positive."

But would this thesis hold up as I quested for quid? My wallet was distressingly light, so Robin's monetary inducement was enough to create the kind of pressure he was looking for. Just to make sure, though, as he introduced the final set of 20 putts to me, he took a face-down piece of paper from his desk and taped it to the wall at the far side of the room, just above my putting target area. "Here are the scores of five people in your handicap group," Robin said. The handwritten table looked something like this:

First place	82 points	£6
Second place	79 points	£4
Third place	75 points	£3
Fourth place	71 points	£2
Fifth place	70 points or less	£1

"Again, on this final set of putts, you will speak your swing thought out loud before every putt you take," Robin said. "After every five putts, I'll call out your score and let you know how you stand. And at the end of this last group of 20 putts, whatever score you get, I'll give you the amount of money in the right-hand column. Okay on all this?"

"What if I score, say, 81 points?" I asked. "Is that worth four pounds or six?"

"Four pounds," Robin answered. "You have to do at least as well as each score to earn the money."

"Fine. Let's go." I admit I was rather nervous.

"Hands forward, accelerate through"—I stroked my first money putt. Three points.

"Hands forward, accelerate through." Bull's-eye, five points.

"Hands forward, accelerate through." The ball shot off the sweet spot of my putter-face and steamed through to the back wall. No points. I never knew my Bullseye *had* a sweet spot—I always used its dead spots the way Larry Bird used the parquet floor of the old Boston Garden. I gritted my teeth.

"Hands forward, accelerate through." Four points.

"Hands forward, accelerate through." Three points.

Robin called out my score: "That's 15 points so far." I mentally multiplied that by four. C'mon, Darren, I told myself—you can do better than that.

"Hands forward, accelerate through." Bull's-eye, five points. And so it continued. At the halfway stage my total had risen to 34.

"Hands forward, accelerate through"—I wanted to kick myself for lumbering myself with a such a stupid swing thought. My back began to ache. Crouching over 80 times in succession will do that to you. I knocked a poor putt that drifted into the two-point zone. Dammit, Darren, think!

"That's 15 putts done," said Robin, "and your score is 52. Nearly finished." His voice had a soothing quality that reminded me of a sadistic dentist I once had.

"Hands forward, accelerate through." I stroked a nice putt into the bull's-eye. Five more points.

"Hands forward, accelerate through." Four points. I had to admit, the swing thought seemed to be working. I couldn't keep a running total of my score in my head.

"Hands forward, accelerate through." Three points. Focus, Darren!

"Hands forward, accelerate through." Five points, bull's-eye! One more to go.

"Hands forward, accelerate through." Three points.

"There, that's it," said Robin. "Your final total is 72 points. Congratulations—that's worth two pounds."

I arched my back and sighed. "I know I could have done better," I said, "but I guess beggars can't be choosers."

Robin grinned and let me in on a secret: he had printed up a variety of different scoring sheets with which to scare his subjects. "There was an element of implicit manipulation in that I said you were putting against five of your peers in the same handicap bracket," he said. "In fact, those scores I just made up completely. No matter how well you did in your baseline score, you'd always be between third and fourth place on the sheet I selected for you." I looked at the sheet again and deduced I must have scored between 72 and 74 points in the baseline round. Robin continued: "If you match your baseline score in a pressure situation, you're supposed to earn two pounds. The key thing is seeing whether people in the control group do worse—the ones not using a swing key—and at the moment it seems that they do. So the manipulation has been working in that respect."

Indeed, as I signed my name and logged the amount of money I'd won into Robin's records, I noticed that a large proportion of those who had gone before me had only earned £1. It finally dawned on me: I hadn't choked! Victory was mine! The guys at Harvard wouldn't have believed it.

FROM THE PSYCHOLOGY department, Robin and I retired to a flowery tearoom on South Street called The Ark. I asked Robin where the prize money came from: "The Royal & Ancient Golf Club" was his unexpected response. "As a postgraduate I get an annual studentship grant," he explained, "but for this experiment I outlined a proposal to David Hill, the Championship Secretary of the R&A, and he and the club agreed to give me a research grant of a thousand pounds." I'll be darned, I thought. I knew the R&A plowed much of its money back into the game it governs, but nevertheless it was nice to have firsthand proof.

Promising though his start had been, Robin knew that he had many more steps to take between his current experiment and any serious conclusions. His immediate goal was to procure a postdoctorate position that would allow him the chance to work directly with specific athletes and teams. I wished him luck, and I meant it— he seemed a very nice guy. He'd run a smooth and efficient experiment that told me something about my golfing self that I hadn't known, and I got paid for the pleasure of participating. He was still a long way from having a career, but with all the money being laundered in today's sports world, I suspected his efforts wouldn't be in vain.

As for me, I skipped Melville dinner that night and took the £2 I'd won from Robin down to JT's Baked Potato Shop, where I bought myself a bacon-egg-and-cheese sandwich on a roll with ketchup. As I bit into it, some of the egg yolk and ketchup dripped out of the roll and ran down my right thumb to my wrist. Mmmmm, I thought, and closed my eyes. Why couldn't Melville food do that?

Chapter 17

BLIND LEADING THE BLIND

❖❖❖

THE DAY AFTER my psychology lesson, my approach at the first hole of the Old Course finished 30 feet from the hole. As I settled over my birdie putt, I instinctively muttered, "Hands forward, accelerate through." I stroked the putt sweetly. The ball hugged the Velcro-like surface of the mottled fescue and ground to a halt six feet short of the hole. I never should have attempted to adapt techniques used on the speedy laboratory carpet to the slow Old Course grass; "Hands forward, accelerate through" is no longer part of my golfing vocabulary.

I *should* have sought other audible swing thoughts: for my full shots, for my pitches, for my sand explosions, for my putts. Robin had demonstrated the science of swing keys to me, and it seemed inherently sound. Perhaps I didn't think my swing and putting stroke were consistent enough at the best of times for ritual swing thoughts to help. But that's an easy excuse; more likely, I was lazy. I'd used

unspoken swing thoughts before, and many of them had worked—
for a round or two. After that, I lost interest in them. I blew subtle
swing keys out of proportion, and their usefulness waned: I remember once wanting to keep my weight forward, toward the balls
of my feet at address, and within a few rounds I was nearly trying
to balance on my toenails. I forgot about swing keys that worked: I
started looking for the mythical "next thing" to correct in my swing
and ignored the lessons of the previous thing. Most maddeningly,
my mind repeatedly wandered from trifling matters like weight dis-
tribution and wrist pronation to questions like "What's on the
Melville dinner menu?" or "What am I going to write that essay
about tonight?" or "What does Heather think about my being on the
golf course all the time?" Fair and weighty questions all, but when
standing to the right of the 13th fairway on the Old Course and trying to cut a 4-iron around a fortress of gorse and land it on a narrow finger of green, clarity of thought was an absolute necessity.

Ill discipline blighted my entire golfing existence in Scotland. I
teetered warily between fascination and obsession with score: at
best, score inspired me and propelled me to play golf as well as I
could; at worst, it drove me into petulance and despair. I enjoyed
golf most, however, when I escaped from score's enslavement altogether. When I thought about how I broke par on the Old Course,
I became selfishly prideful: *I* escaped Shell Bunker, *I* birdied the
12th, *I* shot 71. When I thought about my rounds at Gullane,
Cruden Bay (pre-ace), Brora, Reay, Dornoch Three and the last 13
holes at Machrie, I remembered how the courses and the way I experienced them affected me. These latter epiphanies cleansed me in
a way that the former could not. After experiencing them, I promised myself to take their lessons to heart—increasingly often with

the proviso "And this time, I mean it." But it never lasted. Again and again, I slipped into score's cycle of seeming enlightenment and eventual corruption.

In May I discovered the most consistent golfing form of my time in St. Andrews. In succession I shot 78 on the Old; 78 on the Jubilee, my nemesis; 77 on the New; 76 on the Old; and 73 on the Old. All very good numbers, for me. And yet in the fourth of these rounds I stood in the middle of the 15th fairway on the Old at two over par, blocked a dismal 5-iron to the right of the green, flung my club into the ground . . . and watched the shaft snap. The club repair service at Auchterlonies again beckoned. I recoiled in horror, just as I had at Dornoch, only this time Scott Campbell and two of my Shanty Town teammates were there to see me. I had committed high treason: in front of three good friends, I'd broken a club on the hallowed ground of the Old Course. It felt like a mortal golfing sin.

TOWARD THE END of the autumn I'd begun sporadically to attend meetings of the St. Andrews Christian Union. Heather was the CU's vice president, which speaks volumes about why I went in the first place, but over time I came to enjoy the CU's informal gatherings rather more than I could have anticipated. Then, at one meeting, I happened to confess that I had come to St. Andrews primarily for the golf and not the university. Unbeknownst to me, at the end of that very service, the CU president had a prepared announcement to make. "A call has been made to the CU," she said, "asking if anyone would be willing to guide a blind golfer around one of the courses in St. Andrews. Any volunteers?" She craned her neck and found where I was sitting. People started laughing—all eyes turned to me. I enthusiastically volunteered my services, not that I had much of a choice.

I was given the phone number of a minister at one of the Protestant churches in town, and he patched me through to the golfer, whose name was Pasi. Pasi and I talked on the phone about what he wanted to accomplish: he wanted to play golf on a real golf course—i.e., anywhere but the rudimentary nine holes of the Balgove Course and the flat and undistinguished 18 holes of the Strathtyrum Course, both beginners' courses he had played a few times before. And he craved nothing more than to play a round of golf in St. Andrews with an accomplished golfer. "Failing that, I hope I'm a fair substitute," I told him. I booked a tee time around 11:00 on a quiet weekday morning on the Eden Course and arranged to meet him near the first tee shortly before.

The quickest route to the Eden Course by foot from most parts of town follows the crushed seashell path that bisects the Road Hole and the Old Course Hotel. Many novice golfers, unlearned in the ways of etiquette, walk along this path on their way to the Balgove and Strathtyrum courses or the covered practice range area next to them, unaware that wayward Road Hole drives might crash down upon them at any moment. So I wasn't altogether surprised when I rounded the corner of the old railway sheds and saw a group of golfers waiting on the Road Hole tee to hit their drives while a young man stood still on the path, halfway between the tee and the corner of the sheds, right in the line of fire. He was bushy-haired and mustachioed, he wore a navy blue windbreaker, and he held his golf bag behind him on a trolley. I eased around him silently and made haste to avoid everyone.

As I neared the tee, I heard the waiting golfers grumble in American accents. One of them muttered, "What is that guy doing there?" Another whimsically asked, "How good does he think we are?" A third impatiently shouted, "Get the hell out of the way!" I said a cheery "Hello" as I walked past, and I inwardly sympathized with them. Why *was* he just standing there?

I made it to the crusty Eden practice green with no further incident, but Pasi hadn't showed up yet. I didn't know what he looked like—how would I know when he got there? Then it hit me like a thunderbolt: a *blind* man wouldn't have known when to walk and where to stop back by the railway sheds. I felt like a total idiot and was relieved when Pasi arrived shortly after I did.

"I'm so sorry," I said. "I passed by you back there . . . "

"Yes, I knew I sensed something," he said in a clotted, halting accent. "But it's not a problem. I'm glad you're here."

I stopped and thought for a moment. Something didn't quite compute. "You walked from the center of town all the way out here on your own?"

"Yes, I did." Pasi beamed.

That's a pretty hairy mile to walk blindly, I thought to myself. I resolved not to think of him as handicapped—for it didn't seem as though he was.

While we waited for our tee time, Pasi and I hit a few practice putts. I asked him about his name, and he said he was Finnish, from a town just outside Helsinki. He then explained that he had been visually impaired since birth, but he wasn't totally sightless: he could make out light and dark areas immediately in front of him. His father had a connection to the Finnish national ice hockey team, and as Pasi grew up he discovered that he could identify the contrast between a black puck and a white ice-surface quite well. The same concept applied to putting, in principle: from less than 10 feet, a black hole stands out fairly well against a drab putting surface, and from short distances Pasi seemed quite effective at knocking the ball toward the hole without my help.

Full shots were different. I led Pasi between the tee markers on the first hole. He teed up his ball by himself and remained crouched over to feel the correct relationship between club and ball: one hand held the shaft in place, the other groped for the ball and then twisted the clubface around to meet it. He kept the clubhead and the ball together as he straightened back into an upright position, but his navigational system failed him. He now aimed well to the left of the fairway. I told him this, and he twisted around so his clubhead more or less faced the line of play, but now only the toe end of his driver adjoined the ball at address. I corrected that, and Pasi was now ready to swing away. Almost.

"What does the hole look like?" he asked.

"It's a short par 4, tight, with a rolling fairway and lined with gorse on either side." I wondered how much of that he really needed to know. Maybe I should have told him the fairway was 150 yards wide.

Pasi arched his back, pulled his club back like a hockey player going for a super-slapshot and swung into the ball with the inelegance, if not the running start, of Happy Gilmore. He struck a glancing blow to the ball, and it toppled forward barely an inch.

I cringed. "Don't move," I said. I rushed up to the ball and replaced it on the tee. Pasi smiled, but then a whispered laugh betrayed his nervousness. I hoped it was only first-tee jitters.

He swung again. This time he contacted the ball cleanly, and it soared 180 yards down the middle of the fairway. I didn't think I could give him many lessons, but as long as he could repeat that swing, there wouldn't be much to say. I teed up my own ball,

skanked a 3-iron up the right side of the fairway and walked—
happily enough—alongside my irrepressibly chipper companion. I
noticed a father-son twosome move into position on the first tee,
and I harbored hopes of keeping them at bay.

I rushed ahead to my tee shot, hit a weak 8-iron onto the edge
of the green and marched over to guide Pasi to his ball.

"What does the approach look like?" he again asked.

"You're about 140 yards away from the hole," I said. He reached
for his bag and felt his way from club to club until he found his 7-
iron. I continued: "The pin is in the middle of the green; there's a
large ridge at the front of the green, and the green sort of, um,
curves from left to right, with bunkers front left and front right.
There's a stone wall behind the green, and a big hut behind that, but
none of that should come into play." I liked the first hole on the
Eden Course a lot, and I hoped I'd done it justice.

Pasi bent over, felt around on the ground and pushed his ball
slightly sideways as he grasped for it. I didn't make him replace the
ball. I looked nervously back to the tee, where the father and son
made loud and demonstrative *whooshes* with their practice swings.
Pasi stood up, I rotated him slightly to the right and he swung—
chunking the shot, taking a huge divot and knocking his ball only 50
yards forward.

I wiped my brow. "You go on ahead," I said. "I'll clean up here
and catch up."

Pasi started walking. I replaced his divot for him and rushed
ahead to meet him. At least I didn't have to describe the green again
to him for the next shot.

Pasi chunked that one as well, but his next shot found the green
and he mopped up well once he got near the hole, as promised. I

figured him for a triple-bogey seven, even counting the preliminary whiff. Not too bad, I thought. Objectively, I was very impressed, but still Pasi made me squirm. Flustered, I nearly fluffed *my* first putt and settled for a bogey. I again nervously looked behind me at the father and son now in the fairway. When had I felt like this before?

To the second hole: "A long par 4. Just hit your driver straight," I urged. I meant that to sound like advice, but I think it came out like a command. Pasi hit his drive and his second, third and fourth shots before I reached my tee shot. I eventually marked him down for a 10. At the third, Pasi squirted his first two drives into the gorse in front of the tee and, once in the fairway, dug two deep divots that revealed a rich blackness to the St. Andrews soil I'd never seen before. At the green, I waved the father and son to play through; in retrospect, I'm surprised we'd made it that far without interruption. I ushered Pasi to the side of the green. A foursome replaced the father and son on the horizon, and I donned an extra sweater, as an already gray and dismal May day turned colder.

"Are you warm enough?" I asked Pasi.

He smiled. "I *am* from Finland, remember?" Touché.

The Eden's fourth hole curved from left to right along the Eden Estuary. Pasi drove nicely, but his second shot strayed to the right of the green. The green was elevated well above fairway level, and between the green and the water was a gaping chasm unlike any landscape feature on the Old or New courses, a sort of eight-foot-deep bowl with its highest rim by the side of the green. That's how I'd describe it now, but at the time, when Pasi's shot drifted into it, words failed me. I didn't know what to tell him. His ball sat on very fluffy tufts of grass, and his body battled a 45-degree incline; his mind must have struggled to picture the terrain. No wonder he cut un-

derneath the ball entirely several times, then feebly battered it forward and upward twice. When at last he made solid contact, his ball
pitched onto the far side of the green, trickled over its edge and ran
down another steep slope. I barely suppressed a cry of anguish. I'd
already let the foursome behind us play through, and now a threesome appeared in its place. I hastily calculated that at our present
rate of progress, we'd probably finish the front nine sometime in mid
to late July. At least it might be warm by then, I thought, zipping up
another jacket.

Of course, Pasi then turned around and hit a 7-iron to 20 feet on
the next hole, the par-3 fifth. His par trumped my bogey, but by
then I'd already pretty much surrendered my score to the whims of
fortune. When you're trying to be equal parts forecaddie, swing doctor, navigator, geographer and support group, how much time can
you spend on your duties as a playing partner? I like playing fast, but
zigzagging back and forth across the fairway between two balls—
having to look for both of them by myself when things went awry
—forced me to abandon the game of golf I knew and loved for
something slower and colder. I started to freeze, and we let more
groups play through. I weakly prayed for more patience, but I ran
out by the end of the seventh hole. Once or twice I dipped into the
thin reserves of subtlety I still possessed and suggested to Pasi that
he might-perhaps-possibly-if-he-felt-like-it want to pick up his ball
and move on to the next hole. I was trying my hardest, but after
nearly three hours I hadn't made a par and had begun talking quietly
to myself about good intentions and the road to hell.

Strangely, throughout all of this, Pasi seemed absolutely thrilled.
He gushed over and over again about how wonderful it was to be
playing a real golf course, with a quality golfer alongside him. No

matter how poor his shots were, no matter how much earth he moved, he kept at his task with modesty and intensity. His smile radiated an amazing sense of discovery, like a child's on Christmas morning, and this alone kept me going when he suggested after nine holes that we continue on for a full 18. The nearby Eden changing room offered a handy escape route, and in other circumstances I might have tried to mash Pasi with a niblick and make a speedy getaway. But how could I deny anyone such unbridled joy?

I'm sure I had seen and felt God's presence through golf courses before, but never had I felt so spiritually touched by another human being on a golf course. Rarely if ever had someone else's positive behavior helped me to stop worrying about score, but Pasi did just that. The dropping temperature drove everyone behind us off the course at the turn, and we played on, unhurried for the first time all day. My straitjacket now off, I made four pars in a row. Pasi kept swinging and smiling until we reached the end of the 12th hole, and then even he was ready to turn around. I suggested we cut across to the penultimate tee and play 17 and 18 to get back to the clubhouse. He agreed.

At the par-4 18th, Pasi drove straight down the fairway. "You've got 150 yards to the green," I told him. "It's a tricky dogleg shot over a corner of the gorse to a small green and a narrow landing area—*but don't worry about any of that!*" Pasi chuckled. He felt for his 5-iron, bent over, felt for the ball and stood up again. I turned him only slightly to his left. He whirled away from the ball and crunched into it: the ball flew high and far and well, and it landed just short of the green. Only an unlucky bounce to the left denied him a birdie putt. "Golf shot," I said. "Man, if only you could see that one!"

Pasi made bogey, but that seemed incidental to the afternoon. We finished, shook hands and walked back to town together. Ever since we parted, I've wondered more and more about my preferred policy of playing golf by myself. The eighth hole during my Dornoch One round was magical, and definitely heaven-sent, but only when I manage to capture the love I felt there and share it with other people does that kind of experience actually get me anywhere. My day with Pasi helped me do that, for it reminded me that the game of golf doesn't actually revolve around me. As I walked back to Melville that day, I knew I'd probably soon forget the lessons Pasi taught me. But I haven't forgotten about Pasi, and maybe that's enough.

Chapter 18

LITTLE SHOP OF HORRORS

❖·❖·❖

THE STUDENT UNION mainstage hosted a university production of *Hamlet* less than a week after my round with Pasi, and Heather had landed the plum role of Ophelia. During the winter I'd seen her cameo as a singing nun in a production of *Cyrano de Bergerac,* which, like *Romeo and Juliet* at the Byre Theatre, was performed in full Glaswegian dialect. (I waited in vain for someone in St. Andrews to rewrite *Trainspotting* into Shakespearean English.) Ophelia, however, was the best role of Heather's stage career—and she acquitted herself frighteningly well. I saw Hamlet fling her around the stage like a stuffed animal in Act III, and I feared for her safety. At the start of her "mad" scene in Act IV, she appeared with badly mussed hair and torn tights, and I feared for her sanity. By the end of the scene, I asked myself, "I'm in love with *that?*" I wondered how actors and actresses carry on relationships at all. If Heather could play make-believe that convincingly, what kept her from successful duplicity in real life? I was proud of her and dumb-struck in equal measure.

I hung out with Heather a lot in May, and I wondered what our future might hold. Other than the cost of airfare and telephone calls come July, I couldn't see any reason for us to break up—assuming that "special friends" could technically "break up." Could a *very* long-distance relationship work? Would we even try to have one? I pondered these questions at length, largely because I stayed indoors a lot in May. I wish I could now describe the glories of springtime in St. Andrews, but I can't say I ever saw any. If anything, April and May were colder than February and March. Although I was pleased when the artificial mats were withdrawn from circulation on the Old Course at the start of April, I didn't see why they should have been; Old Course grass didn't start growing just because the Links Trust's timetable said it should. When I did play, the Old Course held most of my attention. I cherry-picked tee times on the rare good days, but otherwise I mostly watched British television, commuted to the other end of town to see my little red-haired girl and philosophized about how I might survive without either.

CHEEKILY, GIVEN MY initial thesis plans, I stalled until a blustery day in early May before I made my first visit to the British Golf Museum. Serious students of the game won't necessarily learn much at the museum, but I enjoyed the hour I spent there. The interactive television displays on the history of the Open Championship were worth the price of admission alone—some highlights you can never watch too many times. And I did discover one very interesting tidbit: not long after the Scots invented golf, they invented golf betting. The history traces back to a match James IV of

Scotland played against the Earl of Bothwell on a wintry day in February 1504. Nobody knows for certain whether they played a straight-up Nassau or a skins game, but royal financial records show that the match cost James 42 shillings—a bit much, given that a contemporary set of clubs and balls would have cost nine shillings, and that green fees on the Old Course weren't collected for another 409 years. (I also laughed when I discovered that the match technically broke the law; James himself had extended the existing ban on playing golf in 1491. Was this, I wondered, golf's first recorded rules breach?)

James was a man after my own heart. I'm normally what the British would call a "mug punter," a man who never met a press he didn't like. My penchant for backing myself into a corner against stiff opposition put several of my Harvard teammates through college, but in Britain I found on-course wagering to be surprisingly rare. One does not propose first-tee stakes in Scotland as a matter of course to "keep things interesting" among one's mates, nor does the absence of financial incentive prevent informal match play from becoming quite spirited. I could join three total strangers on the Old Course, introduce myself and ask them their handicaps, and within seconds teams would be chosen and rudimentary four-ball tactics discussed. On the rare occasions when I was paired with a lone Scotsman of similar ability, we played tenaciously competitive contests at straight match play, as happened on that memorable day in November when I shot 71 and beat David 1-up. I played several three-way Nassaus against friends from Melville, with £1 each at stake for the winner of the front nine, the back nine and the match as a whole. But those matches were few and far between.

I liked to pretend that such betting abstinence showcased

Scotland's inherent code of honor and chivalry. In fact, Scottish on-course virtue probably has a lot to do with the ready availability of off-course vice. Gambling is as legal in Britain as it is in Las Vegas. William Hill and Ladbrokes, Britain's two most prominent book-making houses, were only a toll-free call away, and in most British towns betting shops were nearly as common as pharmacies. And you can bet on *anything* in Britain: horse races, Premiership soccer, the NBA Finals, the Eurovision song contest, the Miss World pageant, the identity of the number one song in the U.K. pop charts on Christmas Day, if it will snow on Christmas Day, if it will rain during the Wimbledon fortnight. You can also bet on the results of professional golf.

Fortunately, the St. Andrews branch of Ladbrokes was situated well to the south of both Melville and the town center, so the temptation to fritter away my meager savings on golf and soccer betting remained distant. I made a few simple "punts" on the Masters—the best of which, a 16/1 pick on Phil Mickelson to win, nearly came off. (He finished third, behind Faldo and Norman.) Apart from that, I stayed away. Nevertheless, in mid-May, in the name of thorough journalism, I put my qualms aside for the duration of the Benson & Hedges Invitational, a European Tour event held at The Oxfordshire Golf Club in Thame, England. All four days of the event were live on BBC television, so I could personally judge the form of the field and instantly see how much money I was losing.

On the Tuesday before the tournament began, I meandered down Bridge Street toward a part of St. Andrews that few visitors ever see. St. Andrews has long streets with rows of semi-detached stucco houses and driveways and gardens with children's bicycles in them, and it has small parks with uneven grass and swing sets and rubbish strewn randomly about. It looks like a normal Scottish town, and Ladbrokes caters to the people who live there.

I entered Ladbrokes in mid-afternoon, and the horse racing crowd—six or seven mostly gray-haired gentlemen with large paunches and distant expressions in their eyes—had gathered to watch and place wagers on the races from Newbury, or Epsom, or Ayr, or wherever it was. Large TV sets mounted on each side of the small, rectangular room showed racing action and up-to-the-minute odds listings in continuous loops. Cigarette smoke penetrated every corner of the room—it stifled my lungs, raised the room temperature by at least 10 degrees Fahrenheit and made the television screens somewhat difficult to see. (Fair enough—I *was* betting on a golf tournament sponsored by a tobacco company.) From carpeted floor to tiled ceiling, hundreds of newspaper clippings climbed the walls like kudzu vines, each offering tips, odds and lineups, most about the races but some pertaining to soccer and more esoteric gambling subjects like cricket, rugby and American sports. Many of the clippings listed odds from betting houses other than Ladbrokes, but to actually place a bet one had to consult one of two special television monitors above the cashier's desk, each of which could be programmed to display in-house odds on any event for which Ladbrokes ran a book.

Naïvely, I tiptoed up to the female cashier and asked about the golf. "What would you like to know?" she asked sweetly.

I panicked. "I'm from an American golf magazine," I said. "I'm doing a story about different ways of gambling on golf." This was true, sort of, but I think I said it because I felt some unease about renewing acquaintances with an old vice, like I was creeping up to the counter at a 7-Eleven to ask for a packet of condoms or an issue of *Penthouse*.

"Okay," she said, "what tournament do you wish to bet on?"

"The Benson & Hedges."

She punched a three-digit code into her keypad, and the following flashed up on one of the monitors:

Faldo	8/1	Brand Jnr	25/1
Montgomerie	9/1	Nobilo	25/1
Woosnam	14/1	Rocca	25/1
Langer	16/1	Coltart	50/1
Torrance	16/1	Jimenez	50/1
Lane	25/1	James	50/1
Gilford	25/1		

On the names went, until there were about 30 on the screen; below that was a notice, "Others available on request," meaning one could bet on any golfer in the tournament. "Those are the odds on each golfer to win, right?" I asked.

"Yes, that's right," she replied, smiling. She was much friendlier than most bookies I could have imagined. Infinitely prettier, too, with short black hair and fair skin.

In the aftermath of my Mickelson bet, I'd been told by one of my Melville pals that straight bets on golfers to win tournaments weren't likely to win me any money. The best way to bet on golf, he said, was to bet "each way": you wager a set amount on a golfer to win, then match that wager with a bet at a quarter odds on the golfer to finish in the top four in the tournament. Had I gone "each way" with Mickelson at the Masters, I would have lost the 16/1 bet to win outright, but I would have won the 4/1 secondary bet to finish in the top four and come out well ahead. Made sense to me.

"Okay," I told the cashier. "I'd like to place a two-pound 'each way' bet on Ian Woosnam to win the tournament." Woosie was my pick to win that week. "How do I do that?"

She grabbed a small, square betting slip from a pile next to her window and wrote down

Woosie, £2 ew (14/1)

She tore off the top copy of the slip for her records and handed me the pink carbon copy underneath. "That costs four pounds, of course. Two on Woosnam to win, and two on him to finish in the top four," she explained. I think I meant to wager £2 in total—or "£1 each way"—but I was so giddy at understanding this complicated system that I let the more expensive bet stand. I rubbed my hands together—now I needed some jackpot potential. I scanned the board and decided to make the same each-way bet on Mark James that I'd just made for Woosnam: £2 to win at 50/1, plus £2 to finish in the top four at 25/2. I took a betting slip myself this time and, using one of many six-inch blue ballpoint pens scattered all over the shop, wrote down the following:

James, £2 ew (50/1)

Step one was now complete. I asked the cashier, "So, what else can I do?"

She punched up another display for me. "This is what we call 'match-betting,'" she said, explaining that Ladbrokes pitted together pairs of reasonably matched golfers and let the bettor choose which would finish better over the course of 72 holes. I was intrigued. Most of the odds were close to 1/1, or "evens," as it's known in the trade. I could also combine bets as "accumulators," wherein the winnings of one bet carry over to the following bet(s), so I made a few calculations and came up with the following wager:

£5 treble:
  –Monty over Faldo (Evs)
  –Coltart over Jimenez (Evs)
  –Riley over Feherty (5/6)

If and only if all three of these bets came good after 72 holes, I'd net £31.67. (£5 at 1/1 becomes £10; £10 at 1/1 becomes £20; £20 at 5/6 becomes £36.67, from which the original stake is subtracted to determine net winnings.)

"Anything else?" I asked the cashier.

"Well, there's also something called 'group betting,'" she said, "which is basically the same as 'match betting' except you pick from five golfers instead of two." She punched another set of numbers into her keypad, and six lettered groups appeared on the monitor. So many choices . . . I was throwing darts at a board now:

McNulty, £2 to win Group E (7/2)

Group E included Andrew Coltart. Having picked Coltart to win a bet earlier, now I picked him to lose. This was just magnificent: I was going to lose my shirt. For me to win all my bets I needed Mark McNulty to finish better than Coltart, who in turn had to finish better than Miguel Angel Jimenez, and meanwhile both Woosnam and James had to finish in the top four. Total potential winnings if I struck four luckies: £170.67. (Yeah, right.) Total likely losses: £15.

The cashier offered me one final, extra-special bet: "I see here that all 12 European Ryder Cup players from last fall are playing in the event this week," she said, pecking again at her magic keypad. Onto the monitor came the "Ryder Cup Special": a single "group bet," with Faldo at the shortest odds and Per-Ulrik Johansson at the longest. I decided I'd done enough for one day.

Before I could leave, I had to pay a "gambling tax." Betting has been aboveboard in Britain since 1961, but government sanctioning for the bettor came at a price; at the time of my bets, that came to an additional 9 percent levy against all wagers made. I had two options: I could let the government tax my original bet or my winnings. Most of my mates emphasized the intelligence of the former, but I'd done a little bit of algebra and figured out that for any bet at longer odds than 1/1, you actually do better to make a slightly larger bet and tax your winnings. For example, take the following winning bet:

£15 at 10/1 = £150 (winnings) –
£1.35 (9% tax on original bet) = £148.65

What if I added the £1.35 onto the original bet and had the winnings taxed instead?

£16.35 at 10/1 = £163.50 (winnings) –
£14.72 (9% tax on winnings) = £148.78

With both these bets, I've paid £16.35 to the bookies at the outset, but the larger bet wins me a few extra pence.

Actually, though, the bookies aren't stupid. They want you to make the larger bet because they think you're going to lose. The professional gamblers at Ladbrokes can identify value better than amateur punters like me—that's a bet you can make every time. And as I staggered out of Ladbrokes, I realized I should have factored another tax into my personal spending power equation: on top of the £15 I paid to Ladbrokes and the £1.35 levied upon me by the House of Commons, I felt compelled to pay an additional 90p for an ice-cream bar at a newsagent's up the street. The fresh air of the outside world hadn't overcome my betting-shop sweating. I felt unclean, and at that moment the concept of sports betting really seemed to stink.

MY WAGERS DID one very good thing, though: they helped me follow the entire tournament with real interest. Once the proverbial smoke had cleared, I knew I had five heroes to cheer (Woosnam, James, Montgomerie, Riley and McNulty) and six villains to jeer (Faldo, Jimenez, Feherty and three of McNulty's four opponents in Group E). As for Andrew Coltart, on whom I'd place bets both for (in my treble) and against (in Group E), I wanted him to finish about 29th. Don't ask me what that means or what it's supposed to feel like from the fan's-eye view, but on Thursday morning that's what I felt like telling him to do. How else can you root for and against the same guy?

I couldn't justify most of my picks. I went against Faldo and Feherty because, as far as I knew, they had played on the U.S. Tour the previous week and were likely candidates for jet lag. I liked Woosnam because he was on form and seemed to have as much chance of winning as anyone, even though he was only third favorite behind Faldo and Montgomerie. Everything else was just coin-flipping. Stupid? Probably, but by tossing the coin often enough I scripted my own television drama. I watched the BBC coverage of the B&H periodically on Thursday and Friday, and it seemed as though I had a vested interest in the performance of every third golfer appearing on my screen.

Several results soon became clear. My Mark James pick was virtually doomed after nine holes: James shot 79 on Thursday and easily missed the cut. By Friday's end, my treble also seemed destined for the trash heap. Feherty had missed the cut, fading as I'd predicted he might and giving Riley an automatic "win" in their match, and Montgomerie was in second place, three shots ahead of Faldo. But Miguel Angel Jimenez shot a brilliant 68-70 in difficult conditions to lead the tournament outright, and Coltart trailed him by seven shots, having opened with a 77. McNulty had missed the cut, so my group bet was dead in the water. Woosnam lurked four shots behind Jimenez, and I still had hopes for him, but on the whole my situation looked pretty bleak.

So on Saturday morning, in a move that wouldn't have been endorsed by Gamblers Anonymous, I went back to Ladbrokes to see if I could sneak back into the black by winning a couple of quick ones. The tournament odds had changed quite significantly since Tuesday, and now Montgomerie was the 5/2 favorite, with Jimenez the second choice at 7/2 and the steady Bernhard Langer third at 4/1. Faldo, though only five shots back of Jimenez, had slipped to 10/1; he had momentum on his side, I thought, and he'd made a hole-in-one on Thursday, so I focused my attention on him:

> Faldo, £2 ew (10/1)

Ladbrokes also now paired the players in each twosome against one another as match bets covering the Saturday round only. I again opted for a treble, looking for multiple successes to bring a fat payday while covering several of my other bets with insurance:

> £3 treble:
>   –Woosnam over Westner (8/11)
>   –Torrance over Faldo (5/4)
>   –Jimenez over Robson (4/6)

Possible net winnings on this one: £19.43. I really liked the "multiples" concept. Obviously, though, I hadn't done my homework.

Much later, I would read the following from a consultant for an online betting house: "If you stick to singles, some selections are allowed to let you down as long as enough others don't. Bookies love multiples, absolutely love 'em. More lovely profit margin, profit margin cubed." Oops.

Anyway, as long as I was lurking at Ladbrokes, I had the cashier flip over to the odds screen for the American PGA Tour. I didn't even know what tournament was taking place, much less what was going on or who was playing well—the U.S. Tour wasn't exactly popular prime-time viewing in the Melville common room. But as a matter of principle I had to have a nibble:

Couples, £1 ew (8/1)

I found out that Rocco Mediate and Wayne Levi were currently leading the Colonial, but Freddie was in sixth place, only three shots back. I liked his odds, even if Ladbrokes still rated him and Mediate as joint second-favorites behind Corey Pavin (who, at 9/2, was two shots off the lead).

I found it tough to reconcile the genteel and staid image I'd had of British life with the realities of its pervasive betting culture. In post–Jimmy-the-Greek America, mainstream broadcasters have to be very careful about mentioning Las Vegas odds and point spreads, but in Britain even the most conservative BBC announcers blithely talk about odds and oddsmakers. In England, it is also perfectly legal for athletes, coaches and owners to place bets on themselves or their teams. (English soccer's governing body, which has recently imposed its own, relatively trifling gambling regulations, is decidedly in the minority.) Pete Rose obviously lives in the wrong country. Imagine a happy-go-lucky golfer like Ian Woosnam feeling good on the morning of a tournament round, assessing his playing partner's form on the practice range and strolling into the Ladbrokes at the tournament pavilion to say, "A hundred thousand pounds at eleven-to-eight on says I'll beat Wayne Westner into a bloody pulp." I bet the bookie taking that one would soil himself.

MY SATURDAY BETS confused me greatly, and I realized I'd crossed an unfortunate line. What was once rooting interest had become perplexed anxiety. I now had two golfers—Faldo and Jimenez—to root both for and against as I watched. I'd also accumulated a hefty stack of pink betting slips on the desk of my room, and I wasn't entirely sure what each of them said at any given moment. During the back nine on Saturday, Jon Robson hit an iron shot stiff on a par 4. Right, I thought, I've got a bet on him . . . but is it for or against? I dumped the papers on my bed and sorted through them, looking for the one with Robson's name on it. After a lengthy trawl I found it, but by then my screen showed Montgomerie driving on a par 5, and Peter Alliss's verbose description of him rang in my eardrums. Robson? What had he done? Was it good or bad for me? I'd forgotten. The pink slips weren't helping me enjoy the golf on television; they were making my head spin. About all I figured out on Saturday was that two of my three one-day treble guesses were hopelessly inept, my each-way bet on Faldo was fading fast and I was sliding ever deeper into the black abyss of student debt.

On Sunday morning I went straight from church to Ladbrokes. I couldn't have been much more desperate. Once more I placed a trifecta of one-day match bets:

£5 treble:
- –Cooper over Robson (11/10)
- –Riley over Ames (5/6)
- –Woosie over Monty (6/5)

Montgomerie, now quoted at 2/5 ("five-to-two on," as the British say it), had opened up a three-shot lead on Woosnam after three rounds. Although I'd wagered against Monty on the treble (figuring that Woosie might just play well enough to keep things interesting), he had been knocking down flagsticks all week and I didn't think he could possibly lose the tournament from such a commanding position. If Woosnam somehow caught and passed Montgomerie, I'd win my initial bet and just about come out ahead for the week. But I figured a bet on Monty to win was still worth my money, and just to keep myself in suspense, I twinned it with something altogether different:

> £3 double:
> –Monty to win the B&H (2/5)
> –Romania to win Group B (4/1)

This final wager brought my total risk for the week to £33.79, including taxes. The latter half of it was a soccer bet; I'd seen Hagi, Raducioiu and company defeat Argentina in World Cup '94, and I liked their chances to spring a mild upset in their first-stage group of the forthcoming European Championships, even against teams as strong as France, Spain and Bulgaria. More to the point, I couldn't resist the sheer silliness of taking a Scottish golfer and an Eastern European soccer team and making a single bet out of them.

I knew I couldn't win this bet before the middle of June, but I could lose it that Sunday afternoon. And as I watched the final round on television, the latter possibility became less and less remote. The weather at The Oxfordshire was appalling; winds gusted up to 40 miles an hour, and the cold made most of the golfers don winter hats and heavy sweaters from the outset. This would have been bad enough at St. Andrews, but on a target-type golf course with ample sand and water hazards in every direction, betting became even more of a lottery; anything could happen. Montgomerie led handily until he reached the turn, and then he collapsed with an embarrassingly inartistic string of double bogeys. He even left a sand shot in a bunker on the 13th, kicking at the sand beneath his feet in frustration as he did so. Woosnam, his playing partner, sheepishly smiled his way to an 82. Faldo, going out earlier, staggered to an 80. The less experienced players I had bet against — Robson, Derrick Cooper, Stephen Ames — retained their composure and kept grinding out pars. For the second day in a row, I missed out on two-thirds of my treble bet. My mental bookie board was a shambles, and with four holes remaining in the tournament I thought I might come away with absolutely nothing.

And then, frustrated and resigned to my fate, I saw Andrew Coltart on television and I remembered something. I rummaged through my wrinkled betting slips, tossing them frantically aside until I found the original treble I'd made on Tuesday. I reevaluated its three components: Riley made the cut and Feherty didn't, so that was a win. For all of Monty's problems, he still led the equally horrid Faldo by four shots with four to play, so that looked like a win. And Jimenez, the Friday night leader, shot 74 on Saturday and went out in 40 on Sunday, fading fast. My Scottish hero from the Alfred Dunhill Cup, Coltart, had done 68 and, astonishingly, 36. With only three holes to play, he now led Jimenez by five shots, and that looked like a win as well. Incredible. Not only was I going to win a bet, but it would be big enough to put me ahead for the week!

I breathed a huge sigh of relief. One moment of brilliance, or blind luck, was going to more than compensate for my otherwise consistent ineptitude. With two holes to go, Monty still led Faldo by four; at this point I left my room and the television to play in goal for Shanty Town FC again. Had the match been scheduled for early afternoon, I almost certainly would have played worse; as it was, I kept a clean sheet (i.e., didn't concede any goals), so I was in a doubly buoyant mood as I returned to my room. I switched the television on to check the final scores and presumably rubber-stamp my victory.

What I saw boggled my mind. Coltart, one shot behind the *real* leader with three holes to go, double-bogeyed 16 and bogeyed 17. In the end, he lost the tournament by four—and only just hung on to beat Jimenez by one. Montgomerie's story was even more amazing: European Tour officials retroactively slapped a two-shot penalty on him for "testing the sand" when he kicked it on 13, because his ball was still within the confines of the bunker. Montgomerie, as if he wasn't already in an ugly mood, then bogeyed 18 to shoot a final-round 84. (I can't imagine that any European Tour third-round leader has ever done worse.) But because Faldo himself shot 80, Monty hung on to pip him by a shot—and keep my bank balance intact. All the same, I broke out in a cold sweat.

The moral of the story is: when you bet on long shots, pick lots of them, because one of them might . . . no, wait, what am I saying? The moral of the story is: golf is a crazy game, and even when you think you've got the knowledge to beat the book, sometimes even the fairest pair of dice can come up snake eyes. Why do professional golfers suddenly get hot for a week (or weeks) at a time? Nobody knows. I wouldn't recommend golf betting to anyone looking to make money. After all, Stephen Ames—who hails from the Caribbean island nation of Trinidad and Tobago, making him the one person in the field I'd expected to be most unsettled by horrendous weather—posted a final-round 72 and won the B&H Invitational by a shot. I could have had him at 16/1 odds to win on *Sunday morning* . . . but I would have been a lunatic to pick him.

As it was, I finished with a small, undeserved profit of £2.88— about $4.50, give or take. I thanked my lucky stars and decided to quit while I was ahead.

Chapter 19

THE FOREIGN INVASION

⋅⊱⋅ ⋅⊱⋅ ⋅⊱⋅

TOWARD THE END of May, St. Andrews reluctantly gave springtime a miss and yielded directly to summer. During our extended winter, Heather had often fantasized aloud about migrating to San Diego, which to her had somehow come to represent a cure for everything she hated about Scottish weather. She seemed to think that 365 days of climate-controlled perfection would make her a better person. For me, the idea of living in San Diego has always had all the appeal of being shot with a tranquilizer dart. All else being equal, when it comes to golf I prefer cloudy weather to sunshine anyway. I detest squinting into the sun to track my ball in flight, reading greens and putting through multilayered shadows, and vainly attempting to wipe the greasy residue of sunblock from my hands before arriving at the first tee.

But I dislike San Diego more for its seasonlessness. The struggle against winter's oppression and spring's ambivalence makes summer what it is. I played many wintertime rounds of golf in St. Andrews because I could, not because I necessarily wanted to. Golfers in Boston hibernate in winter and slog across underripe ground too early in the spring. In St. Andrews they play on through wind and rain all year, but they anticipate the coming of something better no less urgently. When the parole of high spring and summer finally arrives, golf feels like golf again—and the game is blessed with vividness that I don't think longtime Californians or Floridians can properly appreciate. I like the mystical, moody St. Andrews of winter, trapped and turned against itself by cloud, wind and misty rain. Most people don't, but come summer, when the Old Course is bathed in gold and green and purrs with newfound life, only complete curmudgeons could insist that their wait wasn't worth it.

Outsiders flock to this spectacle like moths to a flame. The trickle of tourists coming to St. Andrews in March and April becomes a stream in May and a torrent by June. Luckily for the townspeople, the student population of St. Andrews disperses at the close of May; the town isn't big enough to hold natives, students and tourists all at once. Physically, the town could probably cope, as over 200 different establishments in St. Andrews offer guests at least a bed to sleep in—a pretty impressive total for a town of 16,000 people. But St. Andrews becomes a different place altogether once the student influence wanes and tourists flood the streets and pubs and shops. St. Andreans cope admirably with the changing demographics, but the town would probably implode if overrun by both groups of outsiders at once. I imagine the period between Christmas and New Year's must be wonderful for the locals—no students, no tourists, just peace and cultural unity.

I suffered an identity crisis in May. I wanted to be a native, knew

I was a student and abhorred the thought that I might also be a tourist. Throughout the year I'd studied the Scots and Scotland, and I'd worked hard to overcome my ignorance. By the end of the academic year, I'd been dating a Scot for seven months. I knew the difference between Glaswegian and Yorkshire accents, and could produce identifiable imitations of each. I knew to wear dark socks with brown or black loafers. I knew that the haddock at Joe's fish-and-chip shop was battered to a perfect state of unhealthiness, and that Joe's chips came with ample ketchup on request. I knew why Newcastle United and Heart of Midlothian FC didn't have what it took to win any trophies. I had a competitor's badge to the Scottish Brass Band Championships. And of course I still had my £90 Links Trust season pass and a spot of bump-and-run touch to go with it. But I was still an American, and therefore by definition given to thinking that I knew everything even though I hardly knew anything. Strain though I might, I knew I'd never be more than an honorary Scot at best.

Even the great and good can fit the "ugly American" stereotype. Sam Snead came to St. Andrews in 1946 as one of the few Americans vying for the first postwar Open Championship. During his train ride into town, he noticed to his left "some acreage that was so raggedy and beat-up that I was surprised to see what looked like a fairway amongst the weeds. Down home we wouldn't plant cow beets on land like that." He turned to someone (a royal duke, unbeknownst to Snead) across the aisle and asked, "Say, that looks like an old, abandoned golf course. What did they call it?" Naturally, it was the Old Course. "Until you play it, [the Old Course] looks like the sort of real estate you couldn't give away," Snead said. And although he won the resultant Open by four shots and came to appreciate St. Andrews in golfing terms, Snead never returned to defend his title. "As far as I'm concerned," he later said, "anytime you leave the U.S.A., you're just camping out."

Unfortunately, in my quest to disassociate myself from my more obnoxious countrymen, I became something worse: a cultural snob. I came to believe that most Americans were beneath me, and that Scottish simplicity was in all aspects superior to American brashness. I cringed when a Links Trust starter paired me with Americans. The wrong accent at the wrong time inspired outward selfishness and inward rage.

The day after the Benson & Hedges Invitational, I went to Ladbrokes to collect my winnings, returned to Melville to collect my clubs and walked calmly to the Old Course practice green. In addition to my Coltart-Riley-Montgomerie treble and my Shanty Town soccer match, on Sunday I'd also won a tee time in the Old Course ballot for Monday afternoon, and I felt I needed to get to the putting green 45 minutes early. I was running out of chances on the Old Course, and I had yet to birdie either of the first two holes—largely because I could never judge the speed of their greens.

I had just begun to knock a few balls around the practice green when a loud Missouri drawl boomed into my ears:

"Excuse me—uh, is this the Old Course?"

I turned around. The gentleman had addressed his question to me. He was wearing a yellowish half-zippered windbreaker, a white shirt with razor-sharp lapels, gray slacks, and a white baseball cap from which gray strands of hair extruded in asymmetrical tufts.

"Yes, it is," I said. I started to swivel around again.

"Say, do you know where that hole is where you have to hit over the corner of a building?"

I was dressed as I always was, for where I was and what I was doing: soft collar, sweater, khakis, spikes. These garments apparently conferred upon me some aura of authority.

"Yes, you're talking about the Road Hole," I said impatiently. I waved a finger in the direction of the Old Course Hotel. "It's over there."

"Saw that on television, I did," he said. I turned around, putter still in hand, and crouched over to resume my practice routine, but he wasn't finished

"What are they . . . " he asked aloud before his voice trailed off. Out of the corner of my eye I saw him point in momentary bewilderment at the two foursomes traveling in opposite directions, two white guardrails away. A flash of divine intuition must have come upon him, for he then explained the scene to himself: "Oh, I see. That's the 18th and the first fairway together. Oh, okay."

I could see the cogs slowly turning in his head.

"So . . . are you a caddie?"

I stared blankly at him for a second, shook my head slightly and loaded as much ironic disapproval as I could into an abrupt "No." I returned to my putting, and he drifted away toward Swilcan Burn. Good thing, too, because my thoughts at that moment weren't a model of charity: I'm a golfer, you moron! What is this putter doing in my hand, this glove peeking out of my pocket? Does my voice sound like it could belong to a Scotsman? Do you think I could get a work permit to caddie otherwise? The tourist information office is on Market Street. Could you please go bother everyone there and leave this paid-up Links Trust season-ticket holder alone until you've done a little more homework?

I wanted to loose lightning bolts from my fingers and condemn the gentleman to an eternity of Myrtle Beach. I felt bad about the whole episode later, especially as I bogeyed the first two holes anyway. As much as I'd matured in St. Andrews, I could still be a real schmuck sometimes. But more than that, I wondered, how *do* the Scots put up with us?

SOMETIMES THEY DON'T. One of the Old Course starters told me about a prank he'd played on an American who had taken an excessive number of tentative practice swings with a long iron on the first tee, as though he couldn't quite muster the courage to get his round under way in front of the milling spectators. "I'm sorry, sir," the starter bellowed through his loudspeaker, "there are no irons allowed on the first tee." Terrified, the golfer put his iron away and took out his 3-wood. The starter thundered, "Are you sure that's the club you want to hit, sir?" I thought that was funny, but then I imagined how I might have felt, having just paid nearly $100 for my first Old Course round and on the verge of wetting my pants with nerves, to be thusly abused. It didn't seem so funny after that.

In truth, that pitiable man on the first tee was almost certainly just like me: he'd come to St. Andrews because he wanted to learn and experience something in the Home of Golf. Perhaps he knew less about St. Andrews when he arrived there than I did, and almost certainly he'd have only a day or a week to learn, whereas I had a full year. Should any of that matter? No, I belatedly realized—we were more alike than my ego wanted to acknowledge. I still prefer the St. Andrews of the fall, winter and spring to the St. Andrews most Americans get to see, because the town is full of people totally at home and at ease with their surroundings. But the atmosphere of St. Andrews I saw at the start of summer was highly charged. Students and student life are often apathetic, but tourists trying to maximize their experiences are desperate to absorb all of the many signals St. Andrews sends them.

Tourists can't hope to scratch much more than the surface of St. Andrews in two days and two nights. They *can* see all "the sights" in that time: the faded cathedral and castle ruins; the graveyard and the shrines to Old and Young Tom Morris; the great view from St. Rule's Tower; the cobbled pier jutting from the northeastern corner of town into the North Sea; the West Sands beach immortalized in *Chariots of Fire*; and, lest I forget, the stately quadrangles of the oldest university in Scotland. They might also drink in a few pubs and begin to understand why so many anecdotes emanate from St. Andrews, and why so many writers talk of the town's "character" in hushed tones. But as noted earlier, they can't begin to fathom the depth and complexity of the Old Course in just a couple of days. Not only that, but apart from their crusty Old Course caddies— people paid for their anecdotes as much as their abilities—they are unlikely to meet any of the people who make St. Andrews such a special place for everyone.

In my blindness, I would have gladly ignored these people had I been able to play as a single golfer. As I set out for Scotland, in my then-ideal world I would have had the Old Course to myself, and I would have shared it only with friends and the Old Course's archetypal Scottish patrons, the sorts who famously bring dull rounds to life with dry wit and competitive banter. But St. Andrews did me a great favor. It forced me to play in foursomes, and thereby to discover the final piece of St. Andrews's sociological jigsaw. When forced into an all-foreign foursome, my heart usually sank, but only rarely did I come away disappointed. Once or twice I played with stiff-lipped twits wearing logoed cashmere sweaters who forced their caddies to carry bags they themselves couldn't lift if you spotted them two Schwarzeneggers and a Stallone. Apart from them, I warmed to all my partners quickly—and many of the outsiders taught me things the Scots could not.

A Swedish threesome I met on the New Course introduced me to the phrase *"Djävlar Anammas Förbannade Sattyg"*—I don't know what it means, but I'm told you use it when you miss a short putt and there are no children around. I played with a pair of Italians from South Boston who had never seen the Jubilee Course before, and they poked fun at their own inadequacy, lack of linksland knowledge, accents, everything. I met a trio of troopers from Alaska, big, bearded men who looked like lumberjacks and played their first rounds of the year with me in May, in a chilling rain. "I'm sorry," one of them said to me. "We forgot to pay the import tax on the weather when we brought it over." I also played an extraordinary round on the Old Course with the director of security at the American embassy in Niger, "the poorest country in the world," he told me. He hadn't played golf on real grass (as opposed to oiled sand) in three years, and he had to beg the starter to let him on the Old Course without a handicap card. His wife walked along with us, in bare feet most of the way, and the delight on both their faces moved me greatly.

For such people I learned to serve as a guide, especially on the Old Course and especially when no caddies tagged along. I had refined my Old Course routine pretty well by the end of the academic year; the words always came to me like Chi Chi Rodriguez one-liners. I said them over and over again, but my enthusiasm never flagged, because I always sensed my script was exactly what my audience wanted to hear:

- "Aim left."

- "There are seven bunkers to the right of the fairway here. They're called the 'Seven Sisters,' and the joke is that none of them are virgins, ha-ha."

- "It's the largest green in golf . . . if you can't three-putt these greens, you can't three-putt anywhere."

- "No, aim *really* left."

- "The shot is actually slightly uphill, and you *don't* want to get caught in Strath Bunker."

- "Don't worry, you're in good company. It took Nicklaus five tries to get out of Hell Bunker in the '95 Open, you know?"

- "There's really no need to aim too far over than the corner of the sheds, especially given your usual fade."

At the end of every round, even if the course elicited curious comments and critiques from my companions, they always smiled as if they'd experienced exactly what they'd been led to expect from the Old Course. Because the Old Course means something different to all first-time visitors before they begin, and because that meaning changes significantly somewhere between the first tee and the Valley of Sin, I never learned what that was. Still, I never met an American tourist who indicated it was anything other than an unalloyed joy to be in St. Andrews. St. Andrews isn't every golfer's vision of paradise; I can think of other unspoiled places in Scotland where I might like to pitch my tent and live a peaceful golfing existence for a while (Machrie and Machrihanish come to mind). But St. Andrews is cosmopolitan in a manner that befits the spiritual center of its domain, and it offers the most attractions to the greatest number of people, be they Scots or Americans or Japanese or Swedes. If you can't get something out of St. Andrews, to paraphrase the old

Arnold Palmer USGA commercial, you're probably not a "golfer" but rather someone who merely "plays golf."

You won't get a better description of the Old Course than the one given me by an R&A member who had invited a "large Boston lady" into the Old Course Hotel's conservatory on a fine summer's day. Golfing aristocrat and non-golfing socialite chatted peacefully for a while, and then the lady stood up to survey the spectacle unfolding before her on that hole "where you have to hit over the corner of a building." She paused in thought for a moment, then pursed her lips and, to nobody in particular, announced definitively: "It's shabby, it hasn't changed in 400 years, and it's *very* British." With that, she sat down again.

And that's why I love it so.

IT TOOK ME some time, but I came to realize that St. Andrews wasn't the place I'd expected it to be when I first arrived at Melville in the Overseas Orientation Weekend van. Of course, I didn't know I'd be falling in love or inviting homeless golf fans into my dorm room, but I thought I'd read enough about St. Andrews and Scottish golf in general to give me insight into how it would *feel* to exist in the Home of Golf. For a few months, I let this "insight" govern how I actually felt about St. Andrews. I remember chatting with a member of the St. Andrews Golf Club over post-round drinks back in October, and with very little evidence to back myself up I told him how nice absolutely everyone I'd met had been to me, and how intelligent I thought the local population was relative to society at large. I'd been led to believe these things by everyone from Herbert Warren Wind to the university's public-relations staff, and for a while, I suppose, I willingly allowed their words to subdue my own judgment.

In truth, once I penetrated the façade erected by the golf historians and the tourist boards, I found that St. Andrews had much in common with other Scottish towns of its size. Every family has its 2.3 kids, a dog, maybe a cat. Most adults work hard for eight hours and then watch television or go down to the pub at night; most of them *are* unfailingly friendly, but some of them aren't. The schoolchildren wear uniforms by day and hang around outside the take-away joints during lunch; most aren't truant or deviant, but some of them are. As a university town, scores of very smart people from many walks of life do indeed walk the streets and make great conversation, but there are plenty of low-wattage bulbs to go around, some of which I daresay belong to people affiliated with the university or the local bureaucracy (which by my reckoning includes certain members of the staff on call at the Links Trust).

The town I lived in for nine months was great, good and not-so-good, all at once. True perfection it was not. It took me an embarrassingly long time to discover this, and even longer to emotionally accept it. Still, I'm pretty sure St. Andrews is all the town I could ever want—in this world, surely, if not the next. And anyway, from where I stood for so long, I rarely wondered about what St. Andrews felt like. Much more often, I marveled at what St. Andrews made me feel.

Chapter 20

BEGINNING AT THE END

❖❖❖

FOR THE RECORD, *she* asked to play with me.

And not vice versa.

I don't know what possessed Heather to propose such an unusual date. She had spent nearly five years in St. Andrews without touching more than a putter, and while the Himalayas putting course deserves high praise for what it is, it approximates golf about as well as a penalty shoot-out approximates soccer. I never quite learned how some people in St. Andrews managed to thrive on a lifestyle that excluded golf. Maybe they were bluffing. I would have needed the discipline of a monk, and probably something more besides. Were I to discover that my allotted portion of hell is an eternity in St. Andrews with my access to the linksland blocked by a succession of decrepit starters and rangers, I wouldn't be surprised.

Heather had no such nightmares. Nevertheless, at the end of May, on our final day as official students at the University of St. Andrews, she took it upon herself to join me. I suppose there wasn't much of me left unknown to her. She'd already seen most of my idiosyncrasies, including the time I'd rented a Windows-compatible computer for several months even though I already had a Macintosh, just to play a soccer simulation called "Championship Manager 2." If she could put up with that and still call me her "special friend," she could put up with a lot. With me she had putted on the Himmies, watched golf in person at the Alfred Dunhill Cup, and watched the Masters on television, and I liked to think her progression to the full shots and frustrations of the golfing novitiate was inevitable. I hoped that her conscience had gnawed at her, that she finally understood a true Scot could not live a just and moral life without at least a glimmer of firsthand exposure to the national game. But whatever the reason, I wholeheartedly welcomed her interest, and inquired of the Links Trust about playing the Balgove Course.

Golf in St. Andrews consists of two parallel universes. Most visitors only encounter the Old, New, Jubilee and Eden courses—and fair enough. These 72 holes hold all of St. Andrews's real links subtlety, shot values and difficulty. The other two courses, the Strathtyrum 18 and the Balgove 9, weren't designed with visitor play in mind. Their terrain is Florida-flat throughout, traffic on the adjacent A91 whizzes by with annoying frequency and the soil doesn't even match the quality of the sandy turf between them and the sea. The Strathtyrum and Balgove were built on what had been used as farmland for centuries, and underneath the patchy grasses is a clay base that greatly alters the character of approach shots and short-game play in general.

Most of the holes seem to have been constructed at little expense and with less imagination. Then again, you don't go to the

Strathtyrum or the Balgove to marvel at architectural genius. You go because you're a complete novice and want to learn how to play the game in an easy, unhurried environment. Or you go to practice your swing in wind and weather, or to shoot a confidence-boosting number, or to take a break from the oft-frazzling pace of golf elsewhere in St. Andrews.

I played the Strathtyrum only once, three days before I played the Balgove with Heather, mainly because I wanted to be able to say I'd played every hole in St. Andrews. I wished I'd found it sooner. I played the front nine with an elderly R&A member who condescended to play the course because he could knock the ball about and attempt to score without fear of too many bumps, burns and bunkers. If I needed further proof that golf is a great leveler in St. Andrews, this was it: a reasonably good golfer and a member of one of the world's truly élite clubs came together voluntarily at a venue most tourists shunned with good reason, and we both enjoyed ourselves tremendously. I myself hung around red figures for 10 or 11 holes without breaking a sweat, finished with a one-over-par 70 and felt thoroughly refreshed.

I tried not to expect as much from the Balgove. Heather and I approached the first tee just before six o'clock on a mercifully calm, crisp evening. As summer approached, the days had lengthened, and the Balgove now relaxed in the caramel warmth of the softly rippled sky. The fading western sun, thinly veiled by delicate etchings of cloud, strode calmly toward the horizon, teasing us with the promise of extra, flickering light before slipping out of reach. The course stretched invitingly before us, its fairways and roughs sparsely dotted by patient, plodding twosomes and threesomes. The Balgove didn't take tee times, and as a student without a season ticket Heather paid only £4 ($6) to play it. In truth, were its roughs closely mown, the Balgove would make a better soccer pitch than golf course; the Links Trust ropes off its greens and uses it as a parking lot when the Open comes to St. Andrews. But for a beginner, the terrain was just about perfect. I couldn't imagine a better setting for Heather's baptism of fire.

A threesome of golfers in their twenties—two eager young ladies and a harried-looking young man—reached the first tee moments before we did. The man spoke first: "Please, go on ahead of us."

"Are you sure?" I asked.

"Yes, definitely," he said. One of the ladies had begun stretching on the ground; the other awkwardly held a long-iron and repeatedly swung it, frantically and poorly, into the earth on the far edge of the teeing area.

"I'm not sure you know what you're getting into," I said, chuckling, and nodded at Heather. "This is her first time."

"No, really, you go right on ahead." He smiled wanly. He looked like he'd played the Balgove before.

I gave Heather my 4-iron—we had only my bag of clubs between us—and showed her how to use the ball to drive her tee peg into the ground. She placed the ball on the tee, stood up and took two abbreviated practice swings. "Like this?" she asked. I nodded in approval. She addressed the ball, leaned away from the line of play, dragged the club back with her upper body, tugged the club forward toward the ball . . . and missed. A passing car masked the dim *whoosh* of the club through the air.

My eyeballs bulged, and I shot a quick, grimacing, *I-told-you-so* glance at my equivalent on the far side of the teeing area. He shrugged. He looked neither disappointed nor bemused. (What ungallant pigs we were.)

To prepare Heather for her debut, I'd given her a handful of tees, a ball and her own scorecard; we would exchange cards properly at the end of the round, for I wanted her to meet the great demon "score" up close and personal. But I'd given her only a bare minimum of instruction. Heather had played field hockey for her high school, and I generally trusted her hand-eye coordination. More important, I'd seen many well-intentioned fathers become vicious, sniping ogre-teachers in the presence of their sons and daughters, and I thought Heather deserved a chance of enjoying her evening. I would not mention "swing plane," "angle of attack" or "spine flex," and under no circumstance would I point out her state of "pronation." Even if I thought I could properly explain any of these terms in 50 words or less, I didn't want to clutter her experience with anything more than a garden variety "head-down-and-left-arm-straight" level of assistance. I suspected she had come to the Balgove for two reasons: first, for us to spend time together on a lovely evening; and second, to gain some insight into how I enjoy and play the game. If she learned about the golf swing along the way, and if that knowledge helped to magnify these other experiences, great. Becoming Karrie Webb was not an option.

On the other hand, I imagined my happiness would come from her happiness. I remembered my round with Pasi, and braced myself for a similar performance from Heather. If she was going to take five or six swings for every one of mine, duffing and shanking her way around the course, I'd be far better off checking my A-game at the front door. I could have played the Balgove with intent to score; the course is a 1,530-yard par 30, and I imagined I could have easily shot in the mid-20s. But to optimize my chances of scoring well, I would have had to leave Heather behind in the first fairway, and the choice between remaining on speaking terms with her and breaking par on the Balgove was hardly a choice at all. The New or the Jubilee, maybe, but not the Balgove.

Fortunately, for both of us, Heather's second attempt at her opening drive pinged off the bottom of her club and scuttled 40 yards forward in the general direction of the green. I followed with my driver and skied a weak, sickly drive to the right of my intended line; it plummeted to earth 30 yards from the flag. You can get away with rather a lot on a 220-yard par 4, I thought.

I pitched my ball from the one-inch "rough" onto the green. Much to my surprise, it took Heather only two additional swings to join me there. Even better, she holed a six-foot comebacker to two-putt from 40 feet. I roared with approval, then coyly asked, "You've used that club before, haven't you?"

"Yes, I have," she said, sweetly and modestly.

I was smitten. Smart, attractive, drains six-footers for fun. What more could a guy want?

I two-putted for par and instructed Heather to write "4" down on her scorecard for me. "What are you going to mark me down for?" she asked. I pondered the question: one whiff plus three swings plus two putts equals . . . what? I remembered a story about former USGA official and LPGA commissioner John Laupheimer. During one LPGA event, Laupheimer called a one-shot penalty on his wife of less than six months when her caddie illegally cleaned a ball she'd marked on the apron of a green. What moxie, I thought—but he was right. My code of honor and the integrity of score demanded no less. I looked at Heather, ready to say "Six." Her light blue eyes looked back at me, innocent and pleading. "Five," I said.

Our procession continued. I quickly deduced that superstition trumps intelligence when determining a beginner's club selection. I started Heather with my 4-iron, a neutral choice on my part that favorably combined elements of distance, loft and unshankability. After several solid swings, I tried to groove her down to a 3-iron, but the results were mostly awful so we switched back to number four. I'm not sure Heather fully understood why my bag had to be so heavy ("What club should I use here?" she repeatedly asked). She used the 4-iron from every lie, stance and distance of over 100 yards, and dare I say it, she began to play quite well. Ignoring the occasional whiff, after five holes she had recorded two bogeys, two triple bogeys and a quintuple bogey. She'd even hit the third green in regulation, but from 80 feet she'd done well to three-putt for bogey. She played on quietly and measuredly. She breathed deeply during her quintuple at the second, but otherwise she set about her task with great calmness of spirit. She also complimented my good shots and ignored my bad ones, which pleased me since it meant she could tell the difference. As we reached the fourth tee, I turned around: the threesome we'd initially leapfrogged now lagged a hole and a half behind us. I was unspeakably proud.

The sixth hole changed everything. Pete Dye, Robert Trent Jones, George Crump and Henry Fownes combined could never have created such an evil par 4. The rough on both sides of the fairway was two inches deep, and a road crossed the fairway 60 yards from the green. The hole was 298 yards long, simply abominable for a par 4; it ought to have been labeled a par 6, as the designers surely intended. It even doglegged—to the left! Brutal. A town ordinance should ban the existence of such holes on the Balgove. Heather never stood a chance. She topped her drive, yanked her second shot into the left-hand rough, then gouged her way forward with the laggard consistency of an infantryman crawling from shell hole to shell hole at Gallipoli. Half a yard, half a yard, half a yard onward; our progress slowed, even threatened to come to a standstill. I twitched nervously with each successive whack, and in desperation I yanked the 4-iron away from her and gave her something with more loft. She smiled weakly and silently resigned herself to her fate.

We crawled forward to within 20 yards of the road, where Heather's ball sat nicely on a tuft of rough. I gave her my 7-iron, and with little thought she swung again. The ball shot from the clubface, soared high in the air, landed beyond the green and rolled 40 yards farther. Heather giggled meekly; I flushed with embarrassment. I putted out for par while she played her pitch and three further chip shots, trying to reach the green. (Bobby Jones once said, "There is nothing more trying than the playing of a medal round when one is chipping badly.") From 25 feet Heather two-putted; had she rolled in the first putt, I might have claimed for her a triskaidecouple bogey, but a 14-over-par number on one hole was too big for both my vocabulary and my imagination. Eighteen strokes on one hole. I was unspeakably mortified.

If I had been Heather, I would have sprinted away from golf then and there and thrown myself under the next passing lorry on the A91. But she kept her perspective, even as those about her were losing theirs. She merely yawned, said quietly that she was tiring ever so slightly and continued on to the next hole, a short par 3. There she became stuck behind (and then in) one of the Balgove's few bunkers and made a nine; I knocked a 9-iron to four feet and made birdie. "Well done!" said Heather, in a gushing tone. I couldn't help thinking . . . where was her *frustration*? The spewing of oaths, the throwing of clubs? She'd just played back-to-back holes in 27 strokes—20 over par! And then, in the eighth fairway, I realized: I'd stopped obsessing about my score and started obsessing about hers. I looked to the heavens—score can be *so* satanic—and then looked again at Heather. She kept a graceful equanimity about her, dutifully and diligently completing her assigned task of getting her ball into the hole in as few strokes as possible, with no hints of internal turmoil. I was mesmerized—and, at that moment, probably more envious of her golf game than she was of mine.

Daylight faded as we approached the Balgove's ninth and final hole, another vanilla-flavored par 3 of only 105 yards. I needed a par to break 30, but next to the warm sunset and cool breezes that didn't matter at all. Heather's detachment from the game proved a bewitching therapy, something that loosened the shackles of score. Maybe she'd learned something from our exercise, but I owed her at least as much. On the ninth tee, in the murky half-light she swung again at her ball, loosely and lazily with my too-heavy 4-iron, and it scampered up the fairway. "Not bad, Heather," I said, soothingly. "Not bad at all." From short and right of the green, she played a pitch with my 9-iron, and her ball kicked into a small knob by the green, bounding to the left toward the hole and stopping 20 feet away. I lagged my own approach putt absentmindedly and handed Heather my putter. C'mon, babe, I thought—one time! I wanted the Balgove to thank her for me. She set up over her ball, twitched her wrists, jabbed firmly into the ball, watched it bump and grind along the acned green . . . and saw it disappear into the hole. A par!

"Cool," she said, faintly.

I couldn't believe it—a par! I was so happy for her. I began to congratulate her . . . and then paused. My birdie lag had been woeful. I still had six feet for par myself. Heather wasn't going to *beat* me, was she?

Talk about pressure. As I bent over to read my putt, my palms began to sweat. If I miss this, I thought, I'll never let myself hear the end of it. If 18 years of golf experience can't trump two hours worth nine times out of nine, I should take a long walk off of the short cobblestone pier at the other end of town.

I gathered myself to look at the break again, but my guard was already down. With great effort I'd gradually forced myself to stop worrying about score, and in the gloaming, with the day and our round so nearly finished, I couldn't begin again at a moment's notice. Only Lady Luck could have made that putt for me, and at that moment she clearly favored her own gender. I suppose I could have studied the likely angular deflection of every spike mark between me and the hole, but that would have taken hours; instead I read a line in the neighborhood of right-center, made the inevitable poor stroke and tapped in as speedily as possible thereafter. Bogey.

Heather thanked me for the round as I sheepishly shuffled off the green. At least she was too humble and soft-spoken to razz me for my incompetence. Then again, I'm not sure she knew how unlikely her feat had been: she simply had no right to par a hole in her first round of golf. Costantino Rocca's miracle from the Valley of Sin was definitely more probable, and my hole-in-one at Cruden Bay wasn't much less. But the beauty of the Balgove is that it makes the mythical possible. On any other course in St. Andrews, and on most other courses in the world, it would have taken far more than 66 strokes for Heather to complete her first nine holes. That number, like her three at the ninth, was irrelevant to why we decided to play together, but it said a lot about the nuts and bolts of *how* we played together. She hit a large number of "shots", she pitched and chipped and putted with intent to score, and she suffered through the monotony of failure. But she also experienced the brief thrills of success. In other words, she hadn't merely whacked a ball around a field. She'd played golf. And for a beginner, that's as good as golf can get.

And she didn't lose any of my golf balls, reason enough to justify a celebratory drink in the Jigger, a good golf pub in a great golf location adjacent to the Old Course Hotel. We sat in the back, in a cozy stall from which we could see the contours of the Road Hole fade into darkness. I smiled and congratulated her on a job well done.

She smiled back. "Thanks very much for taking me," she said. "I had a lot of fun."

Fun—how weird. I even think she meant it.

Chapter 21

IF IT'S MONDAY,
IT MUST BE MACHRIHANISH

❖ ❖ ❖

SEVERAL DAYS AFTER our exams had been completed, and after I'd stowed away all my Melville belongings in a broom closet, Heather and I flew to Turkey for what we thought might be our final fling together. We still didn't know what would happen come summer. I was returning to *Golf Digest,* and as part of a missionary organization called Latin Link, Heather was spending a month in Ecuador, completely cut off from phone or e-mail communication. It didn't augur well for our future.

But in the seaside resort of Kuşadasi, Heather and I had a brilliant time together. We baked in the sun by the pool and strolled along the waterfront; we haggled in the marketplace and frequented a Turkish massage parlor together; we exchanged our usual Earl Grey for a flavorsome apple tea I wish I had more of now. We also visited the ruins of Ephesus, where we read to each other from St.

Paul's Letter to the Ephesians while sitting on the steps beneath the façade of what was once a massive library. If anything, our week together was *too* good.

Toward the end of the trip, we defiantly resolved not to let our "special friendship" lapse on account of distance alone. Heather invited me to her St. Andrews graduation ceremony in mid-June. "I know you can't come," she said, "but I thought I'd ask anyway." Our conversation, in a sweaty hotel room by the Mediterranean, had a *Casablanca,* end-of-an-era feel to it.

"Tell you what," I offered melodramatically. "I'll make sure I stay with you one more night, on my way through Inverness."

"Really?" Her chin rose and her eyes opened wide.

"Sure." I sat down beside her on the edge of the bed and draped my left arm around her shoulders. "The guys won't have a choice. And I'll miss you terribly by then." We hugged, and kissed, and kissed again.

ALTHOUGH MY TIME in Turkey with Heather was heart-wrenchingly fantastic in its own way, the two weeks that followed promised an even more definitive conclusion to my year abroad. It would certainly be a more appropriate one. I didn't come to Scotland for the romance, I thought to myself, I came for the golf. If that made me a Philistine, so be it, but three of my former Harvard teammates were joining me in St. Andrews, and I had gone to great lengths to plan the ultimate Scottish golfing extravaganza.

We called it, quite simply, the "Trip." Twelve days. Fourteen courses. Eighteen rounds. Golf until we fell over. Whiskey, if we liked, until we fell asleep. All for the low, low price of £730 (around $1,150), food, drink, petrol and flights not included. What it *did* include was a catalogue of names to savor: St. Andrews (Eden, Old and New), Carnoustie, Blairgowrie, Cruden Bay (twice), Nairn, Royal Dornoch, Shiskine (twice), Machrihanish (twice), North Berwick, Gullane (Nos. 1 and 2) and Southerness (twice). My friends had given me carte blanche to plan this circular route around Scotland, and I tried to combine classical stalwarts, personal favorites and unexplored possibilities that might give each of our disparate personalities something to savor. It also seemed appropriate to start in St. Andrews, but I wondered what it would be like as a tourist. Would I cope? Could I successfully marry life before Scotland to life in Scotland, or would old Harvard habits die hard?

Jack met me first, at Waverly Train Station in Edinburgh. He had captained every Harvard golf team I'd ever played on, but he'd been teaching in Switzerland and had played only two nine-hole rounds of golf during the past six months. Jack was our clean-cut, upper-middle-class, fair-haired, all-American blue-eyed boy: childhood in Maryland, prep school in New England, Classics degree and membership in a Finals Club (our upper-class, super-exclusionary answer to fraternities) at Harvard. After the summer he'd be heading to medical school. Maybe because he was always our leader, he sometimes came across as slightly aloof and distant. But we got off to a good start.

I warmed Jack up with the Eden and Old courses. He played the former well, and the latter for free. I showed my Links Trust season pass to the Old Course starter, who recognized and remembered me. Jack then fumbled through his clothing and told the starter he'd left *his* pass at home by accident. As expected, the starter graciously waved Jack onto the first tee without protestation; he assumed Jack was a student friend of mine who didn't play that often and had forgotten about procedure. I'm embarrassed to admit that this shameless plot was my doing. (I'm donating £60 of the proceeds from this book back to the Links Trust—a student loan, if you will.) But I kept my conscience at bay by beating Jack 4&3 in the afternoon with a three-birdie 78 that guaranteed I'd have happy memories of the Old Course for a long time to come.

We met Joel and Jun at the Glasgow airport the next day. Classmates of mine, they'd cocaptained Harvard while I was in St. Andrews, and they flew out of Boston within hours of their graduation ceremony. I was closer to both of them than I was to Jack. We'd all been "initiated" into the Harvard golf team together (by Captain Jack, among others), an experience which for me involved drinking cocktails of raw eggs, lemon juice and Tabasco sauce. This was part of my "nonalcoholic option," but Joel was so drunk by the end of the evening, he'd memorably grabbed the Tabasco from the table and started to chug it down without a chaser. Some might call this hazing, but for us it had the desired effect. With the possible exception of my father, I'd played more golf with Joel and Jun than anyone else, and the talks we shared on and off the course are among my most treasured golfing memories.

Jun was our humorist. Born in Korea, he had moved to San Francisco as a kid, and his father owned a shop there. Through hard work, Jun became one of the better junior golfers in northern California, and he eventually worked his way onto the junior team at the prestigious Olympic Club, which like most of the clubs in the Bay Area granted junior membership to all its club players. But Jun, like many Harvard players before and after him, saw his swing deteriorate somewhat during his first New England winter, and although he still harbored hopes of becoming a professional golfer, college life had mellowed him considerably. He spent a lot of time in bars, became a superlative darts player, and wrote and distributed a self-deprecating, off-color and exceedingly funny e-mail newsletter called either the *Buddhist Weekly* or the *Vichyssoise*, depending on his mood. The previous summer, Jun had joined me on a two-week, cross-country, 4,500-mile golfing-and-driving orgy for a *Golf Digest* article I was writing. We'd emerged from that experience still on speaking terms, so I couldn't imagine we'd have any problems during the Trip.

On the other hand, I worried about Joel, my ball-striking friend and former college roommate. A rigid thinker, he loved U.S. Open courses, immaculate course conditioning and point-to-point target golf, and he felt lost without a yardage book. Joel had grown up in rural Illinois, and his horizons had remained relatively limited. (He needed to get a passport for the Trip, since he'd never been out of the country before.) But he was very smart, and he had a fantastic work ethic that he applied equally thoroughly to his studies and his golf swing—too thoroughly, I sometimes thought. Occasionally I'd sneak into his half of our two-room dormitory after midnight and catch him still at his desk, his short-cropped red hair seemingly on fire with intensity as he continued to study. "Stop working!" I'd command, but he'd never listen. He even played computer solitaire with an analytical ruthlessness. Joel could have quite a bit of fun when he loosened up, and in that sense I thought exposure to some of the courses on my Trip itinerary might do him some good. But he had taken some convincing before he signed up to join the rest of us. If he bought into the ethos of links golf, I thought, the Trip would surely succeed.

The four of us drove straight from the airport to St. Andrews for our tee time on the New Course. While Joel and Jun fought off their jet lag, and Jack scraped off his remaining ring-rustiness, I shot my third-best score on the New and defeated everyone handily. (Even allowing for the factors inhibiting Jack, Joel and Jun, this was a rare occasion indeed.) I was overjoyed to conclude my St. Andrews career with rounds of 76-78-76. After playing the New, we putted our way around the Himalayas, walked from one end of town to the other and alighted after dusk at the Whey Pat Tavern to reflect on our first day together. Joel professed to have thoroughly enjoyed the New Course as more than just a jet lag cure-all.

I left St. Andrews a very happy man. But on Day Three we segued from the sublime to the ridiculous. Joel—he of the Ben Hogan complex—wouldn't have considered coming to Scotland without a guaranteed tee time at Carnoustie, where Hogan won the Open in 1953. I never would have gone back to Carnoustie on my own; as I'd found out in October, Carnoustie was far too bleak, windy and resistant to score for my liking. But I felt duty-bound to let Joel have his way, and to let Jack and Jun form their own opinions about a course many well-known golfers think to be the greatest in Scotland.

As we arrived, gales caused the North Sea to foam at the mouth like a ravenous tiger, ready to rip us to pieces. Wonderful. I pulled my first drive of the day onto a piece of chewed-up earth near a pond I didn't know existed. To Jack, my match play opponent for the day, I appealed for a ground-under-repair drop. He queried, "I don't know . . . it isn't marked off at all, is it? Joel, what do you think?"

"It's Scotland!" Joel shouted above the wind. "It's Carnoustie! Play it as it lies!"

I could see a manic glint in his eyes, even on the other side of the fairway. Nerves already jangling, I took out my 3-wood and windmilled hopefully into the ball. I nearly whiffed—and embedded the ball in the turf six inches in front of me. Closing my eyes, I pressed my fingers forcefully into my eyelids and breathed deeply. I took a penalty drop (lying three), pitched to the fairway (four), ballooned a poor long-iron high into the air (five), bumped a pitch onto the green (six) and two-putted for an eight. Jack made an eight as well—which frightened me even more. Carnoustie's 391-yard, par-4 first hole had taken all of 15 minutes to hammer my pride, my golf game, and my level of interest in the entire Trip into submission.

I played the first nine holes in 52 strokes: five bogeys, two doubles, one triple and that opening quad. No pars, no birdies. Joel, meanwhile, absorbed Carnoustie's difficulties like an experienced skier on a black diamond run. He birdied the sixth, the par 5 of "Hogan's Alley" fame. On the seventh, a long par 4, he creamed two shots through the wind into the rough just beyond the green. He creamed his downhill chip shot, too—it should have rolled *kilometers* past the hole, but instead it solidly hit the pin and stopped dead, inches from the cup.

"I love this course!" Joel shrieked playfully.

"Shut up!" I responded, less playfully.

Joel reached the turn in 38—and he'd double-bogeyed the first. Unbelievable. He was reaching greens upwind and holding them downwind. To do the same, I would have needed siege towers and catapults. I pondered my nine-hole score and decided that I wouldn't have done much better even if I'd been playing well. But Joel's astonishing play and transparent enjoyment of a course I'd begun to loathe proved that Carnoustie *was* playable. I hated him for that. I could have been on strike against score, but he broke rank. The more inadequate I felt, the more the volcano in me simmered.

On the 12th, I yipped a short putt for what would have been my first par of the day—and unleashed a loud, primal scream of frustration. Immediately I blanched in apology, certain that my cry was audible two holes away, even in the wind. I finally parred a hole, the short 13th, but that respite was short-lived. I double-bogeyed the "Spectacles" 14th, then hit a perfect-looking approach into the 15th that kicked violently to the right and into a bunker. On the impossibly long par-3 16th, I pulled my tee shot and left myself a tricky uphill pitch. I settled over the shot, began my backswing . . . and heard Jack mumble something off to my right. I chunked the shot badly, and in the time it took for the ball to slink back down the hill to my feet, I'd whacked my sand wedge into the base of my golf bag. Surprise, surprise: the shaft snapped in two.

My playing partners, all of whom had seen this act before, shook their heads in dismay. I didn't really care. Get me off this golf course, I thought, or the next thing to break might be Jack's neck. I bogeyed 17 and triple-bogeyed 18 to shoot 97. On the downwind 18th hole, Joel cracked his drive *145 yards* past mine—we paced it off—and lobbed a sand wedge approach to six feet. He made his putt for birdie to shoot 78. I'd seen Joel break par before, but I'd never seen him play better; he, like Jack and Jun, must have thought I should have stayed in St. Andrews.

WHEN I CALMED down, I was allowed to rejoin the chorus of debate about the merits of Carnoustie. Joel declared that it was one of the greatest courses he'd ever seen. Jack and Jun agreed with me that Carnoustie is an excessively demanding and forbidding spectacle, but they also thought it deserved ample praise as one of the world's finest layouts. Their attempts to sway me failed. I still maintain that while Carnoustie is superbly well designed to test the game's best players, the rest of us need hard hats and howitzers. I would have done better to caddie for Joel and save myself the green fee.

My post-Carnoustie hangover lasted for several days. Blair-gowrie's Rosemount Course was a nice enough parkland track but hardly the stuff of seaside glory that I'd remember for years to come. At Blairgowrie, the guys complained for the first time about not being able to play from the back tees, which at British clubs are always reserved for formal stroke play competitions. I understood their frustration—they were bombing tee shots well beyond the bunkers and burns designed to trap players of their length—but such grumbling was *so* American. More alarmingly, it took us four and a half hours to play the Rosemount Course. I'd bragged to everyone about Scotland's rapid pace of play, never expecting that we might become everyone's roadblock. Before we finished, Jack confessed to me, "I'm not really so concerned about playing fast. The key thing is that nobody is holding us up." His narrow-minded attitude nearly set me off again. With barely suppressed fury, I shot a spineless, birdieless 84—nine shots worse than anyone else. I also wasted £30: half to reshaft my sand wedge, half on bets I never should have made. When I switched on my laptop that night, I discovered that someone had snuck into the file of notes I'd been keeping and typed, "Darren goes apeshit for second day in a row. Clubs remain intact."

The prospect of our next day's play now scared me. Neither Joel nor Jack had much fondness for super-quirky golf course architecture, and 36 holes in their company at Cruden Bay figured to be an explosive combination, especially if I kept playing like Gerald Ford. As we bobbed and weaved through the dunes, Joel wound me up by repeatedly declaring his undying love for Blairgowrie. Jun, the type of golfer who should have enjoyed Cruden Bay as much as I did, suddenly lost his swing and struggled mightily to find it. Jack and I shared a weird moment on the 14th hole, an uphill par 4 tucked between a massive sandhill and the sea that has, shall we say, very active fairway contours. I drove up the middle of the fairway, and Jack followed my line exactly; his ball landed several yards beyond mine . . . and kicked dead left, into the rough.

"What!" exclaimed Jack.

"Oh, you hit it in the wrong place," I replied, grinning. (I shot 80-76 at Cruden Bay, and as my golf game improved, I recovered the faintest glimmer of a sense of humor.)

"Ah, so you *don't* want to hit it in the fairway here," said Jack, as though he'd solved the riddle of the sphinx.

Joel and Jun warmed to the theme: "Yep, definitely. Hit it in the shit. In the shit is good."

In general, everyone *did* like Cruden Bay, but this moment with Jack was one of the last laughs we shared for a while. Our daily routine started to wear us down: wake up by eight, force down a heavy Scottish breakfast (eggs, bacon, sausage, toast, grilled tomato, grilled mushrooms, baked beans, black pudding, cereal, fresh fruit, juice, tea and coffee—usually all at once), repack our suitcases and golf bag carriers, find a new way to cram everything into the trunk of the car, check out of our B&B, locate and attack the next spit of linksland, then drive for hours to the next town and fall asleep quickly. Relaxation? Forget about it. I should have given us several chances to stay in the same place for more than one night. My friends became involuntary teetotalers—the worst kind.

We played Nairn in a strange wind that made all the hard holes harder (we collectively played the par-4 fifth in seven over par) and the easy holes easier (at the par-5 18th we had three birdies and an eagle). At the turn, Jun complained, "Have you noticed that none of the holes seem to have bail-out options? I mean, there's gorse *every-where*. Virtually every hole looks the same to me."

I apologized on Nairn's behalf: "If only the wind were normal, you'd see how good a course this really was."

"Great courses do not lose their greatness in 'unusual' weather," retorted Joel. He had a point.

On the road to Inverness, the stench of rebellion permeated the air. Joel questioned my itinerary: "Why didn't we play Lossiemouth instead of Nairn?" He'd heard Lossiemouth's praises extolled by someone at Blairgowrie.

"Because it's nowhere near as good a course as Nairn," I said testily. "Period."

"I don't know, Darren. You weren't originally going to have us play Carnoustie, were you?"

I gritted my teeth. "Look . . . I asked everyone for advice back in March, when I was putting this whole thing together. You said, 'We trust you, Darren, you do what you think is best.' I caved in on Carnoustie because I thought you guys ought to see it. But I think I've done as well as I can here." So give me a break, I didn't say. "It's Dornoch tomorrow—and if you don't like Dornoch, I'll *walk* the rest of the way."

WE DROVE TO Heather's house in Inverness. Heather's parents welcomed us into their living room, and all of us introduced ourselves. For one long, awkward moment of silence, I stood upon the threshold of two completely separate worlds: Joel, Jack and Jun on my left, and Heather, Ian and Alison on my right. Jack spoke first: "Right, well, I guess the rest of us should be going. It's been nice meeting you." The guys shuffled back out to the car. I put my head in my hands.

I needed my night off. But Heather and I hardly had time enough to say hello, much less good-bye. The next morning, she drove me up to Dornoch in her mother's small white hatchback, and we sat in silence much of the way. What more could we do or say? In the parking lot of Royal Dornoch Golf Club, we hugged one final time, and as her car pulled away I throbbed with melancholy. The girl I loved had gone, and I didn't know if I'd ever see her again. A golf course I loved lay before me, but I now thought it rather paled by comparison. And from three guys I really liked, I no longer knew what to expect.

To my great relief, everyone praised Royal Dornoch—finally, a golf course about which we could fully agree. Jack came home in only 34 strokes, proving that quality golf wasn't totally out of our reach. But not even Dornoch's tranquillity could wholly cure our blues. Jun was playing worse than ever. On the 12th tee, he lamented, "What I need is about an hour on the range."

"How about four hours in a car?" asked Jack, maliciously.

"Yeah, I need that about as much as I need an elephant tusk up my ass." I snorted a laugh, but Jun wasn't smiling.

The journey from Dornoch to Tarbert, at the top of the Kintyre Peninsula, actually took six and a half hours—and pushed Joel, Jack and Jun to their respective breaking points. The never-ending sequence of lengthy lochs and intricate inlets, snowcapped mountains and rapeseed-covered hillsides dulled our senses. We talked to each other in strange, pseudo-Scottish accents that strongly resembled pirate-speak. (Joel repeatedly bellowed, "Arrrgh, says I, this ride is a pain in my arse! Arrrgh!") As we rounded our 37th consecutive hairpin chicane on the A816, south of Oban, Argyll, Joel announced that he was about to throw up, although he mercifully refrained from doing so.

And so it went:

JUN: "If you crash, make sure you kill me. I don't want to know about it."

JOEL: "Is this called good planning?"

JACK: "We are driving *so* far."

JUN: "Uh, I think I just saw the Arctic Circle."

I shrugged off most of these comments. But when we finally reached our Tarbert B&B, my colleagues called an impromptu team meeting. "We have got to slow down," said Joel, pressing a hand gently into his still-trembling stomach. I knew what was coming, and I felt sick at heart.

"We're going to need a day off soon," said Jack. "How long is the drive from Machrihanish to North Berwick?"

"Five hours, give or take," I said glumly.

"And you want to play golf that evening?"

"Well, if you'd looked closely at any of the itineraries I e-mailed to you . . . "

"Screw the itineraries!" thundered Jack. We gasped in silence. Jack regathered his composure. "I'm sorry, Darren. But this isn't working at the moment."

I knew where he was going and tried to cut him off before he got there. "But North Berwick is a really fun golf course! Will any of us ever get the chance to play it again?"

"I don't really care," said Jun. "I'm with Jack."

"Me, too," said Joel.

"But we've already paid five pounds each as a booking fee," I said in desperation. "We can't get that back, you know."

"So?"

Jack's question punctured my resistance. I gazed at the floor, dejected.

Joel broke the silence. "I've never been outside America before," he reminded us. "I've flown all the way over here to Scotland, and I'd love to see a castle, or a museum, or *something* that has something to do with history and nothing to do with golf. I vote we go to Edinburgh and do a bit of sight-seeing. How does that sound?"

Jun and Jack nodded in approval. "Okay," I said. "Fine." It wasn't fine, but what could I do?

A wave of irritation washed over me. I felt like I did on the 17th tee at Carnoustie. What else could go wrong? We were all tired, each exasperated in his own way. Jack and I, rooming together for the night, got in a heated and thoroughly unnecessary argument about something ridiculously trivial as he was about to turn off the lights in our room. Things had to change.

DAY EIGHT DAWNED brilliantly. Everyone had slept soundly. The sky was blue, the sun warm and bright. Good thing, too, because we were about to play a golf course that I thought might get me lynched, and I needed all the help I could get.

I'd heard stories about the Shiskine Golf and Tennis Club, near the town of Blackwaterfoot on the island of Arran. Shiskine, I thought, would make Cruden Bay look like the Bonneville Salt Flats. Shiskine is so remote and craggy that Robert the Bruce was said to have fled to a cave adjacent to the present-day fourth hole while hiding out from the English before the battle of Bannockburn. I'd read about the Arran Challenge, a tournament that attracts golf psychopaths from as far away as the States to the freezing winds and rain of Shiskine in *December.* Such stories automatically made Shiskine my kind of place and demanded its inclusion in my *Golf Digest* travel article, but I couldn't tell the guys any of this. They thought it weird enough that we had to ferry our car and possessions to and from a tiny island just to play a course with only 12 holes.

This last number actually excited Jack. "How perfect," he theorized, "to play a course all the way through, have a long and leisurely lunch, then play the course again and still have most of your afternoon free." I could only agree. Our ferry crawled from Claonaig on the mainland to Lochranza, Arran's main port—a dock and a few huddled buildings. In the bright early-morning sunshine, Arran's rocky beauty spangled luminously. For the first time during the Trip, sunblock was mandatory.

Shiskine's rudimentary pro shop was overgrown with shirts and sweaters and tacky, unwanted souvenirs stacked from floor to ceiling. We macheted our way to the back and found its one attendant huddled behind a pane of glass, watching breakfast television. He waved us toward the first tee without so much as a glance of recognition. "Do you have a yardage book of the course we can buy?" I asked.

"No."

"What do you want us to do about our green fees?"

"Dinna worry. Later."

I looked around. Joel shook his head. Jack tried desperately hard not to laugh. "Bizarre," murmured Jun. We turned around and hacked through to the exit.

The puzzle of Shiskine continued on the first tee as we stood around and wondered in what direction to hit our drives. The terrain at which the tee markers pointed us crested quickly and fell away, hiding the hole. The grass mowings didn't give us any clues. Only the road to our left and the shoreline beyond it hinted at where not to go. I studied the primitive course map on the back of the scorecard, and it suggested the tee markers were correctly aligned. But a crooked line on the map also implied that the second shot needed to go straight ahead 50 yards, veer slightly to starboard and bearing 010 degrees, and avoid a clump of eight small black dots on its roundabout way. What could we do? We navigated like sailors of old—by guess and by God.

Some holes at Shiskine defied comparison. The third, for example, was 132 yards long and almost as tall. Called the Crows Nest, it bore the name well; imagine standing on the poop deck of an 18th-century clipper ship and trying to plug the guy in the watchtower with a 9-iron, and you'll have an idea of the hole's working architectural principle. Miss the green five yards to the left, and your second shot—from the ninth fairway—could be almost exactly the same as your first. I'm nearly certain that very few women and senior golfers can hit the ball high enough in the air to finish the hole, which is normally a sure sign of poor design. But the reward for shimmying up the Crows Nest was a scintillating return shot from a clifftop to the green of the short fourth hole, with Kilbrannan Sound, the Kintyre Peninsula and Robert the Bruce's caves in the background. Faces of vertical stone above the caves were creased and cracked like streams of dripping candle wax. Joel, Jack, Jun and I all agreed: Shiskine's panoramas were as beautiful as any we'd ever seen on a golf course.

Shiskine also had more silly blind shots per hole than any course we'd ever played, so as a test of golf it rated somewhat less highly. In fact, it was the complete antithesis of Carnoustie. But it was exactly what we needed. We traipsed from one natural phenomenon to another, hitting our shots with one eye always glued to the horizon. Score mattered little to anyone, especially me, and in no way did our golf spoil such a good walk. After our first 12 holes, we spent an hour in the club's creaky yet eminently functional tearoom, munching on sandwiches and chatting about the transparent weirdness of the "design" elements at work at Shiskine, to use the term very loosely. Everyone smiled broadly; I sighed with palpable relief and satisfaction.

"This is really great," Jack said when lunch came to an end. "Thanks for scheduling this into the Trip."

"You're very welcome," I answered. I'd forgotten what it was like to be complimented.

"Hey, what's that?" Joel got up from the table to study something hanging on the polished oak of the tearoom wall. "It looks a scorecard of the course record round," he said. A light went on in his eyes. "A 40? Only two under par? Is that possible?"

"Yeah, I think so," I said, hesitantly. "It must be." The article I'd read about Shiskine said that its course record was only one under.

"I can shoot that—no problem!" I was afraid Joel was going to say that. "Let's go! Come on—who's with me?" He sounded like John Belushi in *Animal House*.

The thought of consciously trying to play well again so soon frightened me, but I needn't have worried. We now knew where the greens and hazards were, and the afternoon was surprisingly still. About all Shiskine normally had in common with Carnoustie was

the weather, but that wasn't true for us, and we transitioned seam-
lessly from good fun to good golf. Birdies flowed freely between us,
and at the six-hole "turn" our group best-ball score was five under
par. Joel needed only to par his way to the clubhouse to shoot in the
30s.

The eighth hole at Shiskine is listed as a 251-yard par 4 from the
medal tee. Some very sticky vegetation lurks in a crevice just to the
left of a green the size of a throw rug, and the tee shot is made blind
by a downward turn of the fairway, but from our forward tee it
seemed like a cinch birdie. Joel, Jack and Jun attacked the green in
turn with irons. I unsheathed my driver and semi-ballooned a shot
into the air, letting a soft breeze sweep over my right shoulder and
bear my ball over the horizon. We greeted each other's shots with
grunts of affirmation; we thought Jack's was slightly left, and mine
felt like it had come up short, but otherwise we could only nod our
heads in a familiar, blind-hole sort of way.

The ninth hole, Shiskine's lone par 5, runs parallel to the eighth,
and two young Scottish men approached their tee shots to our right
as we marched purposefully forward. One of them, not much older
than the four of us, signaled in our direction and shouted, "You over
there, you in the blue shirt!"

"Me?" I asked. Apparently he could see us from his tee, could tell
us apart as we hit in sequence.

"You just made a hole-in-one!"

THERE IS NO acceptable way to respond to this statement.
None. Here's what raced through my mind in the seconds after I received this astounding report:

OhmyGod OhmyGod OhmyGod. Another ace! An ALBA-
TROSS!!!

Wait a minute—you guys must be lying. No way that ball went in the hole. Did you sneak over and put it there while we couldn't see you?

Never mind that. Joel and Jun have never made an ace. Don't make a fuss, Darren, and they'll be very thankful.

But how can I not? You're such a lucky bastard! How dare you hole a shot so *bad*? Scotland—*I love you!*

Now then, how will I ever afford the drinks bill?

More importantly, with the double eagle, you're now one under par. Even *you* might have a shot at the course record!

Wait a minute—are you trying to suggest that was a real par 4? Playing about, what was it, 220? Downhill and downwind? Get real.

Then again, par is *always* arbitrary—especially in Scotland, the land of match play. And if it wasn't a par 4, what was it? It was never a par 3, that's for sure.

Whatever else you think, Darren, walk quickly. It's not an ace until you see it in the bottom of the cup.

I WAS COMPLETELY flummoxed. I shouted "Thank you!" across the fairway—half for the messenger, half for the message—and walked with ever-tightening muscles toward the green. First we saw the balls belonging to Joel and Jun, both of which had rolled beyond the green. Then we spied Jack's ball, near the crevice on the left. I walked up to the pin, looked down into the hole . . . well, what did I expect to find?

Jun took my picture with my camera four times, just to make sure, as I held the flagstick in one hand and my driver in the other. Unsurprisingly, I didn't make much of a run at the course record—it's hard to make good swings when your knees and intestines are quivering furiously—but Joel holed a 20-foot birdie putt on the final hole to shoot 39. We inquired in the pro shop, and his score only tied the current official record. Joel hardly cared; we all wheeled away from Shiskine with light hearts and happy voices. The Trip *wasn't* dead. Long live the Trip!

WE REACHED MACHRIHANISH well before nightfall and discovered that our beautiful guesthouse was within flop-shot range of the 18th green. Joel and Jack percolated with excitement, and no sooner had we emptied our car than they strolled out to the course to investigate. They walked all 18 holes. After some delay, Jun sprinted over dune and dale to join them, catching up only at the far end of the out-and-back layout. I showed unusual restraint and uncommon wisdom in deciding to stay behind, thinking that my friends might find Machrihanish more magical if I left them to discover it themselves. I was right. They returned together at dusk, singing the course's praises so loudly that we briefly discussed squeezing in an extra round on Sunday morning before we returned to our senses.

Saturday was sunny, and warm, and nearly perfect. We slept late and slurped down another scrumptious plate of cholesterol. We teed off at 10:50 in the morning, and again at our leisure in the afternoon. The whole town was riveted to the England vs. Scotland soccer match in the European Championships, and we had the course almost to ourselves. Each of us broke 80—twice. Our 36-hole scores were 150, 151, 152 and 153. The world of golf was for one day its own isolation tank: we lunched at the club, we dined late at the club and we watched the third round of the U.S. Open on Sky Sports at the club after the outdoor golf was done.

We also made friends at the club—American friends. Gathered

around two tables in the Machrihanish clubhouse were eight golfers from Rome, Georgia. For over a week, they had played 36 holes every day and drunk hard every night. That very day, they had left Gleneagles (in central Scotland, near Blairgowrie) at 6:30 in the morning and somehow had still completed their 36 holes at Machrihanish before we did.

"Is that your big van out in the parking lot?" I asked one of them.

"Sure is," he said.

"How long did the drive from Gleneagles take?" I asked.

"I reckon it was about three and a half hours."

I was flabbergasted. "Are there secret tunnels under the lochs here in Argyll that I don't know about? Or does one of you guys work for NASCAR?"

Jack mischievously suggested to me, "Maybe you should be part of their tour instead of ours."

Right about then Payne Stewart appeared on the television screen, and one of the guys close to the set drawled loudly, "Damn, he sure looks faggoty in them knickers."

Jack turned around. "Or maybe not," he whispered.

About 8:00 in the evening, after several orders of whiskey had passed back and forth, one of the good ol' boys started talking about a four-hole match that they had *begun* at 10:30 at night a couple of days before. "It stays light out for so long here, and we're just enjoying ourselves so much, we just can't stop ourselves," he said. "Hell, we're planning to play some more golf later on."

Jun looked at me, and I at him. Jack looked at Joel—they both looked at us. We all looked out the window, at a sun still shining brightly. I burned with desire. "What do you think?" I asked everyone, hopefully.

"What are we waiting for?" Jun replied.

Next thing I knew, I'd draped my golf bag over my shoulder and was sprinting to the first tee, trying to tie my golf shoes as I ran. When we got there, Jack laid down the rules: "Skins, one pound a hole, with carryovers. As soon as you're out of a hole, pick up. No scorekeeping—yes, Darren, I'm talking to you. We're going to finish all 18 holes, or die trying."

We cracked drives down our 37th fairway of the day and jogged after them, laughing all the way. I felt like a truant schoolboy romping through a meadow. None of that preshot routine, paralysis-through-overanalysis nonsense; this was golf reduced to the knockabout I'm sure its creators meant it to be. We rushed from hole to hole, hitting blind shots with carefree ignorance of all possible consequences. Good shots were quickly congratulated, fetched and hit again. Bad shots disappeared into the dunes forever, but there weren't many of them, and we shrugged them off as a necessary by-product of keeping the match rushing forward. We couldn't have sped around Machrihanish much faster on horseback. I never would have thought I could simultaneously play golf and lose weight, but our dash for the clubhouse was by some distance the healthiest thing we did on the Trip.

Amazingly, I didn't have to pick up once. I knew I was only one over par when the sun dipped beyond the horizon, halfway through the back nine. We pressed on regardless; the glow of the moon, the afterglow of a good day and our Cheshire Cat grins guided us home. On the 18th hole, playing now to only 275 yards, Jack smashed his drive to within 10 feet of the hole. At 10:46 P.M., with seven carryover skins on the line and Joel already in for birdie, Jack lined up his eagle putt in virtual darkness. Jun held the pin so Jack could see the hole. Joel and I hovered anxiously to one side. Jack hit his putt: it caught the right edge of the hole, spun 180 degrees around and twirled away to the left. "NO!" he screamed, and jumped in the air. The rest of us yelled with glee and giggled with excitement. It was that kind of day.

The Georgia boys bought us a final round of drinks in the clubhouse, and we thanked them profusely for egging us on. I settled my scores; even though I'd shot 74-76-72, I'd lost £10 in the evening skins, having birdied only one hole and halved many others, and £30 for the day. The numbers didn't quite add up, but I didn't care. For this experience of what a linksland day among friends could be like, I'd have paid just about anything.

ALTHOUGH I DIDN'T entirely realize it at the time, the up-tight, score-obsessed golfer I had been died some sort of permanent death during that third round at Machrihanish. Everything about it flew in the face of the golfing logic I'd formerly embraced. The round wouldn't have happened were it not for the loud Americans in the clubhouse bar, guys I would have studiously avoided in most other circumstances. It couldn't have worked had I been by myself—I would have had fun, certainly, but not the kind of fun you get when you share the experience with others on the same crazy wavelength. And it certainly wouldn't have felt the same when I bogeyed the 17th had I been obsessed with matching par for 18 holes. I was matter-of-fact about keeping score as we rushed around the course—I kept score, but that didn't mean I had to. I wanted to do well, but I didn't *need* to.

During a quiet moment as we drove away from Argyll on Sunday morning, I realized why my third round at Machrihanish would probably stay with me longer than my third round at Dornoch in November. At Dornoch the setting had demanded that I stop worrying about score altogether. It was a nice feeling, but it wasn't *me*. At Machrihanish score mattered, but in proportion to everything else that happened, it didn't matter much. I liked shooting 72, but the roll of Jack's eagle putt toward the final hole thrilled me much, much more than the tap-in par I'd made. The less I tried to control my own score, the more I allowed myself to delight in the scores of others. It was a lesson in humility I've not forgotten.

WHEN WE FINALLY reached Edinburgh, we shirked the £5.50 entrance fee to the castle and briefly toured Scotland's National Gallery instead. Then we drove on to our North Berwick B&B, where we watched the final round of the U.S. Open for five hours. We decided we'd prioritized the events of our day off just about perfectly, although Joel wasn't pleased when Steve Jones conquered Oakland Hills to win his first major. "You're *not* worthy!" Joel cried at the television set in utter seriousness.

The guys didn't like Gullane No. 1 nearly as much as I thought they would. Then again, I didn't either. The Gullane I'd loved in September defended par with intelligent bunker placement and subtleties of terrain. The Gullane I now manfully fought in June had long, sticky rough and a stiff breeze on its side. It placed a ridiculously high premium on accurate driving. In his book *The Golf Courses of the British Isles*, Bernard Darwin raved that Gullane Hill and its surroundings possessed "the finest, smoothest, and most delicate turf that ever was seen." Why cover it up with cabbage thicker than molasses and stronger than ice plant? At the second hole I blocked my drive into the weeds on the right, never found the ball, agonized about whether or not to return to the well-populated teebox, and decided to drop a new ball just clear of the thick stuff, lying three. By the time I made my putt for a tainted nine, 40 minutes had elapsed since we'd teed off at the first. Did I once say I *liked* the second hole at Gullane No. 1?

The downhill seventh was even goofier. The hole plunges from the lofty heights of Gullane Hill to a green very close to sea level. Its principal hazards *should* be three bunkers bracketing the tee shot landing area and two more guarding against the run-up shot, 55 yards from the green. I loved its challenges in September: the tee set up like the start of a Calvin and Hobbes toboggan run, and the hole thrilled me correspondingly. But with the hole playing into the wind, only a perfect strike could have hit the pencil-thin fairway; punch shots from the tee were impossible, and the wind magnified our errors exponentially. With the grasses tall, anything off-line required a lengthy search. Joel, Jun and I all hit into the deep stuff, so we waved the group behind us to play through, but all four of them hit the ball shorter and even more crookedly so we kept our place. Ten minutes after we started the seventh hole, 16 golfers were strung out between its tee and its green.

The day dragged on and on. After four hours we'd only played 15 holes, I'd recorded every number on my scorecard between three and nine, I was running out of money, and I'd begun to wonder why Gullane Golf Club allowed guest play in June, July and August. I kept persevering, though. With three holes left, I figured I needed two pars and a bogey to break 90. I didn't think I could do it, but I vowed to have fun trying.

On the 177-yard, par-3 16th, the wind blew strongly from behind us and out of the right. I tossed several grass shavings into the air;

parched, browning grass in front of the green suggested a bounced approach would be ideal. I chose my 6-iron and decided to play a small fade, hoping to hold the ball slightly into the breeze. I swung—*perfectly*. The ball fluttered in the wind, wandered right, then left, landed 10 yards short of the green, skipped forward three times, scooted along the green like a magnet into the center of the flagstick and dropped into the hole.

"YES! YES! YEEEESSSS!" I bounced around in circles, pumping my fists and punching the air in my best imitation of Larry Mize at the 1987 Masters. Twice in four days! Flipping heck! And darn it, as much as one can ever *deserve* a hole-in-one, this time I deserved it. I hit a shot that did *exactly* what I designed it to do, exactly how I wanted it to. And I saw it, in flight and along the ground, from start to blessed finish. Unreal.

Joel congratulated me first. "I think you probably know what I thought of your, um, hole-in-one at Shiskine," he said, smiling. He pointed at the green. "But *that* was one hell of a golf shot. Well done."

He shook my hand. Jack and Jun shared similar sentiments. I paused in frivolous thought, and then an idiotic grin came over my face.

"What?" asked Joel.

"A thought has just occurred to me," I said. "Do you realize I've now made as many aces in Scotland as Bobby Jones made in his entire career?"

I ducked before Joel could hit me.

I FINISHED BOGEY-birdie to shoot 86—best damn 86 I've ever shot. The other guys shot 82, 78 and, astoundingly, 74. Jack's three-over-par round rivaled Joel's 78 at Carnoustie for the best Trip performance. He should have done better, too; he double-bogeyed the 18th, a hole the rest of us birdied, and I couldn't believe he failed to birdie the downhill, downwind 17th after his drive. He elected to hit a 2-iron, hoping to stay well short of three steep-faced cross-bunkers set at an angle, 320 yards from the tee. He smashed his ball and it rolled, and rolled, and rolled, and ramped up the inside bank of one of the bunkers, and traversed a 6-foot-long, 12-inch-wide isthmus of land separating that bunker from another, and rolled some more to within 20 yards of the green. I judged this shot luckier than my ace—not least because Jack didn't have to buy drinks for it after the round.

We sleepwalked through Gullane No. 2 in the afternoon . . . until we reached the 15th hole. On the 175-yard par 3, Jack pulled a short-iron that hit a mound to the left of the green and spun sharply to the right, directly at the hole. His ball caressed the rear lip of the cup and stopped inches away.

"Well, I'm not *trying* to have all the fun," I said, laughing.

"Bloody hell," said Jack, picking up on the local lingo. "If that had gone in, it would have been worse than your shot at Shiskine."

"Well, I still don't think it's fair," said Joel, instinctively leaping to Jack's defense. "Why is Darren the only one of us who routinely puts the ball in the hole with clubs other than his putter?" He smiled, but I could tell he was genuinely puzzled.

OUR LAST FULL day began with a splendid three-hour drive to the south, through a series of majestic hills known collectively as the Southern Uplands, but our final course was something of a downer. Southerness has one great hole: the sweeping par-4 12th doglegs around heather and along gorse to the edge of Solway

Firth. Against a soft western sky, its beauty compared favorably to anything we'd seen. But most of Southerness was architecturally uninspiring and visually distasteful. "This is the ugliest course I've ever seen," said Joel.

Jun was even more critical. "You know what it reminds me of?" he asked, rhetorically. "The projects in Washington, D.C."

"A touch of hyperbole there, perhaps?" I tried to put a brave face on it. "It's not *that* bad, chaps. Is it?" But it nearly was. For a course ranked in the *Golf World* Top 100, Southerness was exceedingly flat and dull. And for high summer the course was in terrible shape: the fairways were terribly patchy, and the greens were bumpier than any I'd seen since the ones on the Jubilee Course had been aerated. After all our peaks and valleys, we were disappointed to end the Trip with such an anticlimax.

Still, just as I proved I could find a way to enjoy golf at Gullane No. 1 when I was playing poorly, I had fun at Southerness despite the course's obvious flaws. It helped that we all finished with a flourish of good scoring. In our final round, Jun at last played up to and beyond his ability level—against a par of 69, he shot a six-birdie 67. Jack shot 74 and was completely frozen out of the money, because Joel also notched a 72. I finally did the right thing and begged out of all bets for the first and only time, and after 10 holes I was still one under par. (Go figure.) I tried to choke toward the end; from the tee of the par-3 17th, I hit the Trip's one and only Shank and made triple bogey. But I blasted two big shots on the par-5 18th and reached the green in two. I lagged my 50-footer four feet past the hole. Palms sweating, I homed in on the comebacker and drilled my final birdie putt into the center of the cup. A four-over-par 73—I was very, very pleased. The Trip, and Scottish golf in general, deserved nothing less.

FROM SOUTHERNESS, THE four of us drove to Carlisle, just over the English border, for our final night together. In our B&B, we thought back through the whole Trip, and after careful deliberation each of us ranked the courses we'd all played together from one to 11. I nominated myself to collect everyone's lists and collate them, which was probably a mistake.

"Blairgowrie at number four? Joel, you're on drugs." I just about meant it.

"I could say the same about your pick of Cruden Bay at number two."

"Hey, wait a minute. At least Jun has an excuse for picking Cruden Bay so low—he shot 87-82 there. What's yours?"

"Probably the same one you used to put Carnoustie at number FIVE!"

"Do we need to go through this again? My views on Carnoustie are a matter of public record. Heck, it pains me to rank the New Course at St. Andrews behind it. And Nairn. And Shiskine. And . . . "

"Oh, be quiet, Darren."

Captain Jack had spoken. I did as I was told.

That night, after everyone else had retired upstairs, I snuck down to the sitting room of our B&B to do some packing and watch the highlights of England's 4–1 thrashing of Holland in the European Championships. None of my colleagues cared for soccer—they'd all grown weary of my repeated requests to tune the car stereo to the ever-present matches on BBC Radio Five Live—so I had the room and the television to myself. But even after the highlights were over and I'd switched off the set, I lingered downstairs to think back over the previous two weeks and wonder a little about my golfing future. I couldn't possibly have known then that the lessons I'd learned (and relearned) during the Trip would finally stick, that my club-breaking days would soon be coming to an end, that I would learn to happily say "Yuck!" at my bad shots instead of the word with which it rhymes, that I would become nearly as much at peace with myself on the golf course as I was away from it. But even then, as a wave of exhaustion threatened to swamp me as I sprawled on the sitting room sofa, I sensed that the Trip was a watershed in my golfing career; more than that, it was a transformation that would affect me in ways that transcended the maddening game to which I'd devoted my year in Scotland.

Score, I now realized, wasn't bad in and of itself. Subconsciously, I had believed it *was* bad. I'd seen how the Scots enjoyed match play and I wanted to emulate them, but I knew that I wasn't and probably couldn't be like them. I think I felt ashamed at what I perceived to be a flaw in my character. But really, how could stroke play be anything but morally neutral? Stroke play and match play are apples and oranges, not rotten and ripe. And while excess of any kind is bad, score itself isn't. Besides, I suspect obsessive match play participants come to hate their opponents in the same way that obsessive scorekeepers wind up hating themselves. Stroke play and match play are different variations of the same *game,* and as long as I can continue to keep that simple yet salient word at the front of my mind, I'll do just fine.

The other conclusion I reached about the game was that other people on and around golf courses are not pawns for me to push around. I don't know why I should have subconsciously clung to this foolish notion as long as I did, but it took three of my closest golfing friends to finally disabuse me of it. For far too long I had been using other people, golfers and bystanders alike, as means to the end of increasing my personal golfing enjoyment. I looked for the "right" playing partners and avoided everyone else. Whenever things began to go awry, I retreated into myself and concentrated upon score. Even among friends, I could be quite hideous this way; I think I'd wanted Joel, Jun and Jack to enjoy the Trip as much for the mastery of my planning as for the wonders of Scottish golf itself. What I finally discovered was that by worrying less about my own needs, I could more fully enjoy the company of others. And with something other than score to focus upon, I was able to embrace score more positively than ever before. The Trip only began to gel when I stopped trying to place myself at its center like a manic tour guide. The four of us shared some harsh words and feelings before I accepted this, but by the time we'd finished up at Southerness I knew our anguish hadn't been in vain. Jack, Jun and Joel may have been unwitting agents of my final conversion process, but when I eventually crawled into bed that final night in Carlisle, I silently thanked each of them for the parts they had played in changing me for the better.

The next morning, the four of us drove to Manchester Airport and said our good-byes. I didn't know it at the time, but the Trip was our swan song together. Since we all flew back to the States, I've not been in the same room with, never mind golfed with, more than one of Jack, Jun and Joel at a time. I miss them all tremendously, and I think about them often. I love how the Trip came together at the end, but I remember just as fondly its silly arguments and the slow paces of play and how Joel salivated over the fairways of Blairgowrie. I'd go back to Scotland and have those fights again just to have another trip like that. For what it's worth, I'd even play Carnoustie again. If I had to.

Epilogue

THE ALARM RANG—seven in the morning. My back hurt. My sleeping bag was warm, but the floor was stiff and the carpeting thin and cold even in July. Why did *she* get to sleep in the single bed, again? I contemplated this question at length before remembering something about gallantry and chivalry. Or something like that. Besides, the room belonged to *her* friend. I shook away the cobwebs, peeled myself off the ground, picked up my shaving kit and tiptoed across the chilly hallway to the communal showering facilities on the bottom floor of the Dean's Court postgraduate hall of residence. The murky dawn of another St. Andrews morning crept through the bathroom window's frosted glass.

After showering and shaving, I crossed back to the room in which I'd slept and eased down onto the edge of the bed. "Heather . . . Heather?" I gently shook my wife awake.

"Grbrbrbthhhh . . . huh?" Heather rubbed her eyes. "Oh." She clucked her tongue several times and blinked impulsively.

"Time to wake up. You know we've got a busy day ahead. And for once I've gone and showered first." I winked. "Plenty of hot water still left for you, though." She was just as cute as when I'd first met her. Had it really been almost five years?

She stirred to hug me and rolled out of bed. As she showered and dressed, I packed my rucksack for two: ham-and-tomato sandwiches, sausage rolls, apples, large bottles of water. Plenty of sunblock. By 7:30, we were both ready to go. "Looking good, babe," I said, and kissed her on the cheek. "Now then—let's go watch some golf!"

We emerged from Dean's Court, at the eastern end of Market Street, and slipped down an alleyway over to North Street. Crossing to the far side of the road, onto sunlit cobbled stone recently liberated from the retreating morning shadows, we walked past St. Salvator's Chapel, its amber stone tower sparkling in the molten sunshine, its red-faced clock finally repaired after years of disuse. We instinctively smiled—the clock wasn't working when Heather and I had been married there two Octobers earlier. What a week that was: among our wedding photos is a snapshot of the two of us on Swilcan Bridge, taken as we rushed onto the Old Course between foursomes. Joel was the best man. We both wore kilts, as did Luis and Ed, the cocaptains of my final Harvard golf team; the sight of Luis, a scrawny Guatemalan, in a kilt was by general consensus the funniest thing anyone had ever seen. Ed, Luis, Joel and I played the Old Course in the freezing cold of a pouring rain two days before the service. Luis quit after 12 holes, I shot 99 (with a 15 on the 14th hole), and we loved every minute of it.

I'd played the best golf of my collegiate career under the leadership of Luis and Ed in my penultimate semester at Harvard. A lot of Scottish mysticism had rubbed off on me, too, because I must have holed at least 10 shots from off the green during my senior year. In the autumn, I once chipped in on back-to-back holes, and during our spring trip to Mexico I holed virtually identical 30-yard pitch-and-run shots for birdie on the same difficult par 4 on consecutive days. (I only wished Joel had been around to see me, and to be baffled by me.) On the morning of the wedding, things were no different. I had to stay clear of the town center to make sure I wouldn't see Heather as she rushed around before the service, so several non-golfing friends and family members joined us Harvard men for nine holes on the Balgove. We shared two bags of clubs between seven of us, and I didn't have a putter or a lofted iron, but no matter—I chipped in from 60 feet for an eagle at the first with my *driver.* As we finished the round, a double rainbow sparkled in the gray western sky.

Heather and I now lived in London. We hadn't golfed together since the Balgove, but she'd wanted to come back to St. Andrews with me for this most special of occasions. Once every five or six years, St. Andrews stages its version of Carnival and becomes the spiritual *and* physical center of the game of golf. The Old Course grows upward: green grandstands, distinctive yellow scoreboards, white merchandising and hospitality tents, television cameras and platforms by the gross. Most of the Eden Course survives unscathed, but the Jubilee becomes a practice range, the 18th on the New becomes a chipping green, and the Strathtyrum and Balgove are fertilized with tire treads. The town positively buzzes with energy; everyone who is anyone in the game flocks there, to see more than be seen; upper and lower classes alike gather around newsagents and golf shops, restaurants and hotels. Very few spectacles in all of sport could hope to match the richness and common decency of an Open Championship in St. Andrews.

Heather and I bought tickets for Friday only. All I really wanted to do was say good-bye to the golfing idol of my youth, Jack Nicklaus, who was playing in his final Open at St. Andrews and seemed almost certain to miss the cut. Our battle plan for the day revolved around Jack's arrival at the 18th early in the afternoon. Heather's solitary goal was even simpler: she wanted to see Ernie Els, with whom she'd become strangely infatuated. "He's *soooo* cute and sweet and lovable and nice," she now gushes every time he appears on television back home. I don't complain. At this stage of our golfing relationship, I'm happy for her to take an active interest in *anything*.

In the morning, we paced up and down the first four holes. In one extraordinary 15-minute sequence, three different golfers presented us with masterfully constructed, career-defining vignettes: Colin Montgomerie backed away from his ball on the fourth tee and barked at a bunch of (allegedly) trigger-happy photographers; John Daly shook his head after missing a two-footer and four-putting the second green; and Seve Ballesteros magically appeared behind a large cluster of gorse, several yards away from us, to the right of the second fairway and hacked his ball out of a small bush to the fairway. It was all almost *too* perfect.

We used a crosswalk to get to the Road Hole—and nearly bumped into Padraig Harrington, the fresh-faced Irish golfer, who smiled cheerfully and strode on and up the second fairway as confidently as ever. Heather, who loves to pronounce the name Padraig (with a silent "d" and a rolled "r"), was impressed. "You can really get close to these guys, can't you?" she asked.

I took her over to the vast press tent near the putting green, and we managed to talk our way in. I found a few old friends there—among them Jerry Tarde, still the editor of *Golf Digest* and still just as unfailingly polite and friendly as I'd remembered. I'd gone back to work at *Golf Digest* in the summer after the Trip, but for reasons beyond my understanding, he had used almost none of the material he'd paid me to write, and at the end of the summer we parted ways. No hard feelings.

Jerry introduced me to the great Dan Jenkins, whom I'd never met. "Darren used to work for us, a couple of years ago," Jerry said.

Jenkins turned to me: "And then you went straight?"

On our way back to the course from the press tent, we chanced upon Mr. Els, who was being interviewed by the BBC's Dougie Donnelly near the first tee. Heather craned for a good look. "*Ewww-www*," she concluded, crinkling her nose. "His accent doesn't appeal to me at all." She thought about this and grinned. "Still . . . he's *soooo* cute!"

"You're funny," I said.

Heather and I claimed good seats in the grandstand behind the final green, and ate our sandwiches, and waited. When Nicklaus finally came through, I cheered loudly for him, but he seemed embarrassed by the fawning masses. I admired his forthrightness. He wanted no part of any Jack Nicklaus Memorial Farewell Tour; he'd come to St. Andrews to coax a few good rounds out of his battered body, and when he failed, he didn't want the crowd's sympathy. We gave it to him anyway. Tiger Woods still has some big shoes to fill, I thought.

We waited to watch Tiger and Nick Faldo tee off at the first, and once they were off we walked down to the Road Hole. Heather stayed for an hour and then left; she had to catch an early train to Aberdeen to visit a friend from school. I stayed another five hours. I spread myself out on the grass just behind the wall by the Road, baked my skin under the cloudless sky and watched the Road Hole reduce countless suave and sure professional golfers into gibbering, hollow-eyed casualties of par. With the pin tucked behind Road Bunker, I didn't see a single birdie, and only Lee Trevino and Gary Player, of all people, really came close to making one.

I followed Tiger's progress shot by shot on my Walkman. My old friend Alan Green was up to his usual, highly appealing tricks on BBC Radio Five Live:

> And here's Price, with a six-footer for par . . . he settles over it, he strikes it firmly toward the hole . . . [the crowd groans in the background] and you can probably tell what has happened to the Zimbabwean yet again. I'll tell you what, I haven't been impressed with Price at all today—he's flustered, and to be perfectly blunt, even if he *is* playing with Tiger Woods, this is just not good enough for a golfer of his caliber.

Tiger finally arrived, five and a half hours after he'd started. His approach shot crept just over the green and ran down its bank onto the thin strip of grass between the Road and the seashell path. He nonchalantly flipped his pitch onto the green, using the downward bank of Road Bunker as a backstop to get within 10 of the hole. And against the mellowing, hazy St. Andrews sky, Tiger did exactly what everyone expected him to do—he rolled his putt smoothly into the cup, steadily clenched his right fist close to his body in steely celebration, calmly touched fists with his caddie and strode over to the 18th tee with the arrogance of victory. He'd gone 35 holes without finding a bunker or making a bogey. As far as I was concerned, by seven o'clock on Friday evening he'd won the tournament already.

Tiger and his entourage swirled up and around the 18th fairway, and the current of spectators flowing ceaselessly to and beyond the Road Hole almost immediately slowed to a trickle. My detour to the press tent aside, I'd been watching the Open continuously for 11 and a half hours. I sniffed the air, looked upward and inhaled deeply, savoring the warmth of the evening and the freshness of the seaside atmosphere. I'd seen enough for one day, and for one year. The Open didn't quite beat being out there with my own clubs over my shoulder, but it came pretty close. I thanked St. Andrews for everything it had done, for me and to me. It had shown me its final face, and I felt gloriously sated.

I glanced up at the leaderboard one final time. Tiger led David Toms by three shots, Garcia-Flesch-Roberts by four, Els-Mickelson-Lehman-Couples by five and, among others, Sweden's Pierre Fulke by six. Most of the scores had the number "36" next to them, indicating that they had completed two rounds of play. But Fulke, at five under par, had played only 29 holes. What if he managed to string a bunch of birdies together? He could easily move into second place, I thought. Theoretically, he could still become the halfway leader. I studied my pairings sheet—Fulke, Dean Robertson, and Manny Zerman formed the final threesome of the day. As far as I could tell, they now figured to finish the 18th hole shortly after dark.

After dark. It was my final round at Machrihanish all over again. I looked down for a brief second, closed my eyes, exhaled a small laugh through my nose and shook my head. Then I broke into a sprint. If I hurried, I thought, I might just catch Fulke on the 12th green . . .